MW00809222

Pathways to Their Hearts
Torah Perspectives on the Individual

Rabbi Nachum L. Rabinovitch

PATHWAYS TO THEIR HEARTS
TORAH PERSPECTIVES ON THE INDIVIDUAL

Translated by Elli Fischer

Me'aliyot Press
Maggid Books

Pathways to Their Hearts
Torah Perspectives on the Individual

First Edition, 2023

Maggid Books
An imprint of Koren Publishers Jerusalem Ltd.

POB 8531, New Milford, CT 06776-8531, USA
& POB 4044, Jerusalem 9104001, Israel
www.maggidbooks.com

The publication of this book was made possible
through the generous support of *The Jewish Book Trust.*

This translation was published posthumously and did
not obtain the final approval of the author.

ISBN 978-1-59264-549-7, *hardcover*

Printed and bound in the United States

In memory of our beloved Sabba,

HaRav Nachum Eliezer Rabinovitch zt"l
הרב נחום אליעזר רבינוביץ זצ"ל

*Spiritual giant, outstanding scholar, leader, and teacher
to so many across the globe, as well as being our caring,
loving, and devoted grandfather and great-grandfather.*

*Always ready to listen,
ever kind and sensitive.*

Deeply loved and missed by us all,
הנכדים והנינים, האוהבים ומתגעגעים

Dedicated in memory of our dear parents

ישראל בן יוסף יהודה אריה ז״ל
מאשה בת חיים הכהן ז״ל
דוד מאיר בן משה ז״ל

who, whilst facing considerable challenges,
embodied heartfelt and unwavering dedication to values
of Torah and ḥesed with humility, sensitivity, and kindness.

May the Truth of Torah continue to spring
forth from their rich legacy.

Chaim and Renee Fromowitz
and family

In memory of

HaRav Hagon HaGadol
Rav Nachum Eliezer Rabinovitch

In honor of

Annette Basri

Contents

Foreword

Rabbi Nachum Eliezer Rabinovitch (1928–2020), henceforth "the Rav," was one of the supreme rabbinic scholars of our time, outstanding in a wide range of different fields. As a *posek*, a decisor in Jewish law, he distinguished himself already at a young age, writing the halakha column of *Hadarom*, the journal of the Rabbinical Council of America. In Israel, as dean of the Birkat Moshe Yeshiva in Maaleh Adumim, his true stature as expert in Jewish law was widely recognised within the religious Zionist community, and he wrote many responsa, published in two collections, *Melumdei Milḥama* and *Siaḥ Naḥum*, marked by their clarity, authority, and courage. The philosophy of his approach to halakha is set out in chapter 6 of the present work.

As a talmudic scholar his erudition was vast, as was his ability to find new depth and beauty in ancient texts. His first book, *Hadar Itamar*, consisted of a series of studies linking the end of one talmudic tractate to the beginning of the next. It is a work of dazzling brilliance, covering the whole of the Babylonian Talmud.

As a philosophical *darshan*, an exegete able to draw deep inferences about the human condition from biblical and rabbinic texts, he was one of the finest in our time, to be ranked alongside Rabbi Joseph

---

1. Ed. note: Rabbi Sacks penned this eulogy shortly after the passing of his teacher Rabbi Rabinovitch in May 2020. Sadly, Rabbi Sacks was taken from us only a few months later.

Soloveitchik, as the present volume testifies. To be sure, their methods were different. Rabbi Soloveitchik drew on modern philosophy and phenomenology; Rabbi Rabinovitch was rooted in a Maimonidean worldview, which he was able to present compellingly in the language of our time. Both regarded halakha, Jewish law, not just as a legal system but as the embodiment of a philosophy, yet with this difference: Rabbi Soloveitchik, especially in his works *Halakhic Man* and *The Halakhic Mind*, tended to think of Jewish law as a theoretical system, a way of thinking and feeling. Rabbi Rabinovitch saw it as practical, normative, a self- and society-creating way of acting, based on a philosophy of the human person and of politics and sociology. His theology was at times very dramatic, as I will shortly show.

As a secular scholar, Rabbi Rabinovitch had been a lecturer in mathematics at several universities in North America, culminating in a position at the University of Toronto. He was particularly interested in probability and statistical inference and its history generally and within Judaism. His work in this field earned him a doctorate and was eventually published as a book in its own right. He was, in addition, well versed in all the natural sciences and had a strong sense of history. His account of scientific method and its kinship with certain aspects of Jewish thought is set out in chapter 7 of this work, while chapter 8 deals with the relationship between religion and science.

His supreme achievement, though, was as a commentator of Maimonides. He spent almost fifty years writing *Yad Peshuta*, his multi-volume commentary to the *Mishneh Torah*, Maimonides' law code. This is one of the most extensive modern commentaries to this classic work. The title, *Yad Peshuta*, has an elegant double meaning. On the one hand it means "the *Mishneh Torah* (known as the *Yad* because the word has the numerical value of fourteen, the number of subdivisions of the code) made simple." On the other it refers to God's "hand extended [to receive penitents]." Hence its double purpose: to penetrate to the plain sense of Maimonides' text and to emphasise, as Maimonides himself did, that the main purpose of Jewish law was to create individuals and a society dedicated to the cause of justice and compassion, kindness and peace.

Yad Peshuta is already on its way to becoming a standard work that will endure through the generations, distinguished by vast erudition, lightly worn, and by its lucidity and clarity. The Rav would never favour an ingenious interpretation if the key to understanding was to establish the correct text from a more reliable manuscript than was available to those who produced the traditional printed editions. Its most important distinguishing feature, though, is its insistence on interpreting Maimonides *through* Maimonides – through what he wrote elsewhere, in the *Guide for the Perplexed*, perhaps, or in a responsum, or by way of a comment by his son, Rabbi Avraham, or even by figures like Gersonides, who lived after Maimonides but were peculiarly well attuned to his thought.

Maimonides had availed himself of all the literature available to him at the time, and attempted in his law code to distil every halakha contained in both the Babylonian and Jerusalem Talmuds, as well as the halakhic midrashim *Mekhilta*, *Sifra*, and *Sifrei*. The Rav, who knew the entire rabbinic literature as well as the scientific and philosophical worlds of the Middle Ages, sought above all to put himself in the position of Maimonides, to read texts as he would have read them and make the conceptual connections he would have made. That gives the *Yad Peshuta* its simplicity and depth. There was humility in this approach. The Rav sought to efface himself in the presence of Maimonides. Never did he seek to be clever or to focus attention on his own virtuosity. If any of his students attempted to do so, he would say, "Cute." This was not a compliment. True scholarship for him meant labouring to be open to the truth, not imposing your own views on the material in front of you. That unshakable integrity was a hallmark of everything he did, said, and wrote. That is what will make his scholarship stand the test of time.

* * *

Nachum Eliezer Rabinovitch was born in Montréal, Canada, in 1928. At the age of fourteen, he began studying Talmud with Rabbi Pinhas Hirschsprung, by whom he was ordained as a rabbi. In 1948 he enrolled in Ner Israel Yeshiva in Baltimore, where he studied with and obtained rabbinic ordination from Rabbi Yaakov Yitzchok Ruderman. He also studied mathematics at Johns Hopkins University, where he obtained a master's degree, later completing a doctorate at the University of Toronto.

From 1952 to 1954 he was rabbi of the Orthodox Jewish community in Dallas, Texas, and from 1955 to 1963 he was rabbi of the Orthodox Jewish community in Charleston, South Carolina. He described his time there in the preface to his book *Hadar Itamar*. Though he enjoyed serving the community, he found it less than challenging in its level of Torah scholarship. Toward the end of this period he was offered the position of chief rabbi of Johannesburg as successor to Rabbi Dr. Louis Rabinowitz. He declined, on the grounds that he could not in good conscience live in an apartheid state.

In 1963 he accepted the role of rabbi of the Clanton Park Synagogue in Toronto, as well as teaching at the University of Toronto. In 1971 he came to London to take up the role of principal of Jews' College, Anglo Jewry's rabbinic training centre. His twelve years serving Anglo Jewry were not entirely happy ones. The college had few students, its finances were in poor shape, and the type of Torah scholarship he represented was not, at that time, widely appreciated or even rightfully understood. Prior to taking up the appointment, he had been assured that a yeshiva high school would be created, to act as a feeder for the college. That never materialised. His students during those years were, nonetheless, aware of his greatness, as were a select number of laypeople. He left a lasting mark on those who studied with him.

He had always wanted to live in Israel, and when the opportunity to do so presented itself, he accepted with alacrity. In 1983 he became the head of the hesder yeshiva Birkat Moshe in Maaleh Adumim, founded six years earlier by Rabbis Haim Sabato and Yitzchak Sheilat. It is said that Rabbi Sabato, after hearing Rabbi Rabinovitch for the first time, immediately offered him the position. It was there that he found happiness and fulfilment, taking enormous pride in his thousands of students, both for their intellectual and spiritual achievements and for their courage while serving in the Israel Defense Forces.

* * *

I became the Rav's student in 1973, when I joined Jews' College. By the time I came to study with him I had already studied at Cambridge and Oxford with some of the greatest philosophers of the age. My tutors had included (Sir) Roger Scruton, (Sir) Bernard Williams, and Philippa Foot. Yet in depth and rigor, in knowledge of the many branches of wisdom, in clarity and integrity, he excelled them all. I never met anyone quite like him, not then and not since.

Only when I became his student did I learn the true meaning of intellectual discipline, *shetihyu amelim baTorah*, "laboring in the Torah." To survive his scrutiny, you had to do three things: first, to read everything ever written on the subject; second, to analyze it with complete lucidity, searching for *omek hapeshat*, the deep plain sense; and third, to think independently and critically. I remember writing an essay for him in which I quoted one of the most famous of nineteenth-century talmudic scholars. He read what I had written, then turned to me and said, "But you didn't criticise what he wrote!" He thought that in this case the scholar had not given the correct interpretation, and I should have seen and said this. For him, intellectual honesty and independence of mind were inseparable from the quest for truth, which is what *talmud Torah* must always be.

He and the late Rabbi Aharon Lichtenstein *zt"l* were the *gedolei hador*, the Modern Orthodox/religious Zionist leaders and role models of their generation. They were very different – one scientific, the other artistic, one direct, the other oblique, one bold, the other cautious – but they were giants, intellectually, morally, and spiritually. Happy the generation that is blessed with people like these.

Having Rabbi Rabinovitch as a teacher was a life-changing experience. In my own case, for example, he knew that I had to learn fast because I was coming to the rabbinate late, after a career in academic philosophy. What he did was very bold. He explained to me that the fastest and best way of learning anything is to teach it. So the day I entered Jews' College as a student, I also entered it as a lecturer. How many people would have had that idea and taken that risk?

He also understood how lonely it could be if you lived by the principles of intellectual integrity and independence. Early on, he said to me, "Don't be surprised if only six people in the world understand what you are trying to do." When I asked him whether I should accept the position of chief rabbi, he said, in his laconic way: "Why not? After all, maybe you can teach some Torah." Honor, position, title meant nothing to him. What mattered were learning and teaching, pursuing truth and living it.

He once told me how, having been offered the job of chief rabbi of Johannesburg and turning it down because he refused to live in an apartheid state, he was visited in Toronto by the rabbi who had held the Johannesburg position until then. Looking at the Rav's modest home and recalling his more palatial accommodation in South Africa, he said, "You turned down *that* for *this*?" The Rav would never compromise his integrity and never cared for material things.

* * *

Perhaps the most direct way into the thought of the Rav is through three expositions I heard from him in the years he was in Britain, which had a profound effect on me, shaping my entire understanding of Torah. The first was about Noah.

The Rav pointed out how the tempo and pace of the biblical narrative changes. The story of the Flood begins rapidly. God announces the imminent destruction of life on earth. He orders Noah to build an ark, specifying its precise measurements. Details follow as to what he must bring with him – his family, two (or in the case of pure animals, seven) of all the species of life, and provisions. The rain comes; the earth is flooded; Noah and those with him are the sole survivors. The rain ceases and the water abates.

We expect to read next that Noah emerges from the ark. Instead the narrative slows down, and for fourteen verses almost nothing happens. The water recedes. The ark comes to rest. Noah opens a window and sends out a raven. Then he sends out a dove. He waits seven days and sends it out again. It returns with an olive leaf. Another seven days pass. He sends the dove a third time. This time it does not return, but Noah still does not step out onto dry land. Eventually God Himself says, "Come out of the ark" (Gen. 8:16). Only then does Noah do so.

The Rav then cited this extraordinary midrash:

Once the waters had receded, Noah should have left the ark. However, Noah said, "I entered by divine permission, as it is said, 'Go into the ark' (Gen. 7:1). Shall I now leave without permission?" The Holy One, blessed be He, said to him, "You want permission? Here: you have permission!" as it is said, "Come out of the ark".... Said R. Yehuda bar Ilai, "Had I been there, I would have broken down the ark and taken myself out from there."[2]

The Rav explained that this was the difference between Noah and Abraham. Abraham fought a war to rescue his nephew; he prayed for the people of the plain even though he knew they were wicked; he challenged Heaven itself in words unrivalled in the history of the human encounter with God: "Shall the judge of all the earth not do justice?" The Rav quoted the well-known midrashic comment of R. Yehuda:

> "Noah walked with God" (Gen. 6:9).... R. Yehuda said, this may be compared to a king who had two sons, one grown up and the other a child. To the child he said, "Walk *with* me," but to the adult he said, "Go and walk *before* me." Thus, to Abraham, whose [moral] strength was great, [God] said, "Walk *before* Me and be perfect" (Gen. 17:1). But of Noah, whose strength was feeble, it says, "Noah walked *with* God."[3]

So, the first thing I learned from the Rav was that it takes courage to rebuild a shattered world. The person of faith does not always have the luxury of waiting for divine permission. Faith is the courage to take risks, to walk on ahead. Faith is not certainty; it is the courage to live with uncertainty.

* * *

A second exposition related to the plea of Moshe Rabbenu after the sin of the Golden Calf: "He said, 'If I have gained Your favor, O Lord, pray, let the Lord go in our midst, *because* this is a stiff-necked people. Pardon our iniquity and our sin and take us for Your own'" (Ex. 34:9). The difficulty is obvious. How could Moses ask God to forgive the people

---

2. *Tanḥuma* (Buber), *Noaḥ* 13–14.
3. Genesis Rabba 30:10.

because it was stiff-necked? He should have said: *even though or despite the fact that* they are stiff-necked.

The Rav's answer was remarkable. What Moses was saying, he said, was this: "Sovereign of the Universe, look upon this people with favour, because *what is now their greatest vice will one day be their most heroic virtue.*

"They are indeed an obstinate people. When they have everything to thank You for, they complain. Mere weeks after hearing Your voice they make a golden calf. But *just as now they are stiff-necked in their disobedience, so one day they will be equally stiff-necked in their loyalty.* Nations will call on them to assimilate, but they will refuse. Mightier religions will urge them to convert, but they will resist. They will suffer humiliation, persecution, even torture and death because of the name they bear and the faith they profess, but they will stay true to the covenant their ancestors made with You. They will go to their deaths saying, *Ani maamin,* 'I believe.' This is a people awesome in its obstinacy – and though now it is their failing, there will be times far into the future when it will be their noblest strength.

"Forgive them *because* they are a stiff-necked people," said Moses, because the time will come when that stubbornness will be not a tragic failing but a heroic and defiant loyalty. And so, historically, it came to be.

From this I learned a second fundamental of faith: the importance of defending the Jewish people (*melammed zekhut al Yisrael*). The Rav himself had clearly learned this from Maimonides' *Epistle on Martyrdom (Iggeret HaShemad)*, one of the greatest examples of this in the whole of rabbinic literature. More than once he quoted to me the powerful passage in Pesaḥim:

> The Holy One, blessed be He, said to [the prophet] Hosea: "Your children [the Jewish people] have sinned." Hosea should have replied: "But they are Your children; they are the children of Your beloved ones, the children of Abraham, Isaac, and Jacob. Extend Your mercy over them." Not only did he fail to say that, but instead he said before Him: "Master of the Universe, the entire world is Yours; [since Israel has sinned,] exchange them for another nation."

The Holy One, blessed be He, said: "What shall I do with this old man [who fails to defend Israel]? I will say to him: Go and take a prostitute and bear for yourself children of prostitution. And after that I will say to him: Send her away from you. If he is able to send her away, I will also send away the Jewish people."[4]

It may be the task of the prophet to remonstrate with his generation, but when he speaks to Heaven, he must act as counsel for the defence. Reading this book, or indeed any of the Rav's writings, you will see how deeply he internalized this idea. Rarely did he criticise people directly, even though he may passionately have disagreed with what they did or said. Nor was this because he was in any way hesitant about his beliefs or their justification; quite the contrary: he was bold, clear, and courageous. But he was reluctant to condemn. He relied on the force of argument and truth to win the case, and he never, to my knowledge, engaged in ad hominem attacks.

No less striking was the Rav's quotation from *Sifrei*, which plays a notable part in the present book: " 'A faithful God' (Deut. 32:4) – this means that God had faith in the world and thus created it."[5] To create you must have faith in what you are about to create. Likewise, to lead, you must have faith in the people you lead:

Resh Lakish said: One who suspects the innocent will be afflicted in his body, as it is written: "And Moses answered and said: But they will not believe me and will not hearken to my voice, for they will say, God did not appear to you" (Ex. 4:1). But it was revealed before the Holy One, blessed be He, that the Jewish people would believe. Thus He said to Moses: "They are believers, the children of believers; but ultimately, you will not believe."[6]

Moses was punished, not because he lacked faith in God but because he lacked faith in the people. This was an essential lesson in rabbinic

---

4. Pesaḥim 87a.
5. *Sifrei Devarim* 307, s.v. *HaTzur*.
6. Shabbat 97a.

leadership I learned from the Rav. A rabbi needs faith, not just in God but also in the people of God. The Rav had that faith, and it is reflected in his approach to halakha, his approach to Jewish thought, the way he expressed himself when he spoke and wrote, and the way he related to his students and to all who came to him for advice.

* * *

The third and most radical interpretation I heard from the Rav (it figures in the present volume, in chapter 10) was about the verse in which Moses first encountered God at the burning bush. "Moses hid his face because he was afraid to look at God" (Ex. 3:6). Why was he afraid? Because if he were fully to understand God he would have no choice but to be reconciled to the slavery and oppression of the world.

To be a parent is to be moved by the cry of a child. But if the child is ill and needs medicine, we administer it, making ourselves temporarily deaf to its cry. A surgeon, to do his job competently and well, must to a certain extent desensitize himself to the patient's fears and pains and regard him, however briefly, as a body rather than as a person. A statesman, to do his best for the country, must weigh long-term consequences and make tough, even brutal decisions: for soldiers to die in war if war is necessary, for people to be thrown out of jobs if economic stringency is needed.

Parents, surgeons, and politicians have human feelings, but the very roles they occupy mean that at times they must override them if they are to do the best for those for whom they are responsible. To do the best for others needs a measure of detachment, a silencing of sympathy, an anaesthetizing of compassion, for the road to happiness or health or peace sometimes runs through the landscape of pain and suffering and death.

If we were able to see how evil today leads to good tomorrow – if we were able to see from the point of view of God, Creator of all – we would understand justice but *at the cost of ceasing to be human*. We would accept all, vindicate all, and become deaf to the cries of those in pain. God does not want us to cease to be human, for if He did, He would not have created us. We are not God. We will never see things from His perspective. The attempt to do so is an abdication of the human situation.

From the vantage point of eternity, Moses would have seen that the bad is a necessary stage on the journey to the good. He would understand God but he would have ceased to be Moses, the fighter against injustice who intervened whenever he saw wrong being done. "He was afraid" that seeing heaven would desensitize him to earth, that coming close to infinity would mean losing his humanity.

A Holocaust historian was once interviewing a survivor of the extermination camps. He was a hasidic rebbe, a religious leader. Astonishingly, he seemed to have passed through the valley of the shadow of death, his faith intact. He could still smile. "Seeing what you saw, did you have no questions about God?" she asked. "Yes," he said, "of course I had questions. So powerful were those questions, I had no doubt that were I to ask them, God would personally invite me to heaven to tell me the answers. And I prefer to be down here on earth with the questions than up in heaven with the answers."

There is divine justice, and sometimes, looking back at the past from a distance in time, we can see it. But we do not live by looking back at the past. There is divine justice, but God wants us to strive for *human* justice – in the short term, not just the long term; in this world, not the next; from the perspective of time and space, not infinity and eternity.

God creates divine justice, but only we can create human justice, acting on behalf of God but never aspiring to be other than human. That is why He created us. Creation is empowerment. That is the radical proposition at the heart of Judaism as Rabbi Rabinovitch understands it. The Torah is God's call to human responsibility.

∗ ∗ ∗

The Rav's approach to halakha was part of his total vision of Judaism as understood by Maimonides and by the *poskim* that he admired, figures like Rabbi Yehiel Weinberg (*Seridei Esh*) and Rabbi David Zvi Hoffmann (*Melammed Leho'il*). He believed that the *posek* should have absolute command of the literature, a clear grasp of the underlying logic of the matter at hand, independence of mind, and a deep understanding of the time and circumstance in which the question has been asked. I never heard him refer to the concept of meta-halakhic propositions, but he believed in them profoundly – in those broad statements of value through which the Sages of the Mishna and Talmud expressed their most basic moral commitments.

One example illustrates his approach. I was visiting him just after our first daughter had been born. I told him that I had made the blessing of *Sheheḥeyanu*, in accordance with the ruling of the *Mishna Berura*,[7] but that I found both the ruling and the logic behind it to be uncompelling. The Talmud rules: "If his wife gave birth to a son, he makes the blessing 'Who is good and does good.'"[8] The Talmud makes no mention of the blessing to be said if one's wife gave birth to a daughter, and surprisingly, the early authorities do not address this question. The *Mishna Berura* does, but says that one makes the lesser blessing, *Sheheḥeyanu*, "Who has kept us alive."

"What made you think it was correct?" he asked, and without pausing, said the following: The Rambam includes in the *Mishneh Torah* every halakha in the Bavli, Yerushalmi, and the halakhic midrashim. Yet the Rambam does not codify the law "If his wife gave birth to a son," even though it is stated explicitly in the Talmud. Instead, the Rambam merely codifies the general rule: "In short, one who shares a benefit with others says the blessing 'Who is good and does good.' When he is the sole beneficiary, he recites the blessing 'Who has kept us alive.'"[9]

What, he asked, is the logic behind the absence of this halakha from the Rambam? The reason is that the talmudic passage can be understood in one of two ways: Either (1) there is a specific rule that you make the blessing "Who is good and does good" on the birth of a son, or (2) the Talmud is merely bringing it as an uncontroversial *example* of something that is good for you and for others. A benefit shared with others demands the blessing "Who is good and does good," and the birth of a son is merely cited as an instance, not because it is a son but because there is general celebration.

---

7. To *Shulḥan Arukh, Oraḥ Ḥayim* 223:1.
8. Berakhot 59b.
9. *Mishneh Torah, Hilkhot Berakhot* 10:7.

Not everyone in those days, said the Rav, agreed that having a girl was a blessing: "And Abraham was old, well stricken in age; and the Lord had blessed Abraham with everything (*bakkol*)" (Gen. 24:1) – R. Meir says: The blessing was that he did not have a daughter. R. Yehuda says: The blessing was that he did have a daughter."[10] Consequently, the Talmud cites the example of the birth of a son, but the same would apply in the case of the birth of a daughter, if both parents celebrated the birth.

The fact that the Rambam cited only the general rule, not the specific example of a son, shows that he followed the second interpretation of the passage.[11] Therefore, said the Rav, if you and your wife both wanted a daughter, you should make the blessing "Who is good and does good," which we did when our second daughter was born. It was rulings like these – clear, compelling, courageous – that marked Rabbi Rabinovitch as a *posek* of towering stature, as is clear from his two published volumes of responsa.

Note the combination of factors here: first, his sharp attention to the apparently missing text in the Rambam; second, his understanding of why this was so and its halakhic implications; third, his sensitivity to time and circumstance and the difference they made given the view of the Rambam; and fourth, the meta-halakhic proposition "in order to give pleasantness of spirit to women,"[12] which he saw as one of the shaping principles of the Sages and which he makes clear in chapter 19 of this book.

* * *

And so to the book itself, the Hebrew edition of which he gave the title *Mesilot Bilvavam*, a phrase from Psalms 84:6: "Happy are those whose strength is in You, *in whose heart are [Your] ways*." Judaism is not just a matter of deed. It is also a process of creating "ways in the heart," habits

---

10. Bava Batra 141a.
11. The argument is set out in *Yad Peshuta* on *Hilkhot Berakhot* 10:7 and appears in the penultimate chapter of this book.
12. Ḥagiga 16b.

of intellect and emotion that constitute Judaism's unique religious sensibility. Only thus can we fully help to realise its ultimate goals of loving-kindness, equity, justice, peace, and the manifestation of the Divine that occurs when we make, on earth, a home for the holiness of heaven.

The work is a synthesis of the philosophical positions the Rav had developed over the course of many decades, beginning with his earliest days in the rabbinate. These had been honed and refined over the years but had existed as a series of articles on discrete themes. It was evident that these were the building blocks of a vast overarching structure covering the whole of Judaism, individual and community, ethics and politics, a theological understanding of the Holocaust, and the religious significance of a reborn State of Israel and many other matters besides. Some of these ideas found expression in an extended essay entitled *Darkah shel Torah*, "The Way of the Torah," which was eventually enlarged into a book of the same title. This too, however, was an incomplete expression of the range and scope of the Rav's thought. Hence, *Mesilot Bilvavam*, a work that finally does justice to one of the boldest and most profound religious thinkers of our time.

The current volume, *Pathways to Their Hearts*, is about the individual. There are chapters here on free will and the human condition, the way the Torah's commands interact with moral change, the tension between law and the purposes of law, the difference between religious and secular ethics, the importance of intellectual independence, and the nature of halachic decision making. There is a fascinating comparison between scientific method and the search for the reasons for the commandments, and a powerful chapter on the relationship between Torah and science. There is no opposition between them, argues the Rav, and the belief that there is was imported into Judaism from non-Jewish sources. The conviction, sadly still widespread, that Torah and science are incompatible, has had devastating consequences: "We lost many of our best sons, who never discovered that Judaism never opposed the search for truth and that, on the contrary, disclosing the mysteries of creation leads only to the recognition of God's greatness." Throughout these chapters there is an insistence on choice, personal responsibility, intellectual integrity, and the need for each of us to engage in our own pursuit of truth.

The continuation volume, *Pathways to God*, is about society. It begins with a powerful theological response to the Holocaust, and then turns to a sweeping exploration of the religious significance of the State of Israel, of the role of religion within the state, and of the place of democracy within a Jewish understanding of society. There are strong statements on the importance of collective responsibility, engagement with the wider society, and contributing to the state, especially to its defence. The Rav explains the controversial stand he took on conversion in Israel, and why the openness he adopted is, in his view, the only way of avoiding future tragedy within Israeli society.

Important essays follow on the kind of political structures that halakha would seek in a Jewish state: democratic governance, minority rights, electoral systems, the scope and limits of the Knesset's authority, the relative roles of central and local government, and the proper relationship between religion and politics. There are reflections on what would constitute a Jewish view of economic policy, the balance between personal responsibility and state aid, and how labour relations should be conducted. There is a strong chapter on the place of women in Judaism, and one on the evolving relationship between the Jewish people and humanity as a whole, especially as it has been affected by the rebirth of the State of Israel.

This is an outstanding work, vast in scope, monumental in scholarship, the distilled wisdom of one of the great Jewish minds of our generation. It is a book of strong views, boldly expressed, on topics of vital importance to the future of Judaism and the State of Israel. This is Torah at its most expansive and challenging, and it is as close as we will come to the voice of Maimonides for our time.

Prologue to the Hebrew Edition

We are fortunate to live in the age of the return to Zion and the ingathering of exiles. The events that we are witnessing in our time are beyond anything we could have imagined. Despite all of the threats facing them, the Jewish people and the State of Israel continue to grow and flourish, by the grace of God. Torah study is also on the upswing among our people; in all of history, Torah has never been studied on the scale that it is today. The promises of the Torah are being realized before our eyes.

The Jewish people, though relatively small, has had a profound influence on the nations of the world throughout history, and especially in our day. This influence sometimes arouses hatred toward us, but this is the price we pay for being the bearers of faith in this world, wittingly or unwittingly.

The social, cultural, and scientific changes of the modern age, the return of the Jewish people to its land, and the establishment of the State of Israel are all major historic upheavals that pose new and great challenges to the individual Jew and to the entire nation.

It is the Torah of Israel that shaped the people of Israel's spirit through history and gave us the vision of *tikkun olam*, perfecting the world. However, it is only in the present era of Jewish independence

and of scientific, technological, and cultural progress that circumstances
have made it possible to realize this vision.

For centuries we were forced to invest all of our energies toward
our survival, but now we have been granted the opportunity to realize
the dream of fulfilling the mission of the Torah: kindness, righteousness, justice, peace, and the revelation of God's name on a global scale.
In order to advance toward these goals, we must look to the Torah and
its mitzvot and learn from them how to pave the way to the improvement of man and society.

Almost twenty years ago, the book *Darkah shel Torah* (*The Way
of Torah*), a collection of articles written at different times about various
contemporary issues from a Torah perspective, was published. It is now
long out of print. New articles have been written since then, and new issues
have emerged that require our attention. It was therefore decided to publish
a new volume to collect these new articles, ideas that were articulated in
discourses at Yeshivat Birkat Moshe, as well as the articles that appeared
in *Darkah shel Torah*. In addition, the older articles were revised to reflect
changing circumstances and new material. Significant changes were made
to most of the articles; in some cases new sections were added, and in other
cases sections from the old versions were incorporated into entirely new
articles. In addition, prior to the publication of the Hebrew edition, I held
a series of talks with those who initiated this project and new material was
added to each of the articles based on these conversations.

The volume draws its Hebrew name, *Mesilot Bilvavam*, from the
verse: "Fortunate is the man whose strength is in You, in whose heart are
the paths (*mesilot bilvavam*)" (Ps. 84:6). The Sages explain in a midrash
(Leviticus Rabba 17:1):

> "Fortunate is the man whose strength is in You." One might think
> that this includes all people; therefore the verse states, "in whose
> heart are the paths," in whose heart the path of Torah is well worn.
> "Do good, O Lord, to the good" (Ps. 125:4). One might think that
> this includes all people; therefore the verse states, "to the upright
> in their hearts" (125:4). "The Lord is close to all who call Him"
> (145:18). One might think that this includes all people; therefore
> the verse states, "to all who call Him with sincerity" (145:18).

This midrash teaches us that it is not enough for a person to cling to the Creator with all his might, for "even an ox knows its master, and a donkey cleaves to its master's trough" (Is. 1:3). Man's uniqueness lies in his ability to obtain wisdom of the heart (see Ps. 90:12), and that is accomplished by making the paths of Torah well-worn in his heart – that is, for his mind and will to be shaped by the Torah.

This is similar to what Radak writes (ad loc.) in the name of his father:

> "Fortunate is the man" – my father, of blessed memory, explained that they have strength and wisdom through knowledge of Your oneness, for this is the root of all worship of You. As David said to his son Solomon, "Know the God of your fathers and worship Him" (I Chr. 28:9). "In whose heart are the paths" – they have pathways to knowledge of You in their hearts, and they traverse those paths, growing in strength each day. This interpretation is correct.

This book is divided into two sections: the first section focuses on the individual, and the latter section focuses on society.[1] This division accords with Maimonides' explanation in *Moreh Nevukhim* III:27 of the dual purposes of the Torah: the welfare of the soul and the welfare of the body – that is, society. The common denominator of these sections is the attempt to apply Torah values in accordance with the changing times and their challenges and in light of Halakha and its philosophical underpinnings. For the sake of clarity, we have avoided lengthy halakhic discussions and instead have offered references only to the basic sources. The adept student will fill in the gaps on his own.

It is worth addressing, even if briefly, a major issue in the philosophy of halakha as taught to us by Maimonides: "[One] should seek in all the mitzvot an end that is useful in regard to reality: 'For it is no vain thing' (Deut. 32:47) … The generalities of the commandments necessarily have a cause and have been given because of a certain utility."[2]

---

1. Ed. note: In English, these will be two separate volumes.
2. *Moreh Nevukhim* III:26, 508.

Maimonides rejects those

> who consider it a grievous thing that causes should be given for any law.... What compels them to feel thus is a sickness that they find in their souls.... For they think that if those laws were useful in this existence...it would be as if they derived from the reflection and the understanding of some intelligent being. If, however, there is a thing for which the intellect could not find any meaning at all and that does not lead to something useful, it indubitably derives from God.... It is as if, according to these people of weak intellects, man were more perfect than his Maker; for man speaks and acts in a manner that leads to some intended end, whereas the Deity does not act thus.... Rather things are indubitably as we have mentioned; every commandment from among these 613 commandments exists either with a view to communicating a correct opinion, or to putting an end to an unhealthy opinion, or to communicating a rule of justice, or to warding off an injustice, or to endowing men with a noble moral quality, or to warning them against an evil moral quality. Thus all [the mitzvot] are bound up with three things: opinions, moral qualities, and political civic actions.[3]

In their hearts are the paths!

Here I wish to acknowledge and thank those who undertook this task. Rabbi Gideon Israel initiated and managed the publication of the original Hebrew volume. He worked alongside Rabbi Eli Reif, the volume's editor, who gathered the articles, transcribed the lectures, combined passages that express similar ideas, and worked systematically and meticulously to clarify and elucidate it all. I reviewed everything, of course, so any remaining errors or omissions are my responsibility alone. I am also grateful to Rabbi Mevorach Touito for his assistance during the first stages of work on this volume. Rabbi Binyamin Landau polished the style and language of the book with great skill.

---

3. Ibid. 3:31, 523–24.

"Were Your Torah not my delight, I would perish in my affliction; I will never neglect Your precepts, for You have sustained me through them" (Psalms 119:92–93).

Over two years ago, my world was darkened by the passing of my wife and life partner, the wise-hearted Rabbanit Rachel Malka, may her soul be bound in the bonds of eternal life. If any readers of this volume find it beneficial, I attest that, as Rabbi Akiva said, "Mine and yours are hers."

May the Almighty bless everyone in my family with a long, good, and healthy life. May we merit seeing them all grow up to love God and His Torah, to revere Him. May God light up our eyes with His Torah.

"As for me, may my prayer come to You, O Lord, at a favorable moment. God, in your abundant kindness, answer me with Your sure deliverance" (Psalms 69:14).

Nahum L. Rabinovitch

Sivan 5777

Ed. note (Elul 5782):
We wish to add our thanks to the following people without whose efforts this English edition would not have been possible: translator Rabbi Elli Fischer; translation editor Rabbi Eliyahu Krakowski, who, as Rabbi Rabinovitch's grandson, was privileged to have a close personal relationship with the author; copy editor Sara Henna Dahan; research consultant Rabbi Dr. Zvi Ron; the professional team at Koren Jerusalem – Publisher Matthew Miller, Editorial Director Rabbi Reuven Ziegler, Aryeh Grossman, Caryn Meltz, David Silverstein, Rabbi Michael Siev, and Debbie Ismailoff; Ayal Fishler of Me'aliyot Press; the leadership of Yeshivat Birkat Moshe; and Guido Rauch, for his partnership and his support for this important book.

Most of the essays in this book appeared earlier in other formats and editions. This volume follows the final versions of these essays as they appeared in Rabbi Rabinovitch's *Mesilot BiLvavam* (Maaleh Adumim: Me'aliyot, 2015). This includes articles originally written in English or translated into English; the former were updated to reflect the Hebrew expansions, and the latter were both edited for style and updated to accord with the final Hebrew versions. We acknowledge our debt to the translators of the earlier versions of these articles. Since this volume was published posthumously, the translations did not obtain the final approval of the author.

Note to the Reader

Aᴸᴸ citations of Maimonides' works are to the following editions, unless otherwise indicated:

- *Commentary to the Mishna*: Qafih edition (Jerusalem: Mossad Harav Kook, 1963–1969).
- Introductory essays within the *Commentary on the Mishna* (with the exception of *Eight Chapters*): Shilat edition (Jerusalem: Me'aliyot, 1992).
- *Sefer HaMitzvot*: Qafih edition (Jerusalem: Mossad Harav Kook, 1971).
- *Mishneh Torah*: Where available, the citations are from my edition, *Yad Peshuta* (Ma'aleh Adumim: Me'aliyot, 1990–2011). Otherwise, we use the text of the *Mishneh Torah* Project edition: Y. Makbili, ed. (Haifa: Or Vishua, 2009).
- *Guide of the Perplexed*: Pines translation (Chicago: University of Chicago Press, 1963).
- *Iggerot HaRambam* (with the exception of the *Epistle to Yemen*): Shilat edition (Jerusalem: Me'aliyot, 5750).
- *Responsa of Maimonides*: Blau edition (Jerusalem: Mekitzei Nirdamim, 1958–1960).

- *The Eight Chapters of Maimonides on Ethics: Shemonah Perakim*: Gorfinkle translation and edition (New York: Columbia University Press, 1912).
- *Moses Maimonides' Epistle to Yemen*: Cohen (trans.) and Halkin edition (New York: American Academy for Jewish Research, 1952).

Whenever "*Hilkhot X*" is cited, the reference is to *Mishneh Torah*. References to talmudic tractates in the Yerushalmi are prefaced with Y; if there is no prefacing letter, the reference is to the Babylonian Talmud.

Chapter 1

Grant Our Portion in Your Torah

The Creative Wisdom of Free Will

The uniqueness of man, the Divine image that elevates him above all other creatures, is his power of choice. Our guide for all generations, Maimonides, wrote:

> This is what the Torah means by, "Man has become like one of us, knowing good and evil" (Gen. 3:22). That is, this species, mankind, is unique in the world. There is no other species like man in this respect, in that he autonomously, with his intelligence (*da'at*) and understanding, knows good and evil and does what he wants. None can prevent him from doing good or evil.[1]

---

1. *Hilkhot Teshuva* 5:1. However, see *Hilkhot Yesodei HaTorah* 4:8, where he writes, "the superior intelligence (*da'at yetera*)," which seems to locate man's uniqueness in his intelligence and not his free will, but compare to *Moreh Nevukhim* I:1, where he alludes to the idea of man's intelligence when he writes: "'knowing good and evil'... with his *intelligence* and understanding, [he] knows good and evil and does what he wants." See *Meshekh Ḥokhma* on Genesis 1:26: "The 'Divine image' is the capacity for choice that is free of natural compulsion but rather [derives] from freedom of will and mind.

1

The Creator acts with complete freedom. No inhibition, no coercion, and no duress apply to Him. He decided to create, in the lower realms, a single creature, who would be unique by virtue of the divine quality implanted within him: the power of choice. Yet man, like the other earthly creatures, is limited because he is flesh and blood. Absolute freedom of choice is inconceivable without omnipotence, and man is not all-powerful! Nevertheless, the Creator granted him a space within which he can act freely, as he desires.

To that end, God granted man the awesome powers of wisdom (*ḥokhma*) and understanding (*bina*), whereby he can realize his destiny of building and ruling God's world, as Scripture states: "You have granted him dominion over Your handiwork; You placed everything at his feet" (Ps. 8:7).

There are two types of wisdom: The first is wisdom to observe the world and reveal the natural laws that God prescribed for it. Scripture states: "How manifold are Your works, O Lord; You have made them all with wisdom" (Ps. 104:24). That is, the world was created with wisdom and gives expression to God's wisdom, and God gave man the capacity to disclose nature's mysteries. He created within man intelligence that, in a certain respect, corresponds to the intelligence inherent in creation as a whole. Therefore, by the power of his mind, man can discover some of the hidden wisdom that the world embodies.

The deeper we penetrate, the more we discover, and the more we reveal that the mystery is ever greater. Throughout history, science has progressed both by making new discoveries and by applying this knowledge and these discoveries to human advancement.

The second type of wisdom is the wisdom to choose properly, the wisdom to know good and evil. Man must know his duty in this world and understand how to use his power of choice in order to fulfill his destiny.

Man is a spiritual creature. It is incumbent upon man not only to discover what is, but also to try to imagine what ought to be, and then to make that improved existence a reality. Man was given the ability to create not only in the physical realm, but in the spiritual and moral realm as well. This ability, however, is mere potential. The realization of this potential requires a vast and profound body of wisdom that is utterly unlike empirical science. Forging a moral world is, in essence, a spiritual act, even if it is performed within a reality that is governed entirely by the laws of nature. This is the ultimate fulfillment of man's purpose.

Certainly, both categories of wisdom flow from the same source and stem from the same root: the wisdom of the Creator. But the common root of all wisdom is exceedingly deep, hidden, and beyond our grasp. Therefore, no one may ignore the distinction between these two types of wisdom.

One who ignores man's spiritual destiny sentences himself to imprisonment within the material. Ultimately, he also condemns himself to extinction. One who ignores the wisdom of the natural sciences ultimately condemns himself to the limitation of possibilities, to the point that he will have no control over the physical world and will be unable to achieve even the best and loftiest desires. A complete human being needs both types of wisdom.

As human knowledge expands, so does man's power and control over the world and the forces of nature. Correspondingly, as the ability to dominate the world grows, man's power of choice must contend with an ever-broadening range of possible action, for both good and evil. There are aspects of the universe that man may one day dominate almost completely, and other aspects over which man has less control. All in all, however, man's potential is vast, and he must endeavor to realize that potential, always broadening the realm over which he exercises his free choice. For example, as the natural sciences advance, human beings increasingly dominate the forces of nature and gain the ability to wield them as they see fit. Applied human wisdom leads to a reality in which there are new fields within which man is confronted with choices that earlier generations thought were solely in the hands of Heaven. In fact, sometimes even a single decision can be pivotal. As R. Yehuda HaNasi said, "Some acquire their world all at once."[2]

Only by exercising free will does man realize his essence. One who does not exercise the power to choose – his spirit is dimmed, and he does not embody the Divine image. Conversely, the more one broadens and deepens the scope of his free choice, the more he resembles the One on High, Who created him in His image. Man thus fulfills God's

---

2. Avoda Zara 10b; 17a; 18a.

original design and exhibits the Divine image. All of creation sings his praises: "You have made him a little less than divine; You have crowned him in honor and glory" (Ps. 8:6).

However, it is not choice per se that is demanded of us. Could anyone imagine that the purpose of free will is merely to choose, regardless of *what* one chooses? Freedom of choice enables one to choose darkness over light and evil over righteousness. Is this what brings man his glory? The power to choose is a supreme value only because it is the tool that enables man to actively choose good and reject evil:

> Every person is given power[3] over himself: if he wants to steer himself toward the path of goodness and become righteous – he has that power; and if he wants to steer himself toward the path of evil and become wicked – he has that power.[4]

Since man was given this power: "You have granted him dominion over Your handiwork; You placed everything at his feet" (Ps. 8:7).

Man, endowed with free choice, is the elect of all creatures, yet he is capable of returning the world to primeval chaos. He is worthy of having been created only if he chooses good. However, choosing good is not enough. If one does good but not entirely of his free will, or without using his mind to recognize what is good, then his goodness is not a reflection of the Divine image within him. Only if he *chooses the good because it is good*, not (to the extent possible) due to any external constraints, pressures, or incentives, does he express his true essence through his choices. Only then does he justify the creation and continued existence of the human race.

This is how the Sages expressed the marvel – and risk – inherent in man's ability to choose:

> R. Simon said: When the Holy One sought to create man, the ministering angels divided into factions and groups, some saying he should be created, and others saying he should not be created.[5]

---

3. The Hebrew *reshut* here has connotations of both capacity and authority.
4. *Hilkhot Teshuva* 5:1.
5. Genesis Rabba 8:5; cf. Sanhedrin 38b.

The stakes are high here. Man can only choose good if he is given the power of choice. But what guarantee is there that he will in fact choose good? Yet, if the possibility of choosing evil is withheld from him, then his creation was in vain!

In terms of pure reason, the ministering angels were right to oppose man's creation. Angels, who lack the power of choice, possess only the faculty of critical reasoning, which distinguishes between affirmation and negation, existence and nonexistence – nothing more. Yet freedom of choice is neither of those, as it encompasses both sides of an apparent contradiction: in potential, it entails choosing good and also its opposite.

This is the meaning of the Sages' interpretation of the verse, "The Rock – His deeds are perfect… A faithful God…" (Deut. 32:4):

"The Rock" (*Tzur*) – the Artist (*Tzayar*), Who first shaped (*tzar*) the world and then formed (*va-yatzar*) man within it… "A faithful God" – Who had faith in the world, and created it.[6]

The Holy One is the greatest believer, because only by virtue of faith could He create the world. Only one with the power to choose could have faith in man, who likewise has the power to choose. The Holy One believed in man's purpose, and therefore created him.

In His wisdom, the Almighty created man and imbued in him the power to discover, on his own, the wisdom inherent in the universe – both the wisdom necessary to understand the world as it is and the wisdom to visualize a better world and bring it about. Some things are innate in man, such as how a baby, from birth, knows to suckle. Others, like walking, are learned gradually. There are also things that humanity as a whole requires many generations, and entire epochs, to learn. These things require intense and prolonged effort; yet even after cumulative efforts across generations, we are able to discover only an infinitesimal amount of the wisdom that God embedded within the universe. Nevertheless, the possibility of discovering this wisdom was given to man.

---

6. *Sifrei Devarim* 307.

The wisdom to choose properly is different. Clearly, one who is not prepared to direct and employ his power of choice to seek truth and choose good will not attain either of them. But even one who seeks the proper path can become disoriented. For this reason, mankind requires a long period of growth, education, and maturation; a single lifespan is insufficient. Within the human race, heredity works not only biologically, but also culturally. Each generation acquires knowledge and abilities bequeathed to it by its forebears. Like a dwarf on the shoulders of a giant, it manages to see further. A generation may surpass its predecessors, and it is thus able to train its descendants to go even further.

Throughout history, there have been exceptional individuals who reached elevated spiritual levels, as Maimonides taught us:

> Any individual in the world whose spirit moves him and whose own reason gives him the understanding to set himself apart in order to stand before God, to serve Him and worship Him, to know God; who walks upright, as God created him to do; and who has cast away the burden of the many calculations that people pursue – is sanctified with the utmost holiness. God will be his portion and his inheritance forever and ever.[7]

Nevertheless, history attests to the painful, bitter errors that humanity has made in its search for the proper path. The history of every nation, like the chronicles of all mankind, is a developmental process destined to cultivate virtuous individuals who choose good, and to fashion an entire society that nurtures such virtuous individuals. This is not a one-way process; it has ups and downs. It would have been better if certain generations had never been created, and some exceptional individuals sustain the whole world with their merit. The path is as deep and wide as the sea, and it is paved with hazards. Who will give us instruction? Who can teach us this lesson?

The Crown of Torah

The Holy One did a great kindness for the Jewish people – and not only for the Jewish people, but for the whole world – in giving us His Torah,

---

7. *Hilkhot Shemita VeYovel* 13:13.

thereby enabling us to achieve our spiritual purpose of knowing how to choose the path of God at every juncture. Man is a spiritual being, and as such he needs spiritual wisdom. This wisdom appears in the Torah, and its purpose is to guide human choices. The Torah is the wisdom that enables man to advance toward his destiny – not only the realization of his physical potential, but the realization of his spiritual potential as well: "Beloved is man, in that he was created in the Divine image…. Beloved is Israel, who was given the precious implement…with which the world was created."[8]

It is the destiny of the Jewish people, which has already produced spiritual giants, to advance this process, whose ultimate goal is the construction of a society in which the kingdom of Heaven is realized on earth:

"You shall instruct…the children of Israel that they shall bring you [pure olive oil…for kindling]" (Ex. 27:6) – not that I need [the lamps of the menorah], rather, you shall give light to Me just as I gave light to you…. This can be compared to a sighted man and a blind man who were walking. The sighted man said to the blind man, "Come, and I will support you." And so the blind man went. When they reached home, the sighted man said to the blind man, "Go and light the lamp for me, and give me light, so that you owe me no favors for having accompanied you. That is why I have told you to light." Thus, the sighted man is the Holy One, as it is written: "For the Lord's eyes range over the whole earth" (II Chr. 16:9); the blind man is Israel, as Scripture states: "We grope, like blind men along a wall; like eyeless men, we grope. We stumble at noon as though in darkness." (Is. 59:10)
…Israel said: "'You light my lamp' (Ps. 18:29), and yet You say that we should give You light?" Said He to them: "It is to uplift you, so that you give light to Me just as I gave light to you."
…"The spirit of man is the lamp of the Lord" (Proverbs 20:27). The Holy One said: "Let My lamp be in your hand, and your lamp be in My hand." What is God's lamp? The Torah, as

---

8. Mishna Avot 3:14.

Scripture states: "For the commandment is a lamp, and the Torah is light" (Proverbs 6:23). What is the meaning of "the commandment is a lamp"? One who performs the commandments is like one who lights a lamp before the Holy One. It revives man's spirit, which is called a lamp, as Scripture states: "The spirit of man is the lamp of the Lord."[9]

The Torah, which was given to Israel, molds and shapes the character of Israel in order to attain the ultimate goal, which is the character of Israel to facilitate their attainment of the ultimate goal, which is to realize the Divine image in order to become similar to God in all aspects of one's life. Thus will the vision of the prophet be fulfilled: "I, the Lord, have justly called you; I have grasped your hand, formed you, and made you a covenantal people, a light unto the nations" (Is. 42:6).

Although all of mankind was commanded to observe only the seven Noahide laws, which express the basic religious and moral demands incumbent upon man, and is not charged with the observance of all 613 commandments, Scripture states in a vision for the future: "Many nations shall go and say, 'Come, let us ascend the Mount of the Lord, to the House of the God of Jacob, so that He may instruct us in His ways, and so that we may walk in His path. For Torah (i.e., instruction) shall go forth from Zion, and the word of the Lord from Jerusalem" (Is. 2:3).

The wisdom of the Torah can guide the world to the right path. Indeed, throughout history, the fundamental ideas of the Torah have been disseminated throughout the world and made decisive contributions to the advancement of truth and morality, and to the improvement of man and of society. Yet the road to full realization of this vision, culminating in the prophet's words, "for the earth shall be filled with knowledge of the Lord" (Is. 11:9), is still a long one.

The Torah is there for everyone, ready and waiting. We learn in a mishna: "Rabbi Shimon says: There are three crowns – the crown of Torah, the crown of priesthood, and the crown of royalty."[10] Based on the words of the Sages, Maimonides wrote:

9. Exodus Rabba 36:2–3.
10. Mishna Avot 4:13.

Three crowns were bestowed upon Israel: the crown of Torah, the crown of priesthood, and the crown of royalty. The crown of priesthood Aaron earned…. The crown of royalty David earned…. The crown of Torah is there, ready and waiting for everyone, as Scripture states: "Moses commanded the Torah to us, as the heritage of the congregation of Yaakov" (Deut. 33:4). Anyone who wants it may come and take it. Lest one say that those other crowns are greater than the crown of Torah, Scripture states: "By me kings reign and rulers decree justice. By me princes govern" (Prov. 8:15–16). Thus, the crown of Torah is greater than the crown of priesthood and the crown of royalty. The Sages said: A mamzer who is a Torah scholar takes precedence over a high priest who is an ignoramus…[11]

The three crowns symbolize greatness. The crowns of royalty and priesthood depend on pedigree and are not given to all. Royalty is contingent upon belonging to the Davidic line, and the priesthood was given to the family of Aaron.

Royalty and priesthood, though they express unique social status, are linked to the material world and, as such, represent it. Moreover, they are linked to pedigree, which is material by its very nature. On the material plane, man is a limited creature; many things are beyond his control. In the material world, status is constrained by human limitations. Different people have different strengths; there are differences between male and female, and there are distinct traits that enable specific people to fill specific roles that others, who do not possess those traits, would be unable to fulfill properly. Thus, for example, not everyone can be an elite athlete. By the same token, there are those whose aptitude in scientific thinking enables them to achieve breakthroughs in science.

It is obvious that royalty has a place only in our material world, but in truth, the priesthood, too, belongs to the material world. The priest serves in the Temple, and his service is essentially physical. The physical world can be open to, and influenced by, the spiritual world, but it remains the physical world. This can be compared to someone looking out of a window.

---

11. *Hilkhot Talmud Torah* 3:1–2.

Although the window allows the observer to see another world, it does not really transport him into that world. Thus, even the high priest, who enters the inner sanctum of the Temple, prays for worldly needs. The priest creates a window; the purpose of his service is to draw Israel closer to their Father in heaven, yet his service and actions are within the confines of this world. Royalty and priesthood are of this world, and they have no grasp of eternity. They do not truly characterize man, but merely the material world.

The crown of Torah is different. By means of Torah, one is transported to the spiritual world and becomes rooted in eternity. The Torah belongs to God; it is spiritual wisdom. One who studies and keeps the Torah realizes his soul's potential. His mind, sublimated by God's Torah, creates its own portion in the Torah. "The Torah is his,"[12] and he grasps eternal life. The crown of Torah is available and ready for all, regardless of pedigree. This is the meaning of what the Sages taught: "A mamzer who is a Torah scholar takes precedence over a high priest who is an ignoramus."

The Holy One has given us a perfect Torah. However, as with the wisdom of creation, so too here God has given us only the keys to wisdom, and everything else is dependent on our choice and is the product of our study. Everything else is the product of study. By studying Torah, one realizes the potential of his soul, the Divinity within him.

The Torah is not intended merely to impart wisdom to man, nor even only to teach man to fulfill the commandments. Engaging in Torah enables man to discern – between truth and falsehood, between good and evil, and between various gradations of truth. Understanding that is firmly rooted in the Torah opens, for man, a route to all wisdom and even to the eternal world. The higher the truth one attains, the closer he gets to human perfection, to the point that he is worthy of being described by the verse: "You have made him a little less than divine" (Ps. 8:6). Man studies Torah and wisdom in order to mold himself,[13] true self creation – that is, to form man's very soul.

In *Hilkhot Teshuva* (8:2), Maimonides wrote about the eternal soul in the spiritual existence we refer to as "the World to Come" (*Olam Haba*):

12. Kiddushin 32b. See Rashi, s.v. "*Uvetorato yehegeh.*"
13. See *Hilkhot Yesodei HaTorah* 4:11–13.

The souls of the righteous survive there without exertion or effort. Moreover, the [Sages'] phrase, "with their crowns upon their heads," means: the *de'ah* (mind) with which they know, by virtue of which they attained life in the World to Come, remains with them. It is their crown, as King Solomon said: "The crown with which his mother crowned him" (Song. 3:11).... The crown to which the Sages refer here is *de'ah*.

In these words, Maimonides alludes to a midrashic interpretation: "Ḥizkiyah bar Ḥiya taught: The Torah is a crown upon the head, as Scripture states: 'For they are a graceful wreath upon your head, a necklace around your throat' (Prov. 1:9)."[14] Maimonides explains further in *Hilkhot Yesodei HaTorah* (4:8):

> The superior knowledge found in the soul of man is the "form"[15] of the man whose mind is perfect. Of this form, the Torah states: "Let Us make man in Our image, according to Our likeness" (Gen. 1:26).... This is not the sentient soul of every animal, by means of which it eats, drinks, reproduces, senses, and feels. Rather, it is the mind (*de'ah*), which is the "form" of the soul.

Maimonides uses the term *de'ah* here. Elsewhere – especially in works translated from Arabic – we find the term *sekhel*,[16] as in the expression "disembodied *sekhalim*." Today, the word *sekhel* is generally used to mean "intelligence," which is a more limited sense than the one intended by classical thinkers. It is therefore sometimes difficult to grasp exactly what they are describing. The English word "mind," which has no exact parallel in modern Hebrew, more closely approximates Maimonides' "*de'ah*" and his translators' "*sekhel*" than any modern Hebrew term.

---

14. *Midrash Tehillim* (Buber ed.) 19:15. See also Ta'anit 26b: "'The crown with which his mother crowned him on his wedding day and the day of his heart's rejoicing' – 'his wedding day' refers to the giving of the Torah."
15. The term "form" (*tzura*) is used here in its philosophical sense, and refers to an entity's essential characteristic. See *Moreh Nevukhim* I:1, I:68 and I:70.
16. Maimonides uses the term *sekhel* in different contexts and with various meanings.

Due to this confusion about the term *sekhel*, some think that there is no place in modern thought for Maimonides' statements that *de'ah* grants its possessors everlasting life. That is not so, however. The *de'ah* to which Maimonides refers is not a repository of propositions and proven truths (though, no doubt, they participate in the formation of "*de'ah*"). When Maimonides speaks of *de'ah*, he does not mean the information accumulated in one's brain, as on a hard drive. A computer can contain a great deal of information, but it is not conscious of it. A book may store much information, but a book, even a Torah scroll, has no life-force.

In this context, it is worth citing the comment, well-known amongst Ḥasidim and attributed to the Baal Shem Tov, on the Talmud's discussion of R. Huna's dictum: "Nine plus the ark combine" (Berakhot 47b). That is, according to R. Huna, nine men in a synagogue combine with the holy ark, in which a Torah scroll is stored, to form a prayer quorum. R. Naḥman responds in astonishment: "Is the ark human!?" The Talmud then reinterprets R. Huna's statement. But the question remains: What was the Talmud thinking when it initially stated, "Nine plus the ark combine"?

It is told that the Ba'al Shem Tov explained as follows: The Talmud initially reasoned that in order to establish a prayer quorum, ten are needed because every Jew has his own share in the Torah. Thus, when ten Jews gather, an objective quality of Torah is present, and it is worthy that the Divine Presence devolve upon it. Thus, if only nine are present, and only one share of Torah is missing, why not include the ark, in which the entire Torah can be found?

To this R. Naḥman responds in astonishment: "Is the ark human!?" A Torah scroll, which "sits in a corner,"[17] is not a vehicle of the Divine Presence. Producing a quorum requires specifically human beings, who have their own share in the Torah.

Maimonides identifies *de'ah* with the "form" of the soul. We cannot define precisely what a soul (*nefesh*) is, but wisdom, understanding, knowledge, life experience, mitzva observance, and everything else that one encounters in life – these are all the raw materials that, through man's vigorous desire to serve his Maker, shape the soul. This is, in essence,

---

17. Editor's note: See Kiddushin 66a.

the entirety of man, and this is the perfection that constitutes his share in the everlasting, linking him to the eternal.

The process by which we shape our thought, emotion, and other mental powers according to Torah values manifests the potential of the "form" of man's soul – the Divine, eternal aspect of man.

To Study Torah in Truth

It is not easy to earn the crown of Torah. It demands the intense spiritual effort of studying Torah to discern its truth (*amitah*). On the verse (Deut. 26:16) "The Lord your God commands you *this day* to observe these laws and rules," a midrash states:

> What is meant by "this day"?... Moses said to Israel: "Each day, the Torah should be beloved by you as though you received it on Mount Sinai on that day... R. Yoḥanan said: One who substantiates the Torah (*"oseh Torah le'amitah"*) [i.e., gives substance to the commandments in the physical word by performing them], is considered as though he substantiated (*asah*) himself, as it is stated: "God commanded me at that time to teach you the statutes and laws, so that you perform (*la'asotkhem*) them" (Deut. 4:14). It does not state "to perform" (*la'asot*), but "to make yourselves through them" (*la'asotkhem otam*). We derive from here that he is considered as though he made himself.[18]

The superficial approach to Torah study views it as the absorption of information, like filling a container. In truth, when it comes to Torah study, one cannot rely on the halakhic principle that "listening is tantamount to responding." One must not be content with the passive reception of Torah from his teachers and peers, without acquiring wisdom on his own. The purpose of Torah study is to make the man, and for man to make himself. One of the most painful discoveries is that truth is not something that one person tells another, but rather what a person recognizes as true, drawing from the deepest recesses of a soul which craves knowledge and understanding. As long as one is unable to distinguish

---

18. *Midrash Tanḥuma* (Buber ed.), *Ki Tavo* 3.

between truth and falsehood on his own, truth is not truth, because it is not his own; it is merely something written in a book. Only when the truth becomes part of one's essence is it really truth.

Therefore, one who was not changed or affected by his Torah study has not yet discerned its truth. Man possesses intelligence and mental abilities in potential, and when he realizes their potential by studying Torah to discern its truth, thereby revealing the Torah's wisdom, he is considered self-made. It is as though he has created himself anew.

Torah study is a challenge of intellectual and personal development – a challenge that lasts a lifetime and demands a great deal of investment. Only one who studies the Torah of truth can identify the resonance of God's voice in the world. Only one who truly studies – that is, who develops his logical reasoning and devotes himself to studying with honesty and integrity – attains the Torah of truth.

The midrash cited above teaches two principles. The first is "that day" – each day the Torah should be new to you. The second is that one must study Torah to discern its truth, and doing so renders one "self-made." In actuality, these two principles are two facets of the same idea. The true Torah is the Torah that finds expression in a person who is in constant development, even from one day to the next. If someone is not the same person today that he was yesterday, then the Torah he studies today is also new and is not the Torah of yesterday. If one cannot sense this, then he is not studying the Torah of truth.

Torah study depends on the efforts one makes and on what he inherited and learned from earlier generations. Each generation adds wisdom, which constantly accumulates. Still, there is a difference between empirical wisdom and the wisdom of the Torah. As Rabbi Avraham, the son of Maimonides, wrote:

> Know that it is your duty to understand that anyone who wishes to assert a specific idea, and, in deference to its author, accepts it without examining or understanding its content in order to determine whether it is true or not, exhibits poor character, and this is forbidden by the Torah as well as by logic. It is forbidden by logic because it inevitably results in deficient and defective

thinking about what one must believe. It is forbidden by the Torah because it deviates from the path of truth and straightforward thinking ... to accept an idea and assert it without evidence, out of deference to its author, claiming that he is undoubtedly correct because he is a great man like Heiman, Kalkol, and Darda (I Kings 5:11). None of this constitutes evidence, and it is therefore forbidden [to accept such ideas uncritically].

Accordingly, we have no obligation to defend the ideas and statements of the Sages of the Talmud about medicine, natural science, and astronomy just because of the greatness of their character, the perfect quality of their interpretation of the Torah in all its particulars, and the integrity of their statements explaining its principles and details. We trust their interpretations of the Torah, whose wisdom they possess fully, and which has been given to them so they may instruct man, as it is stated: "In accordance with the instruction (*torah*) that they instruct to you (*yorukha*)" (Deut. 17:11).[19]

Rabbi Avraham explains that we must distinguish between the wisdom of the Torah and empirical wisdom. The wisdom of the Torah has been transmitted to the Sages of our tradition, whom Maimonides calls "the bearers of the teaching" (*ma'atikei hashemu'a*),[20] and who transmit the tradition that began with Moses from one generation to the next. We must make special efforts to learn the wisdom of the Torah at their feet.

However, this is not the case with regard to the natural sciences. The Sages did not disconnect themselves from empirical wisdom, as indeed no one should, but knowledge of the natural sciences is not revealed by God. Rather, each generation must investigate, contemplate, and attempt to advance its understanding of the world; later generations will build on those advances. Sometimes an apparent discovery will be

---

19. "Hama'amar al Derashot Hazal," in *Milhamot Hashem*, R. Reuven Margolies edition (Jerusalem: Mossad HaRav Kook, 1952), 83–84. (The essay also appears as an introduction to the work *Ein Ya'akov*.)
20. Introduction to *Mishneh Torah*, halakha 24; *Hilkhot Talmud Torah* 1:9.

disproven. This, too, is a form of progress. Nowadays, an average person knows things that in the past were unknown to even the wisest of men.

It stands to reason that the Sages' statements about empirical wisdom reflect only the state of science in their time. It does not minimize the honor of the Sages even one bit if today we do not accept what they said about natural sciences like astronomy and medicine. One who follows talmudic medical prescriptions could well harm himself. Rather, one must follow the treatment prescribed by the best doctors of his time and place.

Even with regard to the wisdom of the Torah, although the Torah was given to us at Sinai and is transmitted to us by the *ma'atikei hashemu'a*, in whose footsteps we must follow, nevertheless, every person, in each generation, is commanded to study Torah to discern its truth with his own mind. Thus, for example, Rabbi Avraham, the son of Maimonides, wrote:

> It is possible that something that was not clear to earlier generations will be clarified to later generations. This will happen in most cases, for a member of a later generation receives, in a more understandable form, that which his predecessors worked hard to explain. Thus, he is free to resolve other questions and reach conclusions that they could not because they were preoccupied with other more urgent matters. For that reason, the conventional halakhic presumption vis-à-vis the Sages of the Talmud is that "the law follows the later [authority]" (*hilkheta kebatrai*)[21] – even though they also stated: "The fingernail of the earlier authorities is thicker than the belly of the later authorities" (Yoma 9b). It is not that the later scholar is closer to perfection than the earlier scholar in all cases, rather, the later scholar studies the statements of earlier authorities, builds upon them, and learns from them.... Hence, there is no reason for one with a healthy mind and good

---

21. Editor's note: This rule does not appear in the Talmud itself. See Shai Akavya Wozner, "Hilkheta Kebatrai – Iyun Mehudash," *Shenaton Mishpat HaIvri* 20 (5755–5757), 151–67 (Heb.); Yehuda Zvi Stampfer, "Hilkheta Ke-batrai – Gishot Shonot Betekufat HaGeonim," *Shenaton Mishpat HaIvri* 22 (5761–5763), 176–77 (Heb.).

reasoning ability to reject an opinion expounded and substantiated by a later scholar by saying: "This was not explained thus by your predecessors."[22]

Nahmanides as well, at the end of the introduction to his glosses on *Sefer Hamitzvot*, after vigorously defending *Halakhot Gedolot*'s enumeration of the mitzvot, emphasizes his commitment to truth:

> Yet I, despite my urge and my desire to be a disciple of the earlier [sages], to uphold and reinforce their words, to make them as a necklace for my neck and a bracelet on my arm, I will not always be their book-carrying donkey. I will clarify their path, and I will know their worth. But when they do not contain my ideas, I will contest them from on the ground; I will judge according to what I see. And regarding clear halakha, I will show no favoritism in matters of Torah. For God grants wisdom in all ages and all times. He will not withhold good from those who walk [the path of] perfection.

In recent generations, R. Ḥayim of Volozhin, a disciple of the Vilna Gaon, wrote:

> …It is forbidden for a student to accept the words of his master if he has questions about them. Sometimes the truth will be with the disciple, just as a small twig can ignite a large branch…. This is the meaning of the statement: "Your house should be a meeting place for sages, and you shall become covered in dust (*mit'avek*)" (Mishna Avot 1:4), in the sense of "a man wrestled (*va-ye'avek*) with him" (Gen. 32:25), which refers to wrestling in context of combat…. We are permitted to wrestle and argue about their words, to answer their questions, not to show favoritism to any man, but only to love the truth. However, all of this notwithstanding, one should take care not to speak arrogantly

---

22. *Hamaspik Le'ovdei Hashem* [*A Comprehensive Guide for Servants of God*], Dana Edition (Ramat Gan: Bar Ilan University Press, 1989), 176–77.

or boastfully about finding occasion for dispute, and he must not imagine that he is as great as his master or as the author of the book he is criticizing. He should know deep down that he often does not understand the words or their intent. Therefore, he should be exceedingly humble, saying: "True, I am unworthy, but it is Torah...." Thus, the statement "become covered in dust," as above, is on condition that it is "from the dust of their feet," that is, humbly and submissively, arguing with them from on the ground.[23]

The Torah has been in our hands since Sinai, but it was given to every man so he may toil over it with his mind. Torah study demands courage, self-criticism, and logical reasoning.

The Talmud (Yevamot 62a) recounts:

Moses did three things on his own initiative, and his opinion corresponded to that of God: He separated from his wife, smashed the Tablets, and added one day.

He separated from his wife. What did he expound? He said: "If to the Israelites, with whom the Divine Presence did not speak but briefly, and at a set time, the Torah said: 'Do not approach a woman' (Ex. 19:15), then I, who am singled out to hear God speak at any moment, without a fixed time, should certainly [separate from my wife]." His opinion corresponded to that of God, as it is stated: "Go say to them: 'Return to your tents,' but you stand here with Me" (Deut. 5:26–27).

He smashed the Tablets. What did he expound? He said: "If about the Paschal offering, which is but one of 613 commandments, the Torah said: 'No stranger shall eat from it' (Ex. 12:43), then it should certainly apply to the entire Torah vis-à-vis Israelite apostates." His opinion corresponded to that of God, as it is stated: "That you smashed (*asher shibarta*)" (Ex. 34:1), and

Reish Lakish said: "The Holy One said to Moses: 'More power
to you, for you smashed (*yishar koḥakha sheshibarta*).'"

He added one day [of separation between man and wife
in preparation for the giving of the Torah] of his own initiative.
[Rashi: The Holy One said to him: "Sanctify them today and
tomorrow" (Ex. 19:10), yet he said, "Be ready for three days
hence."] What did he expound? It is stated: "Sanctify them today
and tomorrow." Today is just like tomorrow. Just as "tomorrow"
includes the previous night, so too "today" includes the previous night. But today's night is already past! We thus infer that
the two days exclude today. His opinion corresponded to that of
God since the Divine Presence did not descend until Shabbat.
[Rashi: In Shabbat 86a, we learned that they separated from their
wives on Wednesday, remained separated all Thursday and Friday,
and then the Divine Presence devolved on Shabbat, which was
the third full day. The first day did not count, since its night was
not included.]

How could Moses deviate from God's command on his own initiative?
Why didn't he ask God before acting? We find that the Talmud occasionally asks: "Why do I need a proof text? It makes sense!"[24] That is, when
one studies Torah, logical reasoning must guide him. Moses smashed
the Tablets because he ascertained that the nation was not yet ready
to accept the Torah. A nation that worships a calf, seeks false religious
experiences, and deludes itself, is not yet fit to receive the Torah. One
can attain true values only through readiness to change oneself; one who
believes that good is external deludes himself, distorts the truth, and ultimately worships an idol. This was the sin of the golden calf, about which
the Israelites said: "These are your gods, O Israel, who raised you up out
of the land of Egypt" (Ex. 32:4). Moses understood that if he would give
the Tablets to Israel while they worshipped a calf, they would not attain
the Torah either. Moreover, they would be likely to shatter the Tablets
themselves, and for such a sin, there would be no atonement. Moses did

24. Ketubot 22a; Bava Kama 46b; Nidda 25a.

not need to ask what the law requires. He understood on his own that this was not the time to give the Torah.

The same applies to his separation from his wife. When he heard that one must prepare himself for Divine revelation, it became clear to him that since he must always be ready to serve, he could not be at home in his tent. There was no need to ask a question. This is not a law, but just good sense. So too with regard to God's command, "Sanctify them today and tomorrow." Moses knew that the allotted time would not suffice, and that the results could be harmful. It was thus clear to him that another day must be added, and the Holy One agreed.

One must understand not only what is written in the Torah, but also the goals it sets for us, the aims that it demands we achieve. There are those for whom studying Torah causes fear of independent, logical reasoning. But in fact, one need not always search for an explicit ruling in *Shulḥan Arukh* or other texts. Rather, using logical reasoning, one must constantly reflect on what the Torah commands, what its goals are, and how the Torah's laws can be applied correctly, such that one's actions lead to the ends that the Torah seeks.

This pertains to both Torah study and the observance of mitzvot. It holds true for mitzvot between man and God and even more so for interpersonal mitzvot, because human relationships, by their very nature, cannot be governed solely by the written word. Rather, when determining interpersonal matters, one must employ logical reasoning that originates in an honest, sensitive, and understanding heart. In truth, the same applies to mitzvot between man and God, especially since they too are intended to promote interpersonal relationships as well.[25]

Man's duty to uphold the Torah entails not only acting in accordance with the letter of the law, but also critically assessing the consequences of his actions. To study Torah properly, one must use his intelligence to apply concepts to the real world and to determine what

---

25. See *The Guide of the Perplexed*, translated by S. Pines (Chicago: University of Chicago Press, 1963), III:35, p. 538: "It is known that all the commandments are divided into two groups: transgressions between man and his fellow man and transgressions between man and God...even though in reality these sometimes may affect relations between man and his fellow man."

is true and what is not. This demands effort and experience. One cannot grow in Torah unless he employs all the powers of his mind and heart, and each individual is required to make use of his own unique heart in particular. But even this is insufficient. One must also observe the real world and examine it with open eyes. The book alone is insufficient; to implement the Torah within the real world, one must study and understand the world as it really is.

The Individual and Society

Just as individuals undergo phases of development before reaching spiritual maturity, so too, the Jewish people as a whole progresses through historical eras that parallel the phases of human development. In each of these eras, the Torah serves as our guide and lodestar; the Torah was not given to one generation, but to all generations.

Had God wanted, He could have imbued us with a natural tendency to obey His commandments. Just as He endowed various animals – man included – with instincts for specific behaviors, so too, He could have made a creature that naturally avoids transgression and performs mitzvot. Yet, "if it were His will that the nature of any human individual should be changed because of what He, may He be exalted, wills from the individual, the sending of the prophets and the giving of the Law would have been useless."[26] Fulfillment of the mitzvot has value only if it stems from man's free will. Otherwise, it is meaningless action.

The Torah contains guidance and direction for each phase, from the stages of individual and national infancy, to the highest stages of individual perfection and national development.

Maimonides illustrated this with a parable:

> When teaching children ... one should teach them to serve [God] out of fear [of punishment] or to receive reward.[27]
>
> A young child was brought to a teacher to study Torah .... He said to him, "Study, and I will give you nuts or figs".... He studies hard, not for the sake of the study itself – for he does

---

26. Ibid., III:32, p. 529.
27. *Hilkhot Teshuva* 10:5.

not realize its value – but to get the treat.... When [the student]
grows older and matures, he no longer craves the object that he
once deemed important. Rather, he desires other things instead.
[The teacher] should whet [the student's] appetite again, with
the object that he prefers now.²⁸

This process continues, until one has ascended the steps of wisdom, and
understands that "The sole purpose of truth is to know that it is true. The
mitzvot are truths. Thus, their purpose is their performance [itself]."²⁹

As with the education of an individual, so it is with the education of a nation. The Sages understood that fear was the main motivation during the first stage of the nation's development:

> "They stood beneath the mountain" (Ex. 19:17): R. Avdimi bar
> Hama bar Hasa said: This teaches that the Holy One suspended
> the mountain over them like a barrel and said to them: "If you
> accept the Torah – all is well. If not – there will be your burial.³⁰

Man is endowed with free choice, but he is worthy of being created
only if he chooses good. If there is no one to accept the Torah, which
makes it possible to progress toward the goal of choosing good, then the
whole world is not worthwhile, and it would be fitting for it to return to
the primordial chaos. The Sages expressed this in the form of a threat:
"there will be your grave." As the Talmud further elaborates: "The Holy
One stipulated with creation: If the Israelites accept the Torah, you will
endure; if not, I will return you to primordial chaos."³¹

However, if the Jewish people accepted the Torah based on the
threatened destruction of the world, it was not freely chosen because
it was the good and true choice, but out of fear. Although Israel indeed
proclaimed, "We will do and we will obey" (Ex. 24:7), they likely had

---

28. *Commentary on the Mishna*, Introduction to the Tenth Chapter of Sanhedrin (*Perek Ḥelek*), (Maaleh Adumim: Shilat, 1996) p. 131.
29. Ibid., pp. 131–32.
30. Shabbat 88a.
31. Ibid.

no free choice. A choice made under threat and intimidation has very little value. Thus, the Talmud continues: "R. Aḥa b. Yaakov said: This constitutes a substantial caveat (*moda'a*) against the Torah." A *moda'a* is a declaration that one's future action is being performed under duress, against his will, and without consent; such a declaration constitutes grounds to void an agreement. Thus, according to R. Aḥa, this *moda'a* could have voided the Israelites' acceptance of the Torah.

But, the Talmud continues, "Rava said: Nevertheless, they reaccepted it in the days of Ahasuerus, as it is written, 'The Jews upheld and accepted' (Esther 9:27). They upheld what they had already accepted."[32] Rashi explains: "Out of love for the miracle performed on their behalf." Rava agrees that the acceptance of the Torah at Mount Sinai was not a fully binding acceptance. Rather, the acceptance of the Torah at Sinai was the first stage in the nation's education in the service of God. During this phase, absence of wholehearted will is not a defect, just as fear is the primary motivator during the first phase of an individual's education.

This first phase lasted, according to Rava, a thousand years, through the periods of the judges and kings, through the days of the First Temple and the Babylonian exile, until the miracle of Purim. That entire period, even those generations in which the Torah was sovereign over Israel, was an epoch of fear. In that age, idol worship did not disappear in Israel. Occasionally, the people became aware that their entire existence depended on the Torah, and that if they rejected it, "that would be their grave." In those instances, they returned to the Torah and mitzvot. Nevertheless, since they acted out of fear, their acceptance of the Torah was not considered true acceptance.

The second stage began in the days of Ahaseurus. Like a youngster who studies Torah in order to receive treats, Israel accepted the Torah "out of love for the miracle performed on their behalf." Now, "all the rulers of the provinces... showed deference to the Jews" (Esther 9:3). The Second Temple began a new phase of Jewish history. Idolatry disappeared completely, and Jewish influence began to spread to other nations – through the Septuagint, for example, and by other means.

---

32. Ibid.

This acceptance of the Torah no longer had the status of a coerced agreement. No *moda'a* could be declared, since one who commits to something because he wants to reap its benefits certainly has every intention to keep to the agreement.[33] Yet, though the acceptance of the Torah was now a binding one, it was not yet made out of truly free choice. There was still an element of coercion, and so it does not express the glory of man, the Divine image within him.

Several centuries later, Antigonus of Sokho reckoned that the time had come to announce the end of the second phase of the nation's education. "He would say: Do not be as servants who serve the master in order to receive reward. Rather, be like servants who serve the master regardless of reward."[34] "They meant by this that one should believe in the truth for the sake of truth; and this is the notion of serving out of love."[35] However, the generation was not yet ready; two disciples, Zadok and Boethus, distorted their master's words and went astray. "They rose up and separated themselves from the Torah. Two deviant sects originated with them: the Sadducees (Zadokites) and Boethusians."[36]

Yet throughout those times, there was progress. Outstanding members of the nation attained great heights, and the impact of Torah education was discernible even among the common folk. False notions that had been prevalent among the people gradually vanished. Throughout the First Temple era, despite the revelation of the Divine Presence in the Temple, idolatrous belief remained very strong. Even when those who served God prevailed, idolatry never completely disappeared; it always remained hidden beneath the surface, ready to burst forth at any opportunity. Not so during the Second Temple era. The Men of the Great Assembly eliminated the idolatrous impulse.[37] The efforts of the Great Assembly and its influence prevented idolatry from ever reappearing. A thousand years of Torah had left an indelible mark on the entire Jewish people.

---

33. As stated in Bava Batra 47b: "Self-coercion is different."
34. Mishna Avot 1:3.
35. *Commentary on the Mishna*, Introduction to the Tenth Chapter of Sanhedrin (*Perek Ḥelek*), p. 132.
36. *Avot DeRabbi Natan* 5:2.
37. Yoma 69b; Sanhedrin 64a; Arakhin 32b.

Idolatrous belief was entirely eliminated, uprooted from the hearts of even the least of the Jews. Zadok and Boethus too could not budge the Torah from the center of Jewish consciousness. The Torah became the symbol of Jewish identity; and monotheism was the unique characteristic of the Jews, setting them apart from all other peoples.

Serving God Out of Love

Although our generation, relative to earlier generations, is lacking with respect to faith and mitzva observance, the deepening awareness of individual freedom is a definite advancement over those earlier generations. Until the modern era, an authoritarian worldview which viewed obedience as the supreme value prevailed. Today, freedom is at the top of our priority scale. Only one who is aware of the magnitude of his power to choose can act out of truly free will.

In our times, there has been an increase in the number of people who are not impressed by the notion of reward and punishment. Freedom is what wins hearts today, and people today are willing to sacrifice and suffer greatly for the sake of individual freedom. This very freedom is a necessary condition for preparing hearts to fulfill the purpose of man's creation.

Educating one's child entails guiding him from stage to stage: from fear of punishment, to love of reward, and onward, step by step. The parent's efforts are premised on the belief that, at the end of this lengthy process, when the child reaches maturity, he will exercise his free will and choose the good and the true because they are good and true, not because of any other consideration. This is service out of love. The parent's faith reflects God's faith in humanity, as He "believed in His world and created it."[38] This faith is the axis of all history. And now, in our generation we are approaching national maturity, the age in which the human spirit recoils from any attempt to coerce it. There is no greater guarantee that mankind is on the verge of a great age in which the Divine image within man will appear in all its radiance.

In our day, adherents and teachers of the Torah face a dual challenge. On the one hand, they must acknowledge the greatness of a

---

38. *Sifrei Devarim* 307.

generation that yearns to be free. On the other hand, they must sense the full power of the light contained within the Torah, which, given the chance to shine forth into the world, would permeate every dark corner and awaken hearts to the truth.

Woe to him who flinches from this dual challenge, who is frightened by God's faith in man, who fears the slackening observance of the Torah and does not trust the power of free choice.

Fortunate is one who is familiar with his generation's turmoil, who has experienced, along with his contemporaries, the profound realization that without individual freedom, life loses its meaning. He will recognize that his task is to promote Torah values in such a way that they inspire people to adhere to them freely, not out of coercion. In the words of Ralbag:

> ...Our Torah differs from the precepts and rituals of other nations, for our Torah contains nothing that cannot be derived from logical reasoning and understanding. Accordingly, God-given rituals would attract people to their practice in and of themselves. This is not the case, however, with regard to the rituals of other nations, which are not structured according to logic and wisdom; these rituals are foreign to human nature. People observe them because they are compelled by fear of the regime and the fear of punishment, not in and of themselves.[39]

---

39. Ralbag, *Commentary on the Torah*, Deuteronomy 4, Lesson 14.
Compare this to Maimonides' illuminating words in *Moreh Nevukhim* III:11, pp. 440–41:
These great evils that come about between the human individuals...derive from ignorance, I mean from a privation of knowledge. Just as the blind man, because of absence of sight, does not cease stumbling, being wounded, and also wounding others, because he has nobody to guide him on his way, the various sects of men – every individual according to the extent of his ignorance – does to himself and to others great evils from which individuals of the species suffer. If there were knowledge, whose relation to the human form is like that of the faculty of sight to the eye, they would refrain from doing any harm to themselves and to others. For through cognition of the truth, enmity and hatred are removed and the inflicting of harm by people on one another is abolished. The prophet promised this when he said: "The wolf shall dwell with the lamb, and

Great is His steadfast love toward us. Now, we can provide illumination on His behalf, as He provided illumination for us. The people that returned to its land can now renew its everlasting covenant by a free choice. Only the personal example of true students of the Torah can bring about the dissemination of Torah throughout the Jewish people. The prophet has described the character of such individuals:

> Behold, My servant, whom I uphold; My chosen one, in whom I delight: I have placed My spirit upon him; he will teach justice to the nations. He will not cry out or shout; he will not make his voice heard in the street. He will not break [even] a weak reed or extinguish a dim wick. He will faithfully teach justice. He will not grow dim or weak until he establishes justice on earth; lands across the sea will await his Torah. (Is. 42:1–4)

---

the leopard shall lie down with the kid…and the cow and bear shall graze… and the sucking child shall play" (Is. 11:6–8). Then the text gives the reason for this, saying that the cause of the abolition of these enmities, these discords, and these tyrannies, will be the knowledge that men will then have concerning the true reality of the deity. For it says: "They shall not hurt nor destroy in all My holy mountain, for the earth shall be full of knowledge of the Lord, as the waters cover the sea" (ibid. 9). Know this.

(Compare this to *Mishneh Torah, Hilkhot Melakhim* 11:4; 12:1, 4–5.)

Also see *Mishneh Torah, Hilkhot Teshuva* 9:2: "The king who will arrive from the Davidic line will be wiser than Solomon and a prophet almost as great as Moses. Thus, he will teach the entire people and guide them on God's path…."

Chapter 2

The Role of the Commandments

The Ideal and the Real

Human beings and societies, according to the view of the Torah, are not static and unchanging. On the contrary, certain basic presumptions and assertions about man and his behavior should be considered accurate only in the era in which they were formulated.[1]

The system of Torah and mitzvot shapes society in two ways. On one hand, it imparts ideals that guide us to the highest levels of Divine service and teach us how to mold society into a vehicle for the Divine Presence. On the other hand, the Torah also contains legislation to counteract the evil present within the soul of the individual and the spirit of the nation, thus ensuring that the minimal conditions for spiritual flourishing are present in each generation, whatever its social, economic, and cultural circumstances.[2] To achieve the first objective, the Torah sets lofty goals which remain a challenge throughout time; even the noblest of spirits cannot achieve them in full. At the same time, in order to achieve the second objective, the Torah sets behavioral norms

---

1. See *Moreh Nevukhim* III:29.
2. Ibid. III:32.

and standards that all people are capable of accepting – standards below which the very survival of the individual and his society is threatened and any hope of spiritual advancement is negated.

The 613 mitzvot can be divided into two categories. Some mitzvot retain the same character across all eras; they apply to the end of days as they did to the beginning. Attaining higher levels of moral refinement and intellectual development grants access to deeper understandings of these mitzvot and creates broader horizons for their practical fulfillment. Other mitzvot are primarily aimed at improving society and advancing it to a state that will enable the realization of man's ultimate purpose: creating God's Kingdom on earth.

It is impossible for there to be a legal system that prescribes, in advance, the proper reaction to every possible scenario. Reaching a definitive conclusion in each case based on legal or moral principles would require familiarity with all relevant factors and considerations, including knowledge of human nature and the essence of human existence. These factors remain unknown, and may be unknowable because they are beyond human comprehension. Even were we to possess all the necessary information, it remains possible that there would not be definitive conclusions for every possible scenario.

Consequently, the Torah did not provide principles from which we can deduce the appropriate ruling for each individual case that arises. Rather, the system of mitzvot is constructed primarily from numerous examples. The Sages said: "Scripture speaks in the present,"[3] which means that the Torah describes the common case, but does not intend for the law to apply solely in the case described. Rather, the cases that appear in Scripture are paradigmatic, and the law extends to analogous cases. Specific cases are thus generalized, as Maimonides describes: "What [Joshua] had not heard from Moses in detail he derived by analogy, by means of the thirteen principles that had been given to him at Sinai. These are 'the thirteen hermeneutical principles by which the Torah is expounded.'"[4]

This makes it possible to apply halakha to many cases despite the variability of conditions from one generation to the next. However,

---

3. Mishna Bava Kama 5:7.
4. *Introduction to the Commentary on the Mishna*, p. 28 (Maaleh Adumim: Shilat, 1996).

this path also invites disagreement: "So-and-so draws support from one prooftext, so-and-so draws support from another prooftext, and the like."[5] Hence, there are matters about which there is no clear halakha, and even though "both these and those" opinions originate as "words of the living God,"[6] it is necessary, in some cases, to decide between opposing views. Otherwise, there is a risk that some will practice in one way, another group will practice differently, and the result is a proliferation of factions and disputes.

Additionally, the sages of each generation understood that enactments must be made, based on the needs of the particular time and place, "to benefit interpersonal conduct in a way that does not add to or derogate from the Torah, or to enhance people's welfare as it relates to Torah. The Sages call these enactments (*takanot*) and practices (*minhagot*)."[7] Such enactments are required specifically when a gap has developed between halakha and life's changing conditions.

One of our medieval sages articulated this approach well:

> Our perfect Torah provided general rules for improving human character and behavior. It is written: "Be holy" (Lev. 19:2), which means that one should not be overcome with desires, as the Sages said, "Sanctify yourself with that which is permitted to you."[8] It is similarly stated: "Do that which is right and good" (Deut. 6:18) which means that one should behave benevolently and honestly toward others. It would not have been fitting to command the particulars of all these principles, because the mitzvot of the Torah apply at all times, in every era, and in every situation, and one must perform them no matter what, yet temperaments and manners vary from person to person and from era to era. The Sages listed some useful particular applications of these principles, some of which they enacted as black-letter law, and others as the preferred or pious practice.[9]

---

5. *Introduction to the Commentary on the Mishna*, p. 40.
6. Eiruvin 13b.
7. *Introduction to the Commentary on the Mishna*, p. 42.
8. Yevamot 20a.
9. R. Vidal of Toulouse, *Maggid Mishneh, Hilkhot Shekhenim* 14:5.

Social, economic, and technological innovations and developments open new vistas for legislation that will lead to performance of "that which is right and good." In every era, we must consider and determine what is right and good; this naturally leads to disagreements among our sages.

To illustrate this, we will discuss two topics that relate to society. We can then extrapolate from these straightforward but characteristic examples to other issues.

The Beautiful Captive Woman

Peace is an ideal for which we yearn, but we have not yet been privileged to witness the fulfillment of the prophecy, "Nation will not lift up sword against nation, nor will they train for war anymore" (Is. 2:4); war is still with us. It is our bitter lot that in order to save lives we have had to kill enemies. The yearning for peace and revulsion from war cry out from all of Scripture. The Torah recognizes the necessity of war, but it does not ignore the moral crisis that it generates. To the best of my knowledge, no ancient Near Eastern legal code placed restrictions on how war is waged. This stands in stark contrast to our Torah, which places legal limitations on warfare, to ensure that even as rivers of blood are spilled, no Jewish soldier will erase the Divine image from his soul.

There are numerous halakhot that pertain to warfare. Maimonides summarized these halakhot in chapter 6 of *Hilkhot Melakhim*: "We do not wage war against anyone until we have offered peace" (6:1); "we do not kill women and children" (6:4); "when besieging a city to conquer it, we do not surround it on all sides, but only on three sides, leaving room for fugitives and for anyone else who wishes to flee for his life" (6:7). Even Israel's enemies were aware that Israel espouses different values and does not thirst for blood. Indeed, Scripture recounts how the princes and officers of Aram said to their defeated king: "We have heard that the Israelite kings are magnanimous" (I Kings 20:31).

War, though it has always been part of human history, is wretched. By its very nature, it effects dramatic changes within the souls of its participants. It threatens to evoke in man in general, and soldiers in particular, their basest, most animalistic energies.

Not only does the Torah admonish against turning war into a cruel, murderous rampage; it is also concerned for the soul of the individual soldier, lest he, God forbid, destroy the Divine image within him, and for Jewish military encampments, lest their sanctity be desecrated. The Torah therefore saw fit to offer special guidance for combatants, in recognition of the uniqueness of their circumstances. This guidance operates on two planes: 1) setting aspirational norms; and 2) setting rules from which there may be no deviation.

In order to instill in soldiers that "the Lord your God walks in the midst of your encampment,"[10] and in order to direct them toward proper behavior that will preserve the Divine image within them, the Torah even commands that the sanitary conditions of the encampment be maintained. Maimonides thus rules:

> It is forbidden to relieve oneself inside the encampment or in any open field. Rather, there is a positive commandment to designate a path that will be set aside for relieving oneself, as [Scripture] states: "You shall have an area outside the encampment" (Deut. 23:13). It is also a positive commandment for everyone to have a spike among his gear; he shall go out to that path, dig with [the spike], relieve himself, and then cover it up, as it is stated: "You shall have a spike amongst your equipment" (ibid. 14).... "Your encampment shall be holy" (ibid. 15).[11]

He explains:

> This book also includes the commandment to prepare a [secluded] place and a paddle. For one of the purposes of this Law, as I have made known to you, is cleanliness, and avoidance of excrements and dirt, and man's not being like the beasts. And this commandment also fortifies, by means of the actions it enjoins, the certainty of the combatants that the *Shekhina* has descended among them – as is explained in the reason given for it: "For the Lord your God walks in the midst of your camp." It has also included another notion, saying: "That He see no unclean

thing in you, and turn away from you" (ibid. 14), this being against sexual immorality which, as is well known, is widespread among soldiers in a camp after they have stayed for a long time away from their homes. Accordingly, He, may He be exalted, has commanded us to perform actions that call to mind that the *Shekhina* has descended among us so that we should be preserved from those actions, and has said: "Therefore shall your camp be holy; that He see no unclean thing in you".... Accordingly, everyone should have in his mind that the camp is like a Sanctuary of the Lord, and not like the camps of the Gentiles destined only to destroy and to do wrong and to harm the others and rob them of their property.[12]

There is nothing more hateful than war, which breaks down all inhibitions and makes bloodshed its goal. However, in order to protect Israel from its enemies war cannot be entirely avoided. Thus, due to exigent circumstances during warfare, the Torah relaxed some laws.

The Torah saw fit to be lenient about certain specific temptations that arise in the course of war, when passions flare. If a soldier's impulses get the better of him, and he is unable to withstand temptation – especially in ancient times, when soldiers were away from home for long stretches and when all moral boundaries were breached – the Torah permitted him to take a gentile wife. Yet even in these circumstances, the Torah imposed restrictions on him, to limit his fall as much as possible.

The Torah addresses this case in the passage of the *eshet yefat to'ar*, the beautiful captive woman:

> When you go out to war against your enemies, and the Lord your God delivers them into your hand, and you take captives, and you see among the captives a beautiful woman, and you desire her, and you take her to be a wife. Then you shall bring her into your home, and she shall shave her hair and grow her nails. She shall remove her captive's clothing, and she shall live in your house,

---

12. *Moreh Nevukhim* III:41, pp. 566–67.

mourning her father and mother, for a month. Afterward, you may come to her and cohabit with her, and she shall be your wife. Then, if you do not desire her, you shall set her free. You shall not sell her for money. You shall not enslave her, for you have had your way with her.[13]

The Sages explained:

> The Torah here is addressing the evil impulse [*yetzer hara*]: It is better to eat a properly slaughtered animal, even though it is dying, than to eat it after it has died on its own and become a *nevela* [i.e., even though it is not an ideal situation, the Torah provides a permitted, less debasing alternative].[14]

Maimonides clarified further:

> You know their dictum: "The Torah here is addressing the evil impulse." Nevertheless, this commandment includes an exhortation to noble moral qualities, which excellent men must acquire in a way I shall indicate. For though his desire overcomes him and he cannot hold back, it is necessary for him to bring her to a hidden place; as it says: "into your home." And as [the Sages] have explained, he is not permitted to do her violence during the war. And he is not allowed sexual intercourse with her for the second time before her grief has calmed down and her sorrow has been quieted.[15]

The Sages disagree about when the beautiful captive woman first becomes permitted.[16] Some maintain that she becomes permitted to the soldier only after she has done everything prescribed (shaving her head, etc.) and moved into his home. This is Nahmanides' explanation in his

---

13. Deuteronomy 21:10–14.
14. Kiddushin 21b–22a.
15. *Moreh Nevukhim* III:41, p. 567.
16. Y. Makkot 2:6.

commentary to the Torah.[17] However, according to a second view in the Yerushalmi, it is permitted to cohabit with her during the time of war. This is also the view of the Bavli,[18] and Maimonides rules accordingly: "'You shall bring her' – he brings her into a vacant area and then cohabits with her."[19] Ralbag elaborates on this in his commentary on the Torah:

> The meaning of "you shall take her to be a wife" is that he may cohabit with her, yet the language also suggests that it is unbecoming for him to take her to commit this indecency unless his purpose is to marry her afterward. Thus, the Torah states immediately afterward, "you shall bring her into your home," indicating that it is not proper to treat her lawlessly. Rather, he should bring her into his home or somewhere similar, which they can visit discreetly, and where he may cohabit with her… "you shall bring her into your home" – the Torah explains that it is not proper for him to cohabit with her and then abandon her immediately after he has had his way with her, or to falter with her again. Rather, he is required to bring her into his home.[20]

Even though the Torah permitted something as a concession to man's baser impulses, it regulated it as much as possible and did not permit him to cohabit with her and then abandon her. Rather, it made him responsible for the woman, obliging him to fulfill all of the requirements that appear in the biblical passage. As Maimonides summarizes:

> After his first cohabitation with her, while she is still a gentile, if she accepts upon herself to enter under the wings of the Divine Presence, she is immediately immersed in a ritual bath for the sake of conversion. If she does not accept, she lives in his house for a month, as it is stated: "mourning her father and mother, for a month." She similarly weeps over her religion, and he may not

---

17. Deuteronomy 21:13.
18. Kiddushin 21b.
19. *Hilkhot Melakhim* 8:3.
20. Commentary on Deuteronomy 21:11.

stop her. She grows out her fingernails and shaves her head so that he finds her repulsive. She shall be with him in his home: he sees her when he enters, and he sees her when she leaves, so that he despises her…. If she accepts and he wants her, she shall convert, immersing like all converts…. If he does not want her, he shall set her free.[21]

He further states:

> She may also, for thirty days in public, profess her religion, even in an idolatrous cult, and may not during that period be taken to task because of a belief.[22]

Meiri elaborates further:

> Rather, after he cohabits with her, it is proper for him to speak tenderly to her, to draw her near so she may find shelter under the wings of the Divine Presence…. If she does not accept this, he brings her to his house gently, without reprimand or commotion, and she dwells there for thirty days. He lets her weep over her father, her mother, and her family, and over the abandonment of her religion and culture. He does not withhold this from her.[23]

The Torah further commands: "Then, if you do not desire her, you shall set her free. You shall not sell her for money. You shall not enslave her, for you have had your way with her." That is, because he had his way with her, he must concern himself with her freedom. He must either "marry her [properly,] with a *ketuba* and *kiddushin*,"[24] or liberate her.

There is still more we can learn from studying this mitzva: We must now consider the *category* to which this mitzva belongs.

---

21. *Hilkhot Melakhim* 8:5–6.
22. *Moreh Nevukhim* III:41, p. 567.
23. Meiri on Kiddushin 22a.
24. *Hilkhot Melakhim* 8:5.

Maimonides wrote in *Sefer Hamitzvot*: "...we have been commanded regarding the law (*din*) of the beautiful captive woman."[25] Similarly, in the list of mitzvot that appears at the beginning of *Hilkhot Melakhim*, he writes: "The law (*din*) of the beautiful captive." What is the meaning of this formulation, which categorizes this mitzva as a *din*?

Some mitzvot require that we perform specific acts or refrain from specific acts. There are other mitzvot, of a different sort entirely, that establish legal definitions, and which Maimonides calls *dinim*. They establish, for example, which modes of acquisition are valid and which are not; what causes ritual impurity and what purifies one from such impurity; who can be bound by a particular contract, and who cannot; and so forth.

Thus, Maimonides wrote:

> Understand that whenever I enumerate something as one of the *dinim*, it is not a commandment to perform a specific act perforce. Rather, the mitzva is that we are commanded to apply this procedure to the particular matter.[26]

---

25. Positive commandment 221.
26. *Sefer Hamitzvot*, positive commandment 95. In positive commandment 96, he wrote: Our enumeration of each different type of ritual impurity as a positive commandment does not imply that we are obligated to defile ourselves with such impurities, nor that is it prohibited for us to become defiled, in which case it would be a negative commandment. Rather, the Torah's instruction that one who came into contact with a certain species becomes impure, or that a particular object causes one who touches it to contract a certain level of impurity, is a positive commandment. In other words, this law (*din*) that the Torah commanded is a mitzva, in that we say that one who touches a particular object in a particular manner becomes impure, whereas someone who was in such and such situation does not become impure. Becoming defiled is itself voluntary. If one wants he may become defiled, and if one wants he may avoid defilement.
  And in positive commandment 109:
  When we say that immersion is a mitzva, it does not mean that it is a positive commandment in the sense that anyone who is ritually impure is obligated to immerse, as anyone who dresses himself in a garment is obligated to place tzitzit on it, and anyone who owns a house must build a rail on the roof. Rather, I mean that the *din* of immersion is that we have been commanded that one who wishes to purify himself from defilement cannot do so except by immersing in

The mitzvot that relate to the beautiful captive woman are categorized as *dinim*. Fortunate is the man who is not overcome by his impulse to "eat the flesh of a dying animal" and is not attracted to a beautiful captive woman; the passage of *eshet yefat to'ar* is not addressed to him at all. However, considering the strain of war and the uncontrolled torrent of emotion in battle, the Torah created an exception to the prohibition against cohabiting with a gentile woman, under specific conditions. It established laws to minimize the damage caused by this surge of lust.

Slavery

> The reason man was created alone…is for the sake of peace among men, so no person can say to another, "My father was greater than yours"… and to proclaim the greatness of the Supreme King of Kings, the Holy One, blessed is He – for if a man mints a hundred coins with one mold, they are all alike, but the Supreme King of Kings, the Holy One, fashions every man in the mold of Adam, yet no one is a copy of his fellow. Therefore, everyone can proclaim: "The world was created for me!"[27]

Maimonides explained: "in the mold of Adam – in the form of the species of humankind, that which makes human beings human, which all humans share."[28]

Thus, from the very first chapters of Genesis, the Torah teaches that all men are of equal standing. However, people became depraved and subjugated one another; they created distinctions between men, between slaves and their masters. Yet these differences in status are not grounded in any reality. Before the Creator, all are equal. Only those who sow injustice ignore the fact that all human beings are created in the Divine image. Only an evildoer condemns a slave to subhuman treatment.

---

water…. It does not mean that we require him to immerse. Rather, one who wishes to remain impure…may do so.

27. Mishna Sanhedrin 4:5.
28. *Commentary on the Mishna*, Sanhedrin 4:5.

If I have shown contempt for the rights of my slave, male or female, when they brought complaint against me, then what can I do when God confronts me? When He calls me to account, what can I answer? Did He Who made me in the womb not also make him? Did not One form us both in the womb? (Job 31:13–15)[29]

Nevertheless, the Torah does recognize the institution of slavery. On one hand, the Torah clearly proclaims that the slave, like his master, and the maidservant, like her mistress, are fashioned in God's image. On the other hand, the Torah states: "You shall purchase male and female slaves from them…and they shall be your possession" (Lev. 25:44–45).

To understand this, consider the verse: "God led them not on the road to the land of the Philistines, though it was near, for God considered that the people might have regrets and return to Egypt upon seeing battle" (Ex. 13:17). Maimonides explains the principle derived from this verse:

> Just as God perplexed them in anticipation of what their bodies were naturally incapable of bearing – turning them away from the high road toward which they had been going, toward another road so that the first intention should be achieved – so did He in anticipation of what the soul is naturally incapable of receiving, prescribe the laws that we have mentioned so that the first intention should be achieved, namely, the apprehension of Him, may He be exalted, and the rejection of idolatry.[30]

---

29. Cf. Genesis Rabba 48:3: "R. Isei began: 'If I have shown contempt for the rights of my slave, male or female, when they brought complaint against me, what can I do when God confronts me? When he calls me to account, what can I answer?' R. Yosei's wife would quarrel with her maidservant. He [R. Yosei] contradicted his wife in the maidservant's presence. She said, "Why do you contradict me in the presence of my maidservant?" Said he: "Did Job not say, 'If I have shown contempt for the rights of my slave…'?""

30. *Moreh Nevukhim* III:32, p. 527; see also "Treatise on Resurrection," in *Iggerot HaRambam*, p. 369.

Given the constraints of reality, the Torah conceded the immediate and complete fulfillment of the ideal and instead preferred to advance society step by step, until the goal could be attained in full. This principle applies to the institution of slavery, as made clear in *Torat Kohanim*: "Lest you say...'what shall we use?' Scripture states, 'male and female slaves that shall be yours – from among the nations' (Lev. 25:44)."[31] In the ancient world, it was virtually impossible to sustain a robust economy without massive amounts of manpower, which was generally supplied by slaves. Eminent gentile thinkers, too, could not conceive of a thriving society that was not based on the cheap labor provided by large numbers of slaves.[32] It seemed an economic impossibility. "What shall we use?" was a serious question that could not be ignored.

However, the Torah revolutionized the institution of slavery. It instituted several basic principles that formed a "floor" of sorts, to prevent descent into the depths of depravity that existed in cultures of other nations. Thus, for example, the Torah states, in contrast to the laws that prevailed in the ancient world, that the slave's life belongs not to his master, but to the Supreme Master of all: "If a man strikes his male or female slave with a rod, and he dies as a result, he must be avenged" (Ex. 21:20). Additionally, even though the slave is indeed bound to serve his master, the Torah demonstrates concern for his spiritual life, and he is entitled to partake of Shabbat and its rest. Shabbat is sacred to master and slave alike, as the Torah states: "On the seventh day, you shall desist, so that your ox and donkey may rest, and the son of your female slave and the stranger may be refreshed (*yinafesh*)" (Ex. 23:12). The master must give rest even to his beast of burden, but for the slave, Shabbat offers more than rest and repose from his enslavement. Of him the Torah says "*yinafesh*,"[33] and it is the master's duty to ensure that the slave desists from working on

---

31. *Sifra Behar* 6:3.
32. Aristotle, *Politics* I:5, Stephen Everson, ed. and trans. (Cambridge: Cambridge University Press 1996), 16: "For that some should rule and others be ruled is a thing not only necessary, but expedient; from the hour of their birth, some are marked out for subjection, others for rule." Plato (*Laws* VII:1) describes a state in which the laws clearly distinguish between free citizens and slaves.
33. See *Moreh Nevukhim* I:67, p. 162, which explains: "from the word '*nefesh*'...it means that [his] purpose was perfected and all [his] will realized."

Shabbat. Still, slavery was not abolished, because under the conditions that prevailed then, it was impossible to completely abolish it.

As part of its elevation of the slave's status, the Torah saw fit to make mitzvot obligatory for him[34] and to bring him, in certain respects, under the wings of the Divine Presence. This, however, creates a more acute problem. On one hand, it is unconscionable that a slave who has already had a taste of the mitzvot would be allowed to return to idolatry. It is therefore forbidden to sell him to a non-Jew,[35] and certainly to restore him to his non-Jewish status. On the other hand, entering the covenant of Israel requires *voluntary* acceptance of the mitzvot. If an act of the owner frees the slave, there is no voluntary acceptance. There is also the concern that he would revert to his deviant ways. Furthermore, even if the slave were to proclaim day and night that he desires to become a righteous convert, it is presumably his desire for freedom speaking, not his willingness to serve God.

The emancipation of a large number of slaves who would then become part of the Jewish people, without a way to confirm the sincerity of their expressed desire to become righteous converts, would fundamentally alter the character of Jewish society. Thus, the acceptance of the institution of slavery by the halakhic system generates a paradox: despite the Torah's reservations about slavery, it creates a scenario whereby, at first glance, there is no lawful possibility of emancipation, for any act of emancipation is coercive by definition, and entry into Judaism by means of coercion is unthinkable. How can converts be accepted without evidence that their intentions are to truly assume the yoke of Torah and mitzvot?

Even so, the door was not shut completely. There is a Tannaitic dispute about whether the verse "you shall enslave them forever" (Lev. 25:46) articulates an obligation or merely permission. "'You shall enslave them forever' – this is permission, according to R. Yishmael; R. Akiva says: it is an obligation."[36] Some have indeed ruled in accordance with

---

34. See *Hilkhot Issurei Biah* 13:11, 14:9; *Hilkhot Mila* 1:1, 1:6. There is a type of slave who occupies an intermediate status and does not accept the mitzvot: the temporary slave.
35. *Hilkhot Avadim* 8:1.
36. Sota 3a.

R. Yishmael, explaining that even in his view there is a rabbinic prohibition,[37] yet many *Rishonim* decided in favor of R. Akiva's opinion; in either case, we must note the nature of this law.

Maimonides wrote in *Sefer Hamitzvot*:

> Mitzva 235 is the commandment regarding the law [*din*] of a Canaanite slave. We enslave him forever, and he is not emancipated except as a consequence of [his owner knocking out] a tooth, eye, or any other limb that cannot be restored. This is derived from the traditional interpretation of what the Exalted One said [in the Torah]: "you shall enslave them forever" and "If a man strikes [his slave's eye …]" (Ex. 21:26). In the words of the Talmud in Gittin (38b): "One who emancipates his slaves violates a positive commandment, as it is written: 'you shall enslave them forever,'" and the Torah states that he is emancipated through [the loss of] a tooth or eye.[38]

We have already explained that some mitzvot require us to perform certain acts or desist from certain acts, but that there is another category of mitzvot, called "*dinim*," which set legal parameters. The mitzvot relating to slavery belong to the category of *dinim*. The sum of all of the halakhot pertaining to the Canaanite slave is a single positive commandment: "The *din* of the Canaanite slave." There is no mitzva to purchase a Canaanite slave, and one who owns a Canaanite slave does not fulfill any mitzva thereby. The Torah's statement, "you shall enslave them forever," does not obligate anyone in any specific act, but rather establishes that there is no possibility of emancipation other than the loss of a tooth, eye, or other limb from the master's blow.[39]

Maimonides emphasized the difference between *dinim* and obligations elsewhere in *Sefer Hamitzvot* – in the general summary at the end of the list of positive commandments:

---

37. The opinion of "some commentators," cited in Meiri's commentary on Gittin 38b.
38. Positive commandment 235.
39. See, however, Nahmanides' gloss to *Sefer Hamitzvot*, positive commandment 235. He disagrees with Maimonides and enumerates two mitzvot pertaining to the Canaanite slave.

Some of these mitzvot are *dinim*, as we have explained, such as the
laws of the male or female Hebrew slave, the law of the Canaanite
slave, the law of the unpaid custodian, the law of the borrower,
and others we have mentioned earlier. It is possible for one to live
his entire life without becoming subject to this law or becoming
obligated by this mitzva.

However, even in the case of a *din*, if a legal mechanism to emancipate a
slave were found, it would be considered a circumvention of the law, and
consequently forbidden as a rabbinic safeguard. As Maimonides wrote:

A woman may purchase female slaves but not male slaves, even
minor male slaves, due to suspicion [of licentiousness]. However,
if she purchases them, she owns them, just as a man does…. It
is likewise forbidden for one to emancipate his slave, and one
who does so violates a positive commandment, as Scripture
states: "you shall enslave them forever." However, if he emancipated him, the emancipation is valid, as we have explained. One
may emancipate a slave for the purpose of a mitzva, even a rabbinic mitzva. For example, if there is no [quorum of] ten in the
synagogue, one may free his slave to complete the quorum. The
same applies to similar situations. Likewise, if people are acting
promiscuously with a female slave, and she has become a stumbling block for sinners, we compel her master to emancipate her
so that she may marry, thus removing this stumbling block. The
same applies to similar situations.[40]

Maimonides juxtaposed two halakhot here: the prohibition for a woman
to purchase male slaves, which is rabbinic in origin, and the prohibition
of emancipating slaves. The joining of these two halakhot teaches that
just as the prohibition for a woman to purchase male slaves is rabbinic,
due to suspected licentiousness, so too the prohibition of emancipating
slaves is rabbinic. The reason for the prohibition is that one who eman-
cipates his slave circumvents the law derived from "you shall enslave

40. *Hilkhot Avadim* 9:6.

them forever," which does not establish a procedure for emancipation. However, there is no mitzva from the Torah to enslave someone. Rather, there is a *din* that allows for enslavement, and so it is superseded by any mitzva, even a rabbinic mitzva.[41]

Meiri wrote similarly:

Even though the positive commandment is from the Torah, for the sake of a mitzva, the [Sages] were lenient, since [the commandment] does not apply equally to all, as there is no obligation to purchase a slave in order to fulfill "you shall enslave them forever."[42]

We thus learn that even though the Torah does not specify the possibility of emancipation, such a possibility is indeed implicit in the law, and the Sages revealed it: just as a writ of manumission is effective in the case of a slave that is emancipated due to loss of limb,[43] so it is effective to emancipate any slave. Thus, the Sages decreed that anyone who uses emancipatory language vis-à-vis his slave is "compelled to write him a writ of manumission."[44] Taking account of *why* the Torah made no provision for emancipation, the rabbis recognized that if the community were to be harmed by that omission, the master would be compelled to free the slave or maidservant.

The Sages devoted so much attention to improving the lot of slaves, and the national consciousness became so infused with the doctrine of equality, that at some point it became a Jewish characteristic that enemy regimes attempted to uproot. A *baraita* recounts that at a time of religious persecution, R. Elazar ben Parta was arrested by Roman officials and accused of five "offenses." One of them was: "Why did you emancipate your slaves?"[45] Rashi explains: "They had decreed against this because it was a Jewish religious practice."

---

41. There are *Rishonim* who explain the permit to emancipate the slave as a narrow ruling that cannot be generalized. See, for example, Rashba's commentary on Gittin 38b.
42. Meiri on Gittin 38b.
43. *Hilkhot Avadim* 5:4.
44. Ibid. 8:17.
45. Avoda Zara 17b.

Was this Jewish religious practice innovative? Certainly. Yet it was conceived and cultivated by the Torah's light. Its origins are in Scripture, though the world was not ready for it when the Torah was given. Yet over time, as human knowledge increased, new scientific discoveries and technologies harnessed energies far more powerful than manual labor, thus contributing greatly to general welfare and wellbeing. Divine providence has thus brought about the elimination of slavery in almost every country. Blessed is the One who, through the light of His Torah, has given mankind the understanding to recognize the Divine greatness ingrained in every human being. The abolition of slavery is in fact a partial realization of the ideals taught by the Torah, and it is clear to anyone who has studied a bit of the history of the West that the spread of Torah values was a decisive factor in this historical process.

This process continues to unfold "to improve the whole world so that it will worship God as one, as [Scripture] states: 'For then I will restore pure speech to the nations, so that they may all call God's name and worship Him, shoulder to shoulder (Zephaniah 3:6).'"[46]

The Mitzvot as Educational Values

The *dinim* of the beautiful captive woman and the Canaanite slave are examples of mitzvot that relate to specific circumstances; the goal of the Torah is for us to advance to a state in which these mitzvot are no longer relevant because the circumstances they require no longer exist. In the case of such mitzvot, if historical reality and human society have advanced, clearly we should not strive to turn back the clock.[47] The fact that a mitzva applies in a given circumstance does not imply that this circumstance is ideal. For instance, at the end of the *ḥalitza* (levirate divorce) ceremony, the judges of the rabbinical court say: "May it be God's will that Jewish women nevermore undergo *ḥalitza* or *yibum* (levirate marriage)."[48]

---

46. *Hilkhot Melakhim* 11:4.

47. In this context, many have debated Maimonides' views on animal sacrifice. See my essay, "Society and History: The Uniqueness of Maimonides," in my *Studies in the Thought of Maimonides* (Jerusalem: Yeshivat Birkat Moshe 2010), 214–27 (Heb.). See also below, pp. 174–175.

48. *Shulḥan Arukh, Even HaEzer*, "The Ḥalitza Procedure in Brief" (after §169), section 59. Another example can be found in the prayer of the High Priest in the Holy of

To be sure, these are not mitzvot that were initially given for a specific time and place, like the commands to the Israelites in the wilderness concerning their travels, the manna, water, etc. Maimonides made a count and found more than three hundred commandments that Moses issued to his generation but not to future generations.[49] When the judges pray that Jewish women nevermore have to undergo *ḥalitza*, they are praying that a mitzva that was given for all time never again be fulfilled. Likewise, when we thank God for ridding the world of slavery, we hope that the world never returns to its former state and that this mitzva has forever ceased to be practicable.

This gives rise to two basic questions: The first one relates to the parameters of "a mitzva for all times." According to the ninth of the thirteen principles of faith that Maimonides formulated in his *Commentary on the Mishna*, the eternity of the Torah means that "nothing will be added to it or subtracted from it, neither to its text nor to its interpretation."[50] Maimonides even states as a matter of halakha that: "One who says that the Creator replaced this mitzva with another, or that this Torah has been annulled ... has denied the

---

Holies on Yom Kippur, in which he petitioned: "May Your people Israel not need sustenance from one another" (Yoma 53b; see *Dikdukei Soferim* there, and compare to Maimonides' Laws of the Yom Kippur Service 4:1). In his *Commentary on the Mishna* on Yoma 5:1 Maimonides explains: "He prays for the private affairs of individuals, that God should bring success to every person's labors, and that his dealings and goods thrive, so that he does not need to borrow and beg from another." But if this prayer is accepted, what will become of the mitzva of charity? (See *Moshav Zekeinim* on Deuteronomy 15:4, which poses a similar question.)

Although we are far from the state of "performing God's will" to the point that the promise of "there shall be no poor among you" will be fulfilled (in accordance with *Sifre* 114, on Deut. 15:4), we are nevertheless privileged to have a welfare policy in our independent state such that even the poor do not need to go out into the field to gather the produce that must be given to the poor. Consequently, anyone can now gather fallen sheaves (*leket*), forgotten sheaves (*shikheḥa*), and corners of the field (*pe'ah*) that are left for the poor, since "the mitzva is not to leave them for the beasts and birds, but for the poor, and there are no poor people" (Maimonides, *Hilkhot Matnot Aniyim* 1:10, and see my commentary *Yad Peshuta*).

49. *Sefer Hamitzvot*, shoresh 3.
50. *Commentary on the Mishna*, Introduction to the Tenth Chapter of Sanhedrin (*Perek Ḥelek*), p. 145.

Torah."[51] We may thus ask: If a mitzva is no longer practiced because the circumstances to which it applies no longer obtain, is it considered to have been annulled? If it is, does this contravene the principle of the Torah's eternity?

In his enumeration of the mitzva to wage a war of annihilation against the seven Canaanite nations, Maimonides addresses this question:

> One might think that since the seven nations have ceased to exist, this is a mitzva that is not applicable for all times. Only someone who does not understand the idea of "applicable for all times" would think so. A practice that has ended because its purpose has been achieved, without it being dependent on a specific time, is still considered "applicable for all times" because it applies in every generation in which it can be performed…. We were commanded to kill and eliminate the seven nations, and this war is a mitzva…. And so we did, until their elimination was completed by David, and their remnants were scattered and assimilated among the nations, to the point that they are not identifiable.
>
> Yet although they have been eliminated, the mitzva to kill them is still considered a mitzva for all times, just as we consider the war against Amalek to be for all times even after their elimination and excision, because the mitzva itself is not contingent upon time or place like the special mitzvot given in the wilderness or in Egypt. Rather, it is contingent upon the object of the commandment: as long as they exist, they are the objects of the commandment. The general rule is that one must consider and understand the difference between the commandment and the object of the commandment. There are some commandments that are for all time whose objects have ceased to exist, yet the absence of the object of the commandment does not mean that the mitzva itself is not for all time.[52]

---

51. *Hilkhot Teshuva* 3:8.
52. *Sefer Hamitzvot*, positive commandment 187.

The second question is also fundamental, and the Talmud, in fact, addresses it:[53] What is the use of a mitzva that has no practical application? What purpose does it have? The Talmud sharpens this question even further, asserting that certain mitzvot were never applied in practice and were never even intended for implementation at all.

There are three mitzvot that, according to the Talmud, never happened and never will, even though the Torah describes them in great detail. These three mitzvot shock and frighten all who hear of them. The first is that of the wayward and rebellious son:

> If a man has a wayward and rebellious son … his father and mother shall take hold of him … and say to the elders of the city: "This son of ours is wayward and rebellious. He does not heed our voice; he is a glutton and a drunkard." The people of his city shall stone him to death. You shall purge wickedness from your midst; and all Israel will hear and be afraid. (Deut. 21:18–21)

The Oral Torah explains that this passage refers to a young man who has just reached the age at which he becomes obligated by the mitzvot – thirteen years and one day. There is only a three-month interval during which he can be deemed a "wayward and rebellious son." The severity of the punishment seems completely disproportionate to the severity of the sin; R. Yosei Hagelili addresses this issue in Sanhedrin 72a:

> R. Yosei Hagelili said: For eating half a measure of meat and drinking half a glass of Italian wine, would the Torah send him to court to be stoned to death? Rather, the Torah foresaw what would become of the wayward and rebellious son. He will use up his father's resources and, seeking the lifestyle to which he has become accustomed, he will become a highwayman. The Torah therefore said: Let him die innocent rather than guilty, for the death of the wicked benefits them and benefits the world.

---

53. Sanhedrin 71a.

Yet this law is difficult even with R. Yosei Hagelili's explanation. The law of the wayward and rebellious son brings the attribute of stern justice to bear in a profoundly terrifying way. The passage about the second mitzva, the city led astray, sounds even more frightening:

> If you hear that in one of your cities…wicked men have gone from amongst you to lead the residents of their city astray, saying, "Let us go and worship other gods" that you do not know… and it proves true that this abomination has been perpetrated in your midst, you shall smite the residents of that city by sword. Destroy it and all that is in it, even its livestock, by the sword…. Completely burn the city and all of its spoils…. It shall be a ruin forever. (Deut. 13:13–17)

Finally, in our third mitzva, the mitzva of *tzara'at* of the home, we see that sometimes justice is meted out even against sticks and stones:

> Why are timber, stones, and walls smitten? So that their owners see and repent…. For this reason, the Holy One cautions them by first smiting their homes, so that they repent, as [Scripture] states: "I will inflict a plague of *tzara'at* upon the house on the land you possess" (Lev. 14:34).[54]

The Written Torah explains these mitzvot in great detail, and the Oral Torah adds numerous rules and halakhot. Nevertheless, there are three surprising *baraitot* that relate to these three mitzvot: "There never was and never will be a wayward and rebellious son…. There never was and never will be a city led astray…. There never was and never will be a *tzara'at*-plagued house."[55] The Talmud explains that these *Tanna'im* maintain that the likelihood of all of the conditions

---

54. *Tanḥuma Metzora* §12.
55. Sanhedrin 71a. The Talmud also cites R. Yonatan, who said of the wayward and rebellious son, "I saw one and sat upon his grave," and gives a similar attestation about a city led astray. It is possible that R. Yonatan's testimonies relate to cases of exceptional temporary measures or that were judged when the Sanhedrin was dominated by Sadducees (see the entry in *Megilat Ta'anit* for 28 Tevet, which was a

necessary for these mitzvot to be applied is infinitesimal. So why were they commanded in the first place? "Why was it written? To study it and receive reward."[56]

The very fact that these laws appear in the Torah serves a crucial educational purpose. "Study it and receive reward" means that one who studies these laws cannot but be gripped by panic; it is impossible for him not to be deeply affected. The mere study of these laws can open shuttered eyes and closed ears, fulfilling the verse: "all Israel will hear and be afraid" (Deut. 21:21). There is no reason for these dreadful punishments to ever actually be carried out. The reward for studying them is that they will forever remain purely theoretical. Schoolchildren who are made aware of the laws of the wayward and rebellious son will never adopt his attributes. A community that teaches its members about the city led astray is assured that no idolatrous "root bearing gall and wormwood" will ever flourish there. One who has learned to recognize God's hand in natural phenomena and catastrophes will not need a plague of tzara'at upon his house to contemplate repentance.

The same applies to all mitzvot. Even after they have achieved their goal of bettering human life, they retain their didactic power. Even as humanity has advanced beyond the minimal level that certain mitzvot are there to ensure, studying the particulars of those mitzvot can stimulate new thinking and guide those generations to even greater advancements while preserving past achievements. Even after the idolatrous impulse was eliminated, contemplating the halakhot of idolatry leads us toward recognition of true spirituality. The more we are convinced of the severity of the sin of idolatry, the more we develop the inner longing for true sanctity.

A nation that absorbs the Torah's ideas and values slowly builds up immunity to vulgar temptations. Over the course of time, students of the Torah have developed razor-sharp critical faculties to distinguish between illusion and reality, between fiction and truth, between empty, misleading oracles and the majestic voice of God. Generations that have

---

holiday because it was "the day that the assembly sat in judgment," that is, the day that the Pharisees regained control of the Sanhedrin.

56. Sanhedrin 72a.

been trained by the Torah possess vast stores of spiritual strength with which they can overcome internal and external obstacles to become worthy of the title of our forefather, Israel: "for you have striven with God and man, and prevailed" (Gen. 32:29). This is the meaning of: "Study it and receive reward."

Chapter 3

Mitzvot, Obligations, and Goals

The Fundamentals of Faith as Commandments

The first mitzva enumerated by Maimonides in *Sefer Hamitzvot* is:

> The commandment... to acquire knowledge of the Divine, i.e., to know that there is an Origin and First Cause that brought about all existence. This [commandment] was uttered by the Exalted One: 'I am the Lord, your God' (Ex. 20:2).

In his list of mitzvot at the beginning of *Hilkhot Yesodei HaTorah*, Maimonides included: "To know that God exists." Maimonides' inclusion of knowing God in his list of mitzvot was somewhat revolutionary, as Nahmanides attested:

> I saw that the author of *Halakhot Gedolot* did not enumerate this mitzva as one of the 613.... It seems that the view of *Halakhot Gedolot* is that we only count among the 613 mitzvot God's decrees in which He commanded us to do something or refrain from something. However, belief in His existence, of which He informed us by means of signs, wonders, and the revelation of the Divine Presence

to us, is the root and basis from which the commandments come into being, and is thus not enumerated in these accounts.[1]

Many others objected to Maimonides' inclusion of this mitzva, based primarily on two contentions, as summarized by R. Ḥasdai Crescas:

1. Whoever enumerated the belief in God's existence as a positive mitzva has made a serious error, for the commander is premised; it is inconceivable for there to be a commandment (*mitzva*) in the absence of a commander (*metzaveh*).

In other words, the very willingness to undertake a commandment implies belief in its commander.

2. Given that belief in God's existence is something in which choice and volition do not factor, perforce the word "commandment" does not apply to it.[2]

In fact, Maimonides already preempted both of these objections:

If you belong to those who are satisfied with expressing in speech the opinions that are correct or that you deem to be correct, without representing them to yourself and believing them, and still less without seeking certain knowledge regarding them, you take a very easy road. Indeed, you will find many dull people who can recite by heart statements about beliefs to which, in their representation, they do not attach any meaning whatever.[3]

This, however, is not the intent of the mitzva:

For there is no belief except after a representation; belief is the affirmation that what has been represented is outside the mind

---

1. Glosses on *Sefer Hamitzvot*, positive commandment 1.
2. *Or Hashem*, Introduction.
3. *Moreh Nevukhim* I:50, p. 111.

just as it has been represented in the mind. If, together with this belief, one realizes that a belief different from it is in no way possible and that no starting point can be found in the mind for a rejection of this belief or for the supposition that a different belief is possible, there is certainty. [4]

Thus, we have been commanded to probe, to ascertain, and to verify. This requires constant, serious study, and it is up to man to devote himself to it or to desist from it:

> For these two principles, I mean the existence of the Deity and His being one, are knowable by human speculation alone. Now with regard to everything that can be known by demonstration, the status of the prophet and that of everyone else who knows it are equal; there is no superiority of one over the other. Thus these two principles are not known through prophecy alone. The text of the Torah says: "You have been shown [that the Lord is God, there is no other but Him]" (Deut. 4:35).[5]

Maimonides was not satisfied until he concluded:

> As for someone who thinks about and frequently mentions God, without knowledge, following a mere imagining or following a belief adopted because of his reliance on the authority of somebody else, he…does not in true reality mention or think about God. For that thing which is in his imagination and which he mentions in speech does not correspond to any being at all and has merely been invented by his imagination….[6]

Thus, although God's existence was indeed evident at Mt. Sinai, He nevertheless commanded us to investigate and truly know Him, for

---

4. Ibid.
5. Ibid. II:33, p. 364.
6. Ibid. III:51, p. 620.

knowledge of God has no end or limit. Any capable person can engage in this form of inquiry, and so this goal is attainable to anyone who directs his mind and engages in deep and diligent study.

Nevertheless, though the first principle of faith is the subject of one of the 613 mitzvot, other fundamentals of faith are not associated with any specific commandment. According to Maimonides, there are thirteen fundamentals of the Jewish religion, which he enumerates in his *Commentary on the Mishna*, in the introduction to the tenth chapter of Sanhedrin. Elsewhere in the *Commentary*, in the eighth chapter of his introduction to tractate Avot, he adds another principle, without which "the commands and prohibitions of the Law would become null and void."[7] In *Hilkhot Teshuva*, Maimonides describes this fourteenth principle: "This is a foundational principle, the pillar of the Torah and the commandments"[8] – the principle of freedom of choice.

Some of the principles are themselves mitzvot: knowledge of the Divine and His unity are enumerated as positive commandments,[9] and the prohibition of idolatry is the subject of several negative mitzvot.[10] But some fundamental principles are not mitzvot nor do their subjects relate to any of the mitzvot. Other principles do relate to mitzvot, such as the five principles to which Maimonides alludes at the beginning of *Hilkhot Teshuva*, where he writes: "This mitzva and the principles that follow from it are explained in these chapters." These principles are: God's knowledge of human action, reward and punishment, the advent of the messianic era, the resurrection of the dead, and the foundation of all mitzvot, the principle of free choice. Even though some of these principles can be investigated and logically proven – free choice, for example – there is no specific mitzva to believe or prove them. There is also at least one principle that lies

---

7. *The Eight Chapters of Maimonides on Ethics: Shemonah Perakim*, ed. and trans. by Joseph Isaac Gorfinkle (New York: Columbia University Press, 1912), 87.
8. *Hilkhot Teshuva* 5:3.
9. *Sefer Hamitzvot*, positive commandments 1–2.
10. Ibid., negative commandments 1–10, and more.

outside the domain of logic, as Maimonides wrote in his Letter concerning Resurrection:

> The resurrection of the dead is a miraculous event…. There is nothing to do but believe in it, as it has come to us through an authentic tradition. It is a supernatural matter, and there is no rational proof of it.[11]

However, the fundamentals of Judaism are not solely matters of beliefs; they also have far-reaching halakhic implications. For instance, Maimonides ruled that one who denies one of the thirteen principles has excluded himself from the Jewish people,[12] though, to be sure, in practice this ruling has changed over time, and halakhists have written that modern non-observant Jews are treated as "children who were captured" and thus not excluded.

There are also obligations that derive from these required beliefs. For example, Maimonides ruled regarding the messianic king: "One who does not believe in him or *anticipate his advent* does not deny only the prophets, but also the Torah and our teacher Moses."[13] What is the source for this obligation to anticipate his advent? Where were we commanded to do so? Clearly, this obligation is rooted in the belief in the messiah, though there is no mitzva to anticipate his advent. Thus, even principles which are not commanded can nevertheless create obligations.

Mitzvot vs. Goals

The mitzvot can be grouped by theme. For example, we are commanded to study and teach Torah;[14] there is also a commandment for every Jewish man to have his own Torah scroll,[15] and kings have an additional mitzva in this regard.[16] Obviously, the reason to write a

---

11. *Iggerot HaRambam*, p. 363.
12. *Commentary on the Mishna*, end of the Introduction to the Tenth Chapter of Sanhedrin.
13. *Hilkhot Melakhim* 11:1.
14. *Sefer Hamitzvot*, positive commandment 11.
15. Ibid., positive commandment 18.
16. *Sefer Hamitzvot*, positive commandment 17.

Torah scroll is to study it, as is explicitly stated with regard to the king: "He shall write himself a copy of this Torah ... and it is to remain with him, so he may read it every day of his life" (Deut. 17:18–19). Thus, the purpose of the mitzva to write a Torah scroll is to fulfill another mitzva, studying the Torah. One mitzva – Torah study – is also the purpose of another mitzva – writing a Torah scroll.

There are other groups of mitzvot that have a common theme, but within which no one mitzva is the goal of the other mitzvot. For instance, the Torah specifies that the prohibition of *ḥametz*, the mitzva to eat matza on Passover, and several other mitzvot commemorate the Exodus from Egypt: "So that you remember the day you left the land of Egypt every day of your life" (Deut. 16:3). However, the common purpose of every mitzva in this group – remembering the Exodus daily – was not enumerated by Maimonides as one of the 613 mitzvot, even though the Torah mentions it explicitly. On the other hand, in *Hilkhot Keriat Shema*, he wrote: "It is a mitzva to mention the Exodus from Egypt daily and nightly."[17] How are we to understand this, considering that he did not enumerate this mitzva as one of the 613?

Maimonides preempted this question in his introduction to *Sefer Hamitzvot*, where he lists his rules for determining inclusion in the list of the 613 mitzvot. In the fifth of these rules, he teaches us that the reason and purpose of a mitzva should not be enumerated as a separate mitzva unless the Torah explicitly specified the purpose as a separate mitzva – as in the case of writing a Torah scroll and the mitzva of Torah study, where both commandments are explicit. Maimonides offers a source for this rule:

> This is stated explicitly in the *Sifrei*. Right after the Torah prohibits accepting ransom money for a murderer comes the verse: "and you shall not defile the land" (Num. 35:34), on which the *Sifrei* comments: "This verse teaches us that bloodshed defiles the land." Thus, the *Sifrei* clarifies that "you shall not defile ..." is the reason for the prior prohibition and not a new prohibition.

---

17. *Hilkhot Keriat Shema* 1:3.

The purpose or goal of a mitzva is necessarily broader than the mitzva itself. Mitzvot must be defined by the precise ways in which they are violated or performed. However, the purpose of a mitzva cannot be limited to a specific set of acts, and thus cannot be precisely defined in that manner.[18] Maimonides formulated this rule generally, without distinguishing between positive and negative commandments: "it is not proper to count the reason for a mitzva as a separate mitzva." Although the examples he cites are all negative commandments, it seems that he mentioned only negative commandments because those were the cases in which he disagreed with his predecessors. The rule itself applies to all mitzvot.

Ralbag adopts this rule in his Torah commentary: "The statement, 'You shall recall all of God's commandments' (Num. 15:39) is not a positive commandment; rather, the Torah tells us the function of the mitzva of tzitzit."[19] Maimonides alludes to the same idea in one of his rules at the beginning of *Sefer Hamitzvot*: "The goal of tzitzit is 'so that you remember' (Num. 15:40). Consequently, those things [*tekhelet* strings and white strings] that cause remembrance are collectively counted as one mitzva [and no more]."[20] Had remembering all of the mitzvot been an independent mitzva, we would be obligated to read a list of the 613 mitzvot at least occasionally.

When the Torah reveals that attaining a specific goal is desirable, any action that leads to the attainment of the goal is desirable as well. He who commanded us with regard to the mitzvot also desires that we attain these goals; how can His will not obligate us? However, regarding goals, there are many paths to reach them, but not every path is always suitable for every person. Mitzvot are defined precisely; even mitzvot that have no fixed measurements require one to perform (or refrain

---

18. See also the fourth introductory rule of *Sefer Hamitzvot*: "The Torah contains positive and negative commandments which do not relate to a specific activity, but include all the mitzvot.... There is no place to count such a command as a mitzva on its own, because He did not command the performance of a specific, delimited act, which would make it a positive commandment, nor did he prohibit a specific action, which would make it a negative commandment."

19. Commentary on Num. 15:39.

20. Eleventh Rule.

from) a specific action. However, when it comes to goals and purposes
of mitzvot, it is impossible to specify precisely each and every act that
one must perform or refrain from performing.

Nevertheless, there are a number of actions that the Sages made
obligatory because they saw that they further a desirable goal, and thus
when we perform them, we do God's will. This allows us to understand
Maimonides' views regarding several halakhot that seem to have no
source in any binding Torah commandment but, in Maimonides' presentation, are treated as essential aspects of the Torah. We will address
two examples of this principle:

Healthful Behavior

In his *Hilkhot De'ot*, Maimonides devotes an entire chapter to healthful
behavior. The chapter begins with the following declaration:

> Having a whole and healthy body is a godly path – for it is impos-
> sible for a sick person to know or understand – and so it is nec-
> essary for one to distance himself from things that destroy the
> body and habituate himself to do things that promote health
> and fitness...[21]

It would be futile to search the list at the beginning of *Hilkhot De'ot* for
a specific mitzva that commands healthy living. Maimonides was very
precise in his language: he wrote "it is necessary..." but did not use the
term "mitzva."

Others disagree with Maimonides, maintaining that using
doctors is permitted but not necessary. According to them, if we are
deserving, we would be among those who do not need medicine –
"God's community, whose portion is life," in Nahmanides' words.[22]
Likewise, Rashi explains that King Hezekiah hid the Book of Remedies
"so that people should pray for mercy."[23] Maimonides rejects such
explanations:

21. *Hilkhot De'ot* 4:1.
22. Commentary on Lev. 26:11.
23. Berakhot 10b.

...I have heard an explanation [according to which]Hezekiah
saw that people, in their illnesses, placed their faith not in God
but in the Book of Remedies, so he hid it.... According to what
they imagine... if a hungry person eats bread to alleviate his
hunger pangs... should we say that he no longer has faith in
God?... Just as when I eat, I thank God for creating things that
remove my hunger, nourish me, and sustain me, so too, when
I use medicine, I thank Him for creating remedies that alleviate my illness.[24]

Maimonides therefore explains that the Book of Remedies hidden by
Hezekiah contained prescriptions based on idolatrous elements or
"harmful prescriptions."[25]

As the Gemara states in another context: "It is simple logic –
the one who is in pain goes to the doctor."[26] In keeping with his view,
Maimonides ruled[27] that a Torah scholar may not live in a city that has
no doctor. Using medical science is obligatory, and therefore, halakha
must include basic instructions for healthful living.

Maimonides' source for this obligation is the verse: "'The Lord
commanded us to do all these statutes... that He might preserve us alive,
as it is on this day' (Deut. 6:24).... 'That He might preserve us alive, as
it is on this day' refers to preservation of the body (in good health)."[28]
This dovetails with what he wrote in *Hilkhot De'ot*: "For one cannot
understand an important concept – even if it is explained to him, and
certainly not on his own – while he suffers from pains or from severe
hunger or thirst..."

---

24. *Commentary on the Mishna*, Pesaḥim 4:10.
25. Ibid.
26. Bava Kama 46b. See also Berakhot 60a, where Abaye rejects the statement, "Men
    have no power to heal; it is merely a matter of habit." Rather, they have the power
    and the duty – and the law follows Abaye. See also Maimonides' *Commentary on
    the Mishna*, in the fifth chapter of *Shemoneh Perakim*, where he discusses the value
    of medical science. See also *Yad Peshuta*, my commentary to *Mishneh Torah*, preface
    to chapter 4 of *Hilkhot De'ot*.
27. *Hilkhot De'ot* 4:23, based on Sanhedrin 17b.
28. *Moreh Nevukhim* III:27, pp. 511–12.

The Torah thus states explicitly that one of the goals of the mitz-vot is to attain physical health. This goal is itself binding, and so one is obligated to do whatever furthers this goal. Since the Torah articulates this goal, it is "a Godly path," and so "it is necessary for one to distance himself from things that destroy the body and train himself to do things that promote health and fitness."

Settling the Land of Israel

Maimonides has numerous rulings about settling Eretz Yisrael, through-out *Mishneh Torah*: "One should always live in Eretz Yisrael, even in a mostly gentile city, and should not live outside the land, even in a mostly Jewish city"[29] – and many others.[30] Yet in his enumeration of the 613 mitzvot, he does not list settling Eretz Yisrael. Nahmanides, too, saw all of those laws in the Talmud that explicitly mandate settling Eretz Yisrael, and so he looked for a source for the obligation in the Torah. Thus, in his glosses to *Sefer Hamitzvot*, Nahmanides disagrees with Maimonides' enumeration, and the fourth mitzva on his list of "positive command-ments that Maimonides forgot" is: "We are commanded to possess the land that God gave to our fathers Abraham, Isaac, and Jacob...."

In practice, there is no disagreement between Maimonides and Nahmanides on this issue; after all, Maimonides codifies all of those specific laws that speak of settling Eretz Yisrael. However, according to Maimonides, there is no such distinct mitzva, because the Torah states several times that the goal of many mitzvot is possession of Eretz Yisrael:[31] "Now, O Israel, give heed to the laws and rules that I am instructing you to observe, so that you may live to enter and possess the land that the Lord, God of your fathers, is giving you" (Deut. 4:1); "Keep every mitzva that I am commanding you today, so that you have the strength to enter and possess the land" (Deut. 11:8); and so forth. This goal is

---

29. *Hilkhot Melakhim* 5:12.
30. See, for example, *Hilkhot Melakhim* 5:9–12; *Hilkhot Ishut* 13:19; *Hilkhot Shemita VeYovel* 4:27; *Hilkhot Avadim* 8:6–10; and others.
31. For a broader discussion of this issue and an explanation of the views of Maimonides and Nahmanides regarding the mitzva of settling Eretz Yisrael, see my *Melumdei Milḥama* (Maaleh Adumim: Me'aliyot, 2004), §1, p. 9ff. (originally published as two separate responsa in *Teḥumin* vols. 4 [1983] and 5 [1984]).

binding, and it is thus the source for all of the halakhot, enactments, and decrees made by the Sages pertaining to settling Eretz Yisrael. However, upholding these enactments alone does not absolve us of doing everything we can to further the Torah's goal: "so that you may live to enter and possess the land." Every action that leads toward this desirable goal is a fulfillment of the Creator's will.

We have seen that, according to Maimonides, obligations can originate in sources other than direct commandments: The Torah informed us of the function and goal of certain mitzvot, or of the mitzvot in general, and *since the attainment of this goal is God's will, one should do anything that furthers the realization or attainment of that goal.* However, since these methods are neither defined nor clear-cut, and can evolve due to changing times and circumstances, it is impossible to specify exactly what is obligatory and what is not, and therefore the Torah did not issue an explicit commandment. Even so, when the Sages saw that certain actions lead to the desired results, they made them obligatory, because they clearly fulfill God's will. These obligations are of rabbinic provenance – they were commanded by the Sages, not the Torah, and the Sages, with their enactments, did not exhaust the many ways in which one can serve the Torah's goal.

Improving Society

The entire *Mishneh Torah* consists of halakhot divided into sections. At the beginning of each section, Maimonides lists all of the mitzvot to be discussed in that section. However, there are several sections that are introduced without a single mitzva, positive or negative. For example, *Hilkhot Zekhiya U'Matana*, *Hilkhot Shekhenim*, and *Hilkhot Sheluḥin VeShuttafin*, all in the Book of Acquisition (*Sefer Kinyan*), contain none of the 613 mitzvot. Where does the Torah confer validity on these laws?

In *Moreh Nevukhim*, Maimonides presents the overall goals of the Torah extensively: "It has been explained with utmost clarity that man is political by nature and that it is his nature to live in society."[32] Thus, one of the Torah's most important goals is the improvement of society. He continues:

---

32. *Moreh Nevukhim* II:40, p. 381.

The Law as a whole aims at two things: the welfare of the soul and the welfare of the body.... As for the welfare of the body, it comes about by the improvement of [people's] ways of living one with another. This is achieved through two things. One of them is the abolition of their wronging each other.... The second thing consists in the acquisition by every human individual of moral qualities that are useful for life in society so that the affairs of the city may be well-ordered.[33]

Achieving the goal of improving society requires various forms of social organization and the regulation of commercial and interpersonal relationships. Some of these regulations are explicit in the Torah itself, and some have been enacted by the sages of every generation as they see fit, based on the needs of the time. Some rules of desirable behavior have never been formalized; rather, it is incumbent upon every person to act in a way that improves his society. This was articulated well by R. Vidal of Toulouse, author of *Maggid Mishneh*:

The idea behind a neighbor's right of first refusal[34] is that our perfect Torah provided general rules for improving human character and behavior. It states: "Be holy";.... It similarly states: "Do that which is right and good" (Deut. 6:18), which means that one should behave benevolently and honestly toward others. It would not have made sense to legislate the particulars of all these principles, because the mitzvot of the Torah apply at all times, in every era, and in every situation, and one must perform them, yet temperaments and manners vary from person to person and from era to era. The Sages recorded some effective applications of these principles, some of which they enacted as black-letter law, and others as preferred or pious practice; these are all rabbinic law. Regarding this, it was said: "The words of the beloved

---

33. Ibid. III:27, p. 510.
34. Editor's note: This refers to the rule of *bar metzra* (Aramaic, lit. "the one on the boundary"): A neighbor is granted the right of first refusal with regard to the purchase of adjoining property. See *Bava Metzi'a* 108b.

[referring to the Sages who enacted laws] are more cherished than the wine of Torah, as it is stated: 'For your love is better than wine' (Song. 1:2)."[35]

We have seen that in Nahmanides' view, there is no mitzva to seek medical treatment, and it is thus merely optional, not obligatory. On the other hand, with regard to settling Eretz Yisrael, Nahmanides maintains that there are binding halakhot, because there is a corresponding positive mitzva, which is the source of the obligations. Nahmanides, true to his opinion that obligations must be based on explicit commandments, wrote in his Torah commentary, on the words "Be holy" (Lev. 19:2):

> Therefore, after listing the matters which He prohibited altogether, Scripture followed them up by a general command that we practice moderation even in matters which are permitted: one should minimize sexual intercourse.... One should sanctify himself in this respect until he reaches the degree known as self-restraint.... It is with reference to these and similar matters that this general commandment is concerned, after He had enumerated all individual deeds which are strictly forbidden, so that cleanliness of hands and body are also included in this precept.... For although these are commandments of rabbinic origin, Scripture's main intention is to warn us of such matters, so that we should be clean and pure, and separated from the common people who soil themselves with excessive luxuries and unseemly things. And this is the way of the Torah in such matters, first to list specific prohibitions and then to give a general principle that includes all. Thus, after warning with detailed laws regarding all business dealings between people, such as not to steal or rob or wrong one another, and other similar prohibitions, He said in general, "Do that which is right and good," thus including under a

---

35. R. Vidal of Toulouse, *Maggid Mishneh* on *Hilkhot Shekhenim*, 14:5. Regarding the commandment to "Be holy," compare this to what Maimonides wrote in the fourth introductory rule to *Sefer Hamitzvot*. See also *Hilkhot Shekhenim* 14:5; *Hilkhot Malveh VeLoveh* 22:16.

positive commandment the duty of doing that which is right and agreeing to compromise, as well as all requirements to act beyond the line of justice to benefit one's fellow man.... Similarly, in the case of Shabbat, He prohibited specific classes of work by means of a negative commandment, and then included the prohibition on exhausting activities under a general positive commandment: "you shall rest" (Ex. 23:12).[36]

Nahmanides (in his glosses to the fourth introductory rule in *Sefer Hamitzvot*) agrees with Maimonides that "Be holy" should not be counted as a separate positive commandment, since "generalizations that include all proscriptions are not counted." However, he maintains that general principles that follow several specific prohibitions should be counted: "...the positive commandment to refrain from them is counted as a mitzva, just as the cessation [of labor] on Shabbat and festivals are counted as positive commandments, whereas performing labor on those days violates a negative commandment...."

Accordingly, it would seem likely that "Do that which is right and good" should be enumerated, in Nahmanides' opinion. Yet Nahmanides does not list it among the positive commandments that he adds to Maimonides' count, perhaps because he maintains that it is inclusive of the entire Torah.[37] Either way, it is clear that according

36. Nahmanides on Leviticus 19:2, Charles B. Chavel, trans., (New York: Shilo, 1974), vol. 3, 281 ff. [Subsequent translations of Nahmanides are based on the Chavel translation.]
37. Nahmanides says this in his commentary to that verse (Deut. 6:18; Chavel, vol. 5, p. 88): In line with the plain meaning of Scripture, the verse says, "Keep the commandments of God, His testimonies and statutes, and, in observing them, intend to do what is right and good in His sight only.... Our Sages have a beautiful Midrash on this verse. They have said: "[That which is right and good] refers to compromise and going beyond the requirement of the letter of the law." The intent of this is as follows: At first [Moses] stated that you are to keep [God's] statutes and His testimonies which He commanded you; and now he is stating that even where He has not commanded you, give thought, as well, to do what is good and right in His eyes, for He loves the good and the right. Now this is a great principle, for it is impossible to mention in the Torah all aspects of man's conduct with his neighbors and friends, and all his various transactions, and the ordinances of all societies and countries. But since He mentioned many of

to Nahmanides there is a specific command that grants validity to the halakhot of a neighbor's right of first refusal, the laws of honest behavior, and the like.

Thus, although Nahmanides does not disagree with Maimonides in practice, he nevertheless clearly espouses the view that there must be an explicit command "[to do] that which is right and agreeing to compromise."

Nahmanides highlights the command to "do that which is right and good" as a principle that encompasses "the detailed laws regarding all business dealings between people," since these details do not sufficiently explain everything. Maimonides formulates the same expectation, but differently. At the end of *Hilkhot De'ot*, after a thorough discussion of several basic interpersonal mitzvot, he concludes with the goal of the negative commandment against bearing a grudge (Lev. 19:18), which is likewise the reason for all mitzvot of this sort:

> The Torah condemned holding a grudge, [requiring] one to wipe the wrong from his heart entirely, without remembering it at all. This is the correct temperament, which sustains civilization and all human interactions.[38]

That is, according to Maimonides, the goal and purpose of the mitzvot generates a comprehensive, overarching framework, rendering an explicit

---

them – such as "do not spread slander" (Lev. 19:16); "do not take vengeance or bear a grudge" (ibid. 18); "do not curse the deaf" (ibid. 14); "rise before the aged" (ibid. 32), and the like – he reverted to state in a general way that, in all matters, one should do what is good and right; including even compromise and going beyond the requirements of the law. Other examples are the Sages' ordinances concerning the neighbor's right of first refusal, and even what they said [concerning the desirability] that one's youthful reputation be unblemished and that one's conversation with people be pleasant. Thus [a person must seek to refine his behavior] in every form of activity, until he is worthy of being called "good and upright."
The implication is that this command indeed relates to the entire Torah, and it is therefore not counted as a separate positive commandment – and is very similar to "Be holy."
38. *Hilkhot De'ot* 7:8.

command unnecessary, contra Nahmanides. Perhaps Maimonides maintains that "do that which is right and good" cannot be interpreted as a command; even Nahmanides admits that, according to the plain meaning of Scripture, it is not a specific commandment.

With respect to the improvement of society, Maimonides asserts[39] that the Torah has a threefold approach, consisting of three groups of mitzvot: "the commandments concerned with preventing wrongdoing and aggression, which are included in the Book of Torts [*Sefer Nezikin*]"; then, "the commandments concerned with punishments, as for instance laws concerning thieves and robbers.... The utility of this is clear and manifest, for if a criminal is not punished, injurious actions will not be abolished at all and none of those who design aggression will be deterred"; and finally, "the laws of property concerned with the mutual transactions of people." He later explains at greater length:

> The commandments...enumerated in the Book of Torts are all concerned with putting an end to acts of injustice and with the prevention of acts causing damage. In order that great care should be taken to avoid causing damage, man is held responsible for every act causing damage deriving from his possessions or caused by an act of his, if only it was possible for him to be cautious and take care not to cause damage. Therefore we are held responsible for damage deriving from our beasts, so that we should watch over them; and also for damage from fire and from a pit, for these two belong to the works of man, and he can keep watch over them and take precautions with regard to them, so that no harm is occasioned by them.[40]

In accordance with his recognition that one of the basic goals of the Torah is "the prevention of acts causing damage," Maimonides ruled: "One may not cause damage and then pay for the damage he caused;

---

39. *Moreh Nevukhim* III:35, p. 536.
40. Ibid. II:40, p. 555.

causing damage is also forbidden."[41] Many commentators have asked: Where does the Torah prohibit causing damage?[42]

Based on the approach articulated above, the source of the prohibition is clear. The very fact that the Torah punishes someone who causes damage teaches us that the Torah requires us to keep our possessions from causing damage.[43] According to Maimonides, where damage was likely, the Sages enacted preventative measures, because by doing so they furthered the Torah's goals. This is the meaning of Maimonides' later statement in *Hilkhot Nizkei Mamon*: "Therefore" – that is, since it is forbidden to cause damage – "the Sages forbade raising flocks in areas of Eretz Yisrael where fields and vineyards are cultivated, only [permitting it] in its forests and wildernesses."[44]

"In All Thy Ways, Know Him"

Maimonides wrote in *Hilkhot De'ot*:

One must direct all of his actions solely toward knowing God. When he rests, rises up, or speaks, it should be to this end. For example, when he engages in commerce or labor for profit, he should not be thinking solely about accumulating money. Rather, he should engage in these activities so that he obtains his bodily

---

41. *Hilkhot Nizkei Mamon* 5:1.

42. The prohibition is already explicit in Geonic writings; *She'iltot DeRabbi Aḥai Ga'on* (*Mishpatim* §61) states: "It is forbidden for one to damage another's property..." (and see also §111). However, the question remains: Where does the Torah prohibit this?

43. Cf. *Zevahim* 66a: "Since [Scripture] says, 'the owner of the pit shall pay,' it is incumbent on him to cover it." Maimonides cites this passage in the eighth introductory rule to *Sefer Hamitzvot*. In contrast to capital punishments and excision (*karet*), the presence of monetary punishment does not grant a prohibition the status of a negative commandment enumerated among the 613 mitzvot (see Maimonides' statement at the end of the introductory rules of *Sefer Hamitzvot*). Nevertheless, the same idea applies to all forms of punishment: if the Torah imposed a punishment for a certain action, such as failure to cover a pit, it is clearly prohibited, even though not every prohibition is counted as one of the negative commandments. See my introduction to *Hilkhot Nizkei Mamon* in *Yad Peshuta*, where I further explain Maimonides' view of the prohibition of causing damage.

44. *Hilkhot Nizkei Mamon* 5:2.

needs: food, drink, a home, and a wife…. He should be scrupulous about keeping his body whole and strong, so that his mind can focus on knowing God, for one cannot understand or contemplate the sciences if he is ill or if one of his limbs hurts…. One who follows this path throughout his life serves God constantly, even while engaged in commerce…. Even while sleeping, if he sleeps in order that his mind and body rest…then his sleep is in service of God. Concerning this, the Sages commanded (Mishna Avot 2:15), "all of your actions should be for the sake of heaven." This is also what [King] Solomon said, in his wisdom: "In all thy ways, know Him, and He will smooth your paths" (Prov. 3:6).[45]

Maimonides' ruling is not based on any specific mitzva; his prooftexts are a mishna in Avot and a verse in Proverbs, not a commandment of the Torah. Moreover, one cannot say that there is any mitzva that one fulfills while sleeping!

Yet, in *Shemonah Perakim*, Maimonides wrote about the virtue of one who attains this level:

Know that to live according to this standard is to arrive at a very high degree of perfection, which, in consequence of the difficulty of attainment, only a few, after long and continuous perseverance on the paths of virtue, have succeeded in reaching. If there be found a man who has accomplished this…I would place him in a rank not lower than that of the prophets.[46]

Are we really commanded to be prophets? Certainly not, yet it is clear that the goal of the mitzvot is for us to serve God always, and since this is the goal, we must do everything that brings us closer to that goal, even sleep.

The examples cited demonstrate that aside from obligations based on commands, there are obligations that are derived from the goals and purposes of the mitzvot. Sometimes the obligation to realize the goal is

---

45. *Hilkhot De'ot* 3:2–3.
46. *Shemoneh Perakim*, chapter 5, pp. 72–73.

expressed in specific laws, but there is also a wide range of activity that furthers the goal *that has not been defined and cannot be defined.* Within this range of activity, each individual has the freedom to serve God according to his personality and talents.

Beliefs as Goals

We have seen that beliefs are obligatory even if they are not the subject of a command, and that the purposes and goals of the mitzvot are likewise obligatory without a command. Are these two different categories? Must we explain their binding nature separately?

Maimonides provides the answer to this question:

> The Law as a whole aims at two things: the welfare of the soul and the welfare of the body.... Know that between these two aims, one is indubitably greater in nobility, namely, the welfare of the soul – I mean the procuring of correct opinions – while the second aim – I mean the welfare of the body – is prior in nature and time. The latter aim consists in the governance of the city and the wellbeing of the states of all its people according to their capacity. This second aim is the more certain one, and it is the one regarding which every effort has been made to precisely expound it and all its particulars. For the first aim can only be achieved after achieving the second one. For it has already been demonstrated that man has two perfections: a first perfection, which is the perfection of the body, and an ultimate perfection, which is the perfection of the soul.... It is also clear that this noble and ultimate perfection can only be achieved after the first perfection has been achieved....
>
> The true Law then, which as we have already made clear is unique – namely, the Law of Moses our Master – has come to bring us both perfections, I mean the welfare of the states of people in their relations with one another.... I also mean the soundness of the beliefs and the giving of correct opinions through which ultimate perfection is achieved. The letter of the Torah speaks of both perfections and informs us that the end of this Law in its entirety is the achievement of these two

71

perfections. For He, may He be exalted, says: "And the Lord commanded us to do all these statutes, to fear the Lord our God, for our good always, that He might preserve us alive, as it is at this day' (Deut. 6:24). Here He puts the ultimate perfection first because of its nobility; for, as we have explained, it is the ultimate end. It is referred to in the dictum: "for our good always." You know already what [the Sages], may their memory be blessed, have said interpreting His dictum, may He be exalted: "That it may be well with you, and that you may prolong your days" (Deut. 22:7). They said: "That it may be well with you in a world in which everything is well and that you may prolong your days in a world the whole of which is long."[47] Similarly the intention of His dictum here, "for our good always," is this same notion: I mean the attainment of a world in which everything is well and [the whole of which is] long. And this is eternity. On the other hand, His dictum, "That He might preserve us alive, as it is at this day," refers to the first and corporeal preservation, which lasts for a certain duration and which can only be well ordered through political association, as we have explained.[48]

Thus, the ideas and beliefs that the Torah teaches are themselves the very purposes and goals toward which the Torah and mitzvot lead. There is a hierarchy of goals; there are proximate goals and goals that are more remote, all the way up to the ultimate goal. He Who commanded specific mitzvot wants us to achieve these goals. Each individual can observe mitzvot according to his ability and environment, thereby fulfilling his obligation to a certain degree, through specific actions; the goals, however, are boundless. As one progresses, he comes closer to knowing God, but such knowledge is infinite and immeasurable. It is for this reason that goals are not defined as commands. There are many paths leading to the goals, even to the secondary goals – too many to count or specify. And they are all desirable. One must constantly consider his actions

---

47. *Midrash Tanna'im* on Deut. 22:7; see Kiddushin 39b.
48. *Moreh Nevukhim* III:27; pp. 511–12.

and ways in order to guide them toward the desired goals. About this, Scripture states: "to him who keeps to the path I will show the salvation of God" (Ps. 50:23).[49]

Yet we have seen that the commandments and their goals are not completely distinct. There are mitzvot that serve as the purpose and goal of other mitzvot. By definition, a mitzva that also serves as the goal of other mitzvot is broader and less precisely defined. We have seen that the mitzva of Torah study is the goal of the mitzvot to write a Torah scroll. The latter are well-defined; once one has written a proper Torah scroll, he has fulfilled the mitzva. There is certainly room for "beautifying the mitzva" (*hiddur mitzva*), but the essential content of the mitzva is limited.

This is not the case with respect to the mitzva of Torah study, which has no quantitative or qualitative limit. Only its negation can be defined precisely: "'Because he has despised the word of the Lord' (Num. 15:31) – this refers to one who paid no heed at all to the words of the Torah."[50] The positive formulation is necessarily imprecise: "Every Jewish man is obligated to study Torah.... He is obligated to set a time to study Torah daily and nightly, as it is stated: 'meditate on it by day and by night' (Josh. 1:8)."[51] There is an obligation to set a time, even only a very short time, to study Torah.[52] One has transgressed this commandment only if he completely neglects it.

The ultimate goal of all mitzvot likewise blends with a specific mitzva – the very first mitzva, to know that God exists. Here too, the specific mitzva is defined by its negation:

---

49. See *Shemonah Perakim*, end of chapter 4, p. 68, where Maimonides quotes the Sages' interpretation of this verse (Mo'ed Katan 5a) and explains: "If a man will always carefully discriminate as regards his actions, directing them to the medium course, he will reach the highest degree of perfection possible for a human being, thereby approaching God and sharing in His happiness." Cf. Laws of Temperaments 1:4.
50. *Hilkhot Talmud Torah* 3:14.
51. Ibid. 1:8.
52. See Menaḥot 99b: "Even if one merely reviews one passage in the morning and one in the evening, he has fulfilled the mitzva of 'this book of the Torah shall not depart from your mouth.'"

This is what the prophet says: "The Lord is the true God" (Jer. 10:10). He alone is the truth, and no other is true in the way that He is true. This is also what the Torah says: "there is none else besides Him" (Deut. 4:35) – that is, there is no true being like Him besides Him.[53]

One who thinks, God forbid, that the existence of God's creations is as true as the existence of God Himself negates this mitzva. However, the fulfillment of this mitzva is endless: "The truth of this matter cannot be grasped or fathomed by the human mind."[54] Since the goal of all mitzvot is included in this mitzva, the mitzva perforce has no distinct parameters. Aside from duty, we have seen that even sleep, when done for the right reasons, furthers knowledge of God. Clearly, though, one who goes to sleep without such lofty intentions has not transgressed this positive commandment.

The principles of faith that were not included in specific mitzvot are themselves "correct opinions through which ultimate perfection is achieved."[55] Since inculcating these beliefs is the goal of the mitzvot as a whole, they are obligatory. Moreover, the fact that the Torah teaches and inculcates these views proves its divine origin:

> If, on the other hand, you find a Law all of whose ordinances are due to attention being paid, as was stated before, to the soundness of the circumstances pertaining to the body and also to the soundness of belief – a law that takes pains to inculcate correct opinions with regard to God, may He be exalted, in the first place, and with regard to the angels, and that desires to make man wise, to give him understanding, and to awaken his attention, so that he should know the whole of that which exists in its true form – you must know that this guidance comes from Him, may He be exalted, and that this Law is divine.[56]

---

53. *Hilkhot Yesodei HaTorah* 1:1.
54. Ibid. 7.
55. *Moreh Nevukhim* III:27, p. 511.
56. Ibid. II:40, p. 384.

Mutual Responsibility

We have seen that some obligations are rooted in explicit commands, whereas other, more general obligations are based on the Torah's *goals* for individuals and for society. Yet we have still not exhausted everything that the halakhic system obligates. There are several more fundamental Torah principles we need to examine in order to identify the source of these additional obligations.

Maimonides cites the following general halakhic principle:

> For all transgressions in the Torah, retribution is exacted from [the perpetrator], but here it is exacted from [the perpetrator] and from his family who give him cover; moreover, he causes retribution to be exacted from all of Israel's enemies,[57] *for all Israel is responsible for one another*, as it is stated: "Swearing, dishonesty, and murder...," and it is written thereafter: "therefore the land mourns, and all who dwell therein languish" (Hos. 4:2–3).[58]

Although Maimonides mentions the principle that "all Israel is responsible for one another" explicitly only in the same context that the Talmud mentions it,[59] the principle itself applies to the entire Torah and has manifold ramifications,[60] to the degree that:

> One who removes himself from the ways of the community, and even if he has not transgressed, but has separated himself from the congregation of Israel and does not perform mitzvot together with them, does not share in their troubles, and does not fast on their fast days; rather, he goes his own way... as though he is not one of them – he has no share in the world to come.[61]

---

57. [A euphemistic reference to Israel itself – ed.]
58. *Hilkhot Shevuot* 11:16. The context is the warnings against swearing in vain that are issued before an oath is administered in court.
59. Shevuot 39a.
60. See *Melumdei Milḥama* §4.
61. *Hilkhot Teshuva* 3:11.

Maimonides emphasizes that the person he describes "has not transgressed." It is possible that he even performs mitzvot, but he does not
join the rest of Israel in performing them.[62] This is surprising: Is there
a mitzva to feel Israel's pain? Where are we commanded to share Israel's
troubles and fast on its fast days? What is the source of the obligation
to share the communal burden and of the terrible punishment for one
who separates himself from the community?

    Yet Scripture makes it clear:

> [You are standing here] in order to enter the covenant of the Lord
> your God, and into His oath, which the Lord your God is making
> with you today, so that He may establish you today as His people....
> Not only with you do I make this covenant and this oath, but with
> those standing here with us this day before the Lord our God and
> with those who are not with us here this day. (Deut. 29:11–14)

In addition, Scripture states: "for you are a holy nation to the Lord your
God" (ibid. 7:6). In his *Epistle to Yemen*, Maimonides explained that the
Torah's goals are fulfilled only through the chosen nation, not through
individuals, and that this is the greatness of the Torah:

> [By means of these commands] the Godly community[63] becomes
> pre-eminent, reaching a two-fold perfection. By the first perfec-
> tion I mean, man's spending his life in this world under the most
> agreeable and congenial conditions. The second perfection would
> constitute the achievement of intellectual objectives, each in
> accordance with his native powers.[64]

The "holy nation" is the "Godly community." The purpose of the Exodus
from Egypt and the giving of the Torah was to fashion and unify this

---

62. See my *Yad Peshuta, Hilkhot Teshuva* 3:11.
63. Cf. *Moreh Nevukhim* III:27 (pp. 510–12). There Maimonides does not mention the
national dimension explicitly, but it is self-evident, and Maimonides does not state
the obvious.
64. *Moses Maimonides' Epistle to Yemen* (Halkin and Cohen ed.), (New York: American
Academy for Jewish Research, 1952), iv.

nation, with whom God made an everlasting covenant. The covenant is binding on all generations of Israel. Anyone who separates from Israel separates from life itself, and anyone who removes himself from the community of Israel removes himself from the covenant with God. The covenant formed the nation, and so one can join the nation only by entering the covenant:

> By means of three things Israel entered the covenant: circumcision, immersion, and a sacrificial offering…. So it is for all generations, when a gentile wants to enter the covenant and dwell beneath the wings of the Divine Presence, and accept the yoke of Torah, he must undergo circumcision, immersion, and the atonement of an offering.[65]

It is not possible to come beneath the wings of the Divine Presence and accept the whole Torah without entering the covenant, which defines the nation of Israel. One who wishes to come beneath the wings of the Divine Presence is told: "'No one is completely righteous except for a wise man who performs these commandments and knows them.' And we tell him: 'Know that the next world is reserved only for the righteous people, and they are Israel.'"[66]

The covenant differs from commandments, since the covenant binds the Commander in addition to those He commanded. Maimonides emphasizes this, too, in his Epistle to Yemen:

> We are in possession of the divine assurance that Israel is indestructible and imperishable, and will always continue to be a pre-eminent community. As it is impossible for God to cease to exist, so is Israel's destruction and disappearance from the world unthinkable, as we read: "For I the Lord change not, and you, O sons of Jacob, will not be consumed" (Mal. 3:6). Similarly He has avowed and assured us that it is unimaginable that He will reject us entirely even if we disobey Him, and disregard His

---

65. *Hilkhot Issurei Biah* 13:1–4.
66. Ibid. 3–4.

behests, as the prophet Jeremiah avers: "Thus says the Lord: 'If heaven above can be measured, and the foundations of the earth searched out beneath, then will I also cast off all the seed of Israel for all that they have done,' says the Lord" (Jer. 31:36). Indeed this very promise has already been given before through Moses our Teacher who says, "And yet for all that, when they are in the land of their enemies, I will not reject them, neither will I abhor them, to destroy them utterly, and to break My covenant with them; for I am the Lord their God." (Lev. 26:44).[67]

The verse, "The hidden things belong to the Lord our God, but the things revealed belong to us and to our children forever, so that we may do all the words of this Torah" (Deut. 29:28) is explained as follows by Targum Yonatan, based on the Talmud:[68] "The secret things are revealed to the Lord our God, and He will exact retribution for them; but the things revealed will be given to us and our children forever to bring to justice, so as to uphold all the words of this Torah." Accordingly, Rashi explains: "They became responsible for one another." *Mutual responsibility stems from the covenant* and obligates all generations. The goal of the Torah is to shape Israel and make it unique, and it is therefore clear that we have a duty to further this goal. Moreover, the obligation of the covenant includes an aspect of acceptance – our forefathers accepted it upon themselves and upon all future generations with an oath.

Serving Out of Love

Realizing the goal of the Torah and mitzvot "is what gives the individual true perfection...and it gives him eternity; through it man becomes man."[69]

This ultimate goal has no equal, to the extent that

all the actions prescribed by the Law – I refer to the various species of worship and also the moral habits that are useful to all

---

67. *Moses Maimonides' Epistle to Yemen* (Halkin and Cohen ed.), pp. v–vi.
68. Sanhedrin 43b.
69. *Moreh Nevukhim* III:54, p. 635.

people in their mutual dealings – that all this is not to be compared with this ultimate end and does not equal it, being but preparations made for the sake of this end. Hear verbatim ... a text in Genesis Rabba (35:3). It is said there: "One scriptural dictum says: 'And all things desirable (*hafatzim*) are not to be compared to her' (Prov. 8:11). Another scriptural dictum says: 'And all things you can desire (*hafatzekha*) are not to be compared to her' (ibid. 3:15). '*Hafatzim*' refers to commandments and good actions; while *hafatzekha* refers to precious stones and pearls. Neither *hafatzim* nor *hafatzekha* are to be compared unto her."[70]

Certainly this does not mean that the mitzvot are ever rendered null, God forbid. Rather, the perfected man has been refined by the observance of the Torah and its mitzvot until his entire life is in the service of God, his very essence is defined by closeness to God, and none of his thoughts, utterances, or actions stray from his service of God. Everything he does opens new avenues to knowing God. No longer is there any difference between a commanded act and a permitted act: all is service.

God indeed wished to make Israel meritorious, and so He gave them Torah and mitzvot in abundance. Each day brings more mitzvot. However, the perfected man finds many more ways to serve, for knowledge of God is limitless.

The perfection of man ... is the one acquired by him who has achieved, in a measure corresponding to his capacity, apprehension of Him, may He be exalted, and who knows His providence extending over His creatures as manifested in the act of bringing them into being and in their governance as it is. The way of life of such an individual, after he has achieved this apprehension, will always have in view loving-kindness, righteousness, and judgment, through assimilation to His actions, may He be exalted.[71]

---

70. Ibid., pp. 636–37.
71. Ibid., p. 638.

Once a person has achieved this perfection, he is motivated not only by God's command, but by God's will, which he discerns.

Maimonides describes "one who serves out of love" as such: "[He] occupies himself with Torah and mitzvot and follows the paths of wisdom, not to not for any personal gain.... Rather, he does that which is true *because it is true*."[72] The order he presents is marvelously precise. First, he occupies himself with Torah and mitzvot. Then, once he has realized the goal of the Torah and mitzvot – namely, true perfection – he "follows the paths of wisdom" and constantly discovers new ways to serve his Creator and do what pleases Him. Truth is what the Holy One desires. There are truths that our minds can discover and understand, or at least approximate, with minimal contemplation. Such are the rational mitzvot. There are other truths that may only become comprehensible to us because they have been commanded to us. Still other truths remain beyond us completely, though we trust that the Giver of the Torah commanded truth. Such are the mitzvot that, "were it not for the Law, they would not at all be considered transgressions."[73] However, when a person attains true perfection, the truth that pervades all existence is revealed to him, and the entire universe shimmers with God's light. The soul of one who loves God pours out in longing for Him, without limit or restraint. His love flows not only into specific, defined actions, but also into every thought and every gesture. Correspondingly, the light of the truth which is God's seal breaks forth. At the beginning of the path, we see the mitzvot as points of light in a pervasive darkness. However, of those special individuals who achieve perfection, it is said: "The people that walked in darkness have seen a great light; upon those who dwelt in the land of the shadow of death, the light has shined" (Is. 9:1).[74]

---

72. *Hilkhot Teshuva* 10:2. It is self-evident that this recognition of the truth, which is the lot of one who "follows the paths of wisdom," is completely different from the "judiciousness" (*"hekhra hada'at"*) that Maimonides mentions in *Hilkhot Melakhim* 8:11. The latter does not constitute recognition of the will of the Creator. It seems that Maimonides' "judiciousness" is similar to the idea of *lex naturalis* (natural law).

73. *Shemonah Perakim*, chapter 6, p. 77.

74. This verse concludes the last chapter of *Moreh Nevukhim* (III:54, p. 638), and the work as a whole.

Chapter 4

Natural Morality and the Morality of the Torah

Does Natural Morality Exist?

The perplexing question of natural morality has occupied many thinkers throughout history. Those who espouse the idea of natural morality believe that man has a certain innate moral inclination. Thus, for example, some maintain that man has a natural sensibility that finds expression in the dictum: "What is hateful to you, do not do unto others."[1] Moreover, in their view, human beings – whose very existence hinges on their ability to obtain, through collective effort, the means of survival – have a tendency to cooperate for the mutual benefit of all contributors. They claim that this tendency appears not only among humans, but also, to an extent, among certain species of animals that exhibit group effort and mutual aid, although the tendency is more developed among humans. Recognition that society must be built on a foundation of mutual responsibility develops from awareness of, and sensitivity to, the interdependence of human beings.

Yet in light of the abundance of criminals and thieves, as well as other evidence, some contend that there is no such thing as natural

---

1. Based on Shabbat 31a.

morality. Some even maintain that man is innately wicked and can only be restrained by coercive means.

In practice, we see that even the most primitive cultures have traditions of mutual assistance. The family is the foundation of society, and families are fundamentally relationships of mutual concern. Moreover, we see the same phenomena amongst animals. Of course, one can contend that even mutual assistance developed from mere utilitarian interests such as obtaining food, protection, and the like. It is possible that the moral conduct that we see as natural in fact stems from social and cultural norms and from indoctrinated values; and it is possible that a different society or culture, which does not inculcate those values, would not have the same moral conduct.

Maimonides maintains that man does have a natural moral inclination to avoid injustice. He explains that this is why the generation of the Flood was punished even though they had not been given the Torah or mitzvot: since there are basic moral values that man can grasp on his own, failure to apply those values and conduct oneself accordingly constitutes sin. Even without a teacher or guide, one is obligated to recognize immorality and corruption, and to recoil from them.

> For Him, may He be exalted, justice is necessary and obligatory; namely, that an obedient individual receives compensation for all the pious and righteous actions he has accomplished, even if he was not ordered by a prophet to do them, and that he is punished for all evil acts committed by him, even if he was not forbidden by a prophet to do them; this being forbidden by the inborn disposition – I refer to the prohibition against wrongdoing and injustice.[2]

Maimonides further explains:

> [Regarding] things which all people commonly agree are evils, such as the shedding of blood, theft, robbery, fraud, injury to one who has done no harm, ingratitude, contempt for parents, and

2. *Moreh Nevukhim* III:17 (p. 470); see also Ḥizkuni on Genesis 7:21.

the like…there is no doubt that a soul which has the desire for, and lusts after, the above-mentioned misdeeds, is imperfect, and that a noble soul has absolutely no desire for any such crimes.[3]

Maimonides' view is based on Scripture and statements of the Sages. Man is expected to understand on his own not only that he should "turn away from evil," but also that he should "do good."[4] Of Abraham, who had not been commanded and had not received the Torah, God attested: "For I know him, that he will command his children and his household after him to keep the way of the Lord by doing righteousness and justice" (Genesis 18:19).[5] The Sages expressed this in their dictum: "No father taught him; he had no teacher. Where did he study Torah? The Holy One appointed his two kidneys to be like two rabbis, and they would gush forth and teach him Torah and wisdom. His kidneys gave him counsel."[6]

The Talmud asks rhetorically, "Is there anything that is permitted to a Jew but forbidden to a gentile?"[7] That is, something that is demanded of a gentile even though he has not received the Torah is obligatory by virtue of the demands of natural morality, even if it is not mentioned explicitly in the Torah. Its violation constitutes a serious transgression. It is thus demanded of Israel as well.

The Sages further stated:

> "Obey my laws" (Lev. 18:4): these are the things that were written in the Torah that, had they not been written, it would have been fitting to write them. For example: had theft, incest, idolatry, blasphemy, and bloodshed not been written, it would have been fitting to write them.[8]

---

3. *Shemonah Perakim*, chapter 6, p. 77.
4. See Psalms 34:15.
5. See also Rashbam on Genesis 26:5, s.v. "*ḥukotai vetorotai.*"
6. Genesis Rabba 61:1.
7. Ḥullin 33a; and see Rashi on Sanhedrin 59a: "When they left the category of gentiles, it was to become holy, not to make things easier." See also *Tosafot* ad loc., s.v. "*leika midam.*"
8. *Sifra, Aḥarei Mot* 13:10.

Man is expected to learn, on his own, not only to refrain from harming others, but also to conduct himself virtuously, as the Sages say: "Had the Torah not been given, we would learn modesty from the cat and theft from the ant."[9] Moreover, he faces an even greater challenge: refraining from idolatry, which is allowing falsehood to gain control of one's conceptions.

The Sages averred that a healthy individual has a moral sense that originates in the depths of his soul. This view was espoused by the Geonim and Maimonides. Thus, for example, Rav Nissim Gaon writes: "All of the mitzvot that depend on reason and on the heart's understanding have been obligatory for every person from the day that God created man on earth."[10]

Natural Morality, Religious Command, and the Binding of Isaac

The complexity of the idea of natural morality has another dimension: even if man possesses a degree of innate morality, this does not mean that each individual will act in accordance with what is best for society. The fact that man is a social animal who requires the aid of others can also lead him to the nefarious attempt to control others by force. However, even if man acts in consonance with an innate moral sense, and even in a society that has developed effective rules of conduct, the question remains as to how far these rules go, and whom they include. It is possible, for example, that man has a natural aversion to murder and even an emotional impulse of mercy for one who is suffering; but how much effort must one expend, and what must one sacrifice, for the sake of this natural moral claim? Even if one has a natural feeling of respect or generosity toward others, does natural morality guide man to give everyone what he needs? How can the demands of natural morality be quantified? What if moral expectations conflict with one another?

---

9. Eiruvin 100b.

10. Introduction to *Sefer Mafte'aḥ* (which is printed before Berakhot, as an introduction to the Talmud, in standard versions of the Babylonian Talmud). See also Rav Saadia Gaon's commentary on *Beḥukotai* (cited in M. Zucker's introduction to his edition of *Rav Saadia Gaon's Commentary on Genesis* [New York: The Jewish Theological Seminary of America, 1984], 18,) as well as his *Emunot VeDe'ot*, third treatise, chapter 8.

There is an episode in the Torah – *Akedat Yitzḥak* (the Binding of Isaac) – which teaches us that natural morality is insufficient, for man's intelligence can deceive him. The episode is an uninterrupted flow of questions and perplexities, but one main question emerges: how could Abraham be commanded to sacrifice his son? Does the Torah require man to subordinate his moral universe to religious dictate?

The prophet reproves his contemporaries: "For they have forsaken Me…and they have filled this place with the blood of the innocent…to put their children to the fire as burnt offerings to Baal – which I never commanded, never decreed, and which never came to My mind" (Jer. 19:4–5). The Sages expounded this verse:

> "Which I never commanded" – this refers to the son of King Mesha of Moab, as it is stated: "So he took his first-born son, who was to succeed him as king, and offered him as a burnt offering" (II Kings 3:27); "never decreed" – this refers to Yiftah; "and which never came to My mind" – this refers to Isaac, the son of Abraham.[11]

The mention of *Akedat Yitzḥak* together with the acts of Mesha and Yiftah is astonishing. How can they be compared? What is the common denominator between Isaac, the Moabite prince, and Yiftah's daughter? More perplexingly, how can Yiftah and Mesha be compared to Abraham? What are the Sages trying to teach by equating them?

Maimonides explains that *Akedat Yitzḥak* teaches us two major lessons, which are fundamental to the Torah:

> One of these notions consists in our being informed of the limit of love for God, may He be exalted, and fear of Him…
>
> The second notion consists in making known to us the fact that the prophets consider as true that which comes to them from God in a prophetic revelation. For it should not be thought that what they hear or what appears to them in a parable is not certain or is commingled with illusion just because

---

11. Ta'anit 4a.

it comes about in a dream and in a vision…and through the medium of the imaginative faculty. Accordingly, [Scripture] wished to make it known to us that all that is seen by a prophet in a vision of prophecy is, in the opinion of the prophet, a certain truth, that the prophet has no doubts in any way concerning anything in it, and that in his opinion its status is the same as that of all existent things that are apprehended through the senses or through the intellect. A proof for this is the fact that [Abraham] hastened to slaughter, as he had been commanded, his son, his only son, whom he loved, even though this command came to him in a dream or in a vision. For if a dream of prophecy had been obscure for the prophets, or if they had doubts or incertitude concerning what they apprehended in a vision of prophecy, *they would not have hastened to do that which is repugnant to nature*, and Abraham's soul would not have consented to accomplish an act of so great importance if there had been a doubt about it.[12]

The same Abraham who did not shrink from confronting the Creator when Sodom's fate was sealed, demanding justice for His creation and claiming, "Shall not the Judge of all the earth deal justly?!" (Gen. 18:25) did not ask for mercy on his own behalf. Rather, he accepted God's decree and rose with alacrity to do the will of his Maker.

But what "will" was there, really? The prophet attests that the sacrifice of Isaac "never came to My mind"! This was not what God wanted! How could it be that Abraham's greatest trial was based on a misunderstanding?!

A midrash expands upon the above-cited passage from the Talmud, and the additional material helps us understand its meaning:

Scripture states: "The fruit of the righteous is a tree of life; and one who is wise wins lives" (Prov. 11:30)…. "The fruit of the righteous is a tree of life" – this refers to Torah, for one who is a *ben Torah* (possesses Torah knowledge) will learn how to win lives,

12. *Moreh Nevukhim* III:24, pp. 500–502 (italics added).

as it states: "one who is wise wins lives," that is, if one vows the value of a life, he learns from the Torah how to do so. If he has no Torah, he has nothing. This is what we find with respect to Yiftah of Gilad: since he was not a *ben Torah*, he lost his daughter.[13]

The midrash goes on to explain that had he been a *ben Torah*, he would have read the Torah and learned that his vow to sacrifice his daughter was not valid. The midrash says the same of King Mesha of Moab:

> "Which never came to My mind" – this refers to King Mesha of Moab, of whom Scripture states that when he fell into the hands of the King of Israel, "he took his first-born son, who was to succeed him as king, and offered him as a burnt offering." What caused him to sacrifice his son? The fact that he was not a *ben Torah*. Had he read the Torah, he would not have lost his son, for the Torah says, "When anyone explicitly vows ... if it is a male the equivalent is ... and if it is a female the equivalent is ..." (Lev. 27:2–4). Thus, "one who is wise wins lives."

In other words, the Torah establishes standards that apply even to prophecy. This is quite straightforward: when a prophet, even an established prophet, addresses a group, the law is that if the prophet states "that God sent him to add or subtract a mitzva or to interpret a mitzva in a manner that has no tradition from Moses ... he is a false prophet."[14] This applies not only to the prophet's audience, but even to the prophet himself: just as when an individual hears a friend speak, his understanding reflects his own judgment no less than the clarity of the speaker's formulation, so too with respect to prophecy. This is evident from the initial prophecy of Samuel, who did not know who was speaking to him. A prophet who hears the word of God will likely not understand his vision properly without the Torah's guidance.

Maimonides, when speaking about Abraham, states: "He did not have a teacher or source of information, rather ... his heart would explore

---

13. *Tanḥuma Beḥukotai* 5:1.
14. *Hilkhot Yesodei HaTorah* 9:1.

and understand things until he ultimately comprehended the way of truth and understood the contours of righteousness through proper thinking."[15] Abraham discovered the Maker of the world through passionate longing and drew wisdom from the depth of his intellect, until the gates of heaven opened before him and he attained prophecy. Abraham blazed the trail to worshipping God and heeding His commands by means of his own intellect. Yet the Torah, which is not a product of human intelligence, he did not possess.

Abraham heard God's voice and was certain that the voice was God's, unlike the novice Samuel, who did not initially know who was speaking to him. However, Abraham grew up in an environment in which it was accepted that deities crave human sacrifice. It is true that Abraham recognized the worthlessness of his native society's deities, but in such a cultural environment, natural morality did not shield him from his trial! Abraham heard God's command, and it was indeed difficult for him, but he understood that, since God is the God of truth, no human consideration could compete with God's command.

Yet the youngest school child among his descendants knows that the Torah says: "You shall not act thus toward the Lord your God, for they perform for their gods every abhorrent act that the Lord detests; they even offer up their sons and daughters in fire to their gods" (Deut. 12:31). The notion that a human being would sacrifice his son on an altar certainly never "came to God's mind." How do we know this? Because the Torah says so explicitly, in the verse cited above. Abraham, however, did not know this, and had no way of knowing it, because he did not receive the Torah.

The Holy One said to Abraham: "raise him up there as a burnt offering (*ha'alehu sham le'ola*)" (Gen. 22:2). Abraham understood this according to the plain meaning: he must sacrifice his son Isaac as a burnt offering, as all the other nations do, as was common at the time. Certainly it was difficult for him, but Abraham said to himself: "Who am I to challenge God?" And so he asked no questions. His absolute loyalty to the Creator left no room for doubts, questions, or hesitation.

---

15. *Hilkhot Avoda Zara* 1:3.

On the other hand, the Sages said[16] that *Akedat Yitzhak* is juxtaposed to the death of Sarah because when Sarah heard that her son almost died, her soul departed. Sarah had no prophetic vision. She did not hear God's voice speaking to her. But nevertheless she knew, from the very depth of her soul, that God could not possibly desire human sacrifice. How did she know what Abraham did not? Perhaps because a mother's connection with her child, the closeness she feels toward him, is stronger than the father's connection. It stands to reason that this, in turn, is related to the natural bond between a child and his mother, who carries him in her womb and gives birth to him. As Moses said: "Did I conceive all this people? Did I bear them, that You should say to me, 'Carry them in your bosom...'?" (Num. 11:12).

What was the purpose of this trial? It was not only to test Abraham's faith, but also to teach him that in order to understand the truth of a prophetic vision, one needs Torah. Why did God test him this way? So that Abraham would comprehend that one cannot rely on natural morality and human reason alone; Torah is also needed. Torah is the prophetic revelation to all Israel, not the revelation to an individual prophet.

After Abraham withstood the test and demonstrated that he was persuaded by the truth of his prophecy, the Holy One blessed him: "All the nations of the earth shall bless themselves by your descendants, because you have heeded My voice" (Gen. 22:18).

The Sages say:

> The Holy One, blessed be He, said to him: Your descendants will sin against me in the future, and I will sit in judgment of them on Rosh HaShana.... Fortunate are you, O Israel, for God showed His love for you, which He did not do for any other people or nation. [Scripture] states: "He told His people the power of His works" (Ps. 111:6); and it is written: "He told His words to Jacob, His laws and statutes to Israel" (ibid. 147:19); and it is written: "He did not do so for any other nation; of such laws they know not" (ibid. 20).[17]

---

16. Genesis Rabba 58:5.
17. *Midrash Tanhuma* (Buber ed.) *Vayera* §15.

That is, the Torah was given to Israel in Abraham's merit. They further stated:

> "All the nations of the earth shall bless themselves by your descendants" – had Israel not accepted the Torah, the world would have been destroyed. So too, all the goodness that comes to the world is for Israel, who accepted the Torah.[18]

Abraham broadened the boundaries of love for God to the point of unquenchable yearning, to the point of ultimate devotion, and therefore, quid pro quo, it was determined that God would forever love his descendants;[19] God taught us His laws and statutes, and by virtue of the Torah, these descendants will find the path to God even when darkness covers the earth and when there is no prophecy.

The Holy One came to teach Abraham that human understanding alone is not enough. Even if man can discover his Creator and understand His will, human intelligence is nevertheless limited in what it can grasp; it can grasp only what it can comprehend through habits of speech, culture, and language. Therefore, Abraham could only learn the real meaning of the command, "Take your son ... and raise him up there as a burnt offering" (Gen. 22:2), through a powerful, despair-inducing experience.

If it is true of prophetic revelation that a prophet cannot penetrate the full meaning of the message communicated to him unless he considers it in light of the Torah, then with regard to other forms of knowledge, which are not communicated to man directly from the Source of wisdom, this is certainly the case. If it is true of a giant like Abraham, then it is certainly true of other men, even the wisest of them.

---

18. Ibid. §18. See also *Maimonides' Epistle to Yemen* (Halkin and Cohen ed.), p. vii:
    Isaiah, the herald of the national redemption, has already stated that Israel's indestructibility is the result of a Divine pact betokened by the perpetuation of the Torah in our midst, and our devotion to its tenets and teachings, as he says, "And as for Me, this is My covenant with them, says the Lord; My spirit that is upon you, and My words which I have put in your mouth, shall not depart out of your mouth, nor out of the mouth of your seed, nor out of the mouth of your seed's seed, says the Lord, from henceforth and for ever" (Is. 59:21).
19. See Nahmanides on Genesis 22:16.

There are two sides to this equation: On one hand, the Torah aims to guide man along the straight path, instructing him as to his moral duties and responsibilities. On the other hand, one who has not developed a high level of moral sensitivity will not know how to act properly, in accordance with the Torah.

The giving of the Torah broadened, deepened, and enhanced the rise of the natural moral inclination, first and foremost in Israel, and later among all peoples.

The Septuagint, the translation of the Torah into Greek, was completed during the Second Temple era. Scripture has since been translated into virtually every human language. There are several languages that had no written form, for which translators created a script so that audiences might be able to access Scripture in their native tongue.[20] It is a matter of historical fact that the translation of Scripture into English helped bring the Torah's moral values into Western culture, thus laying the foundation for democracy and for individual freedoms. The Torah indeed attests of itself: "it is your wisdom and discernment in the eyes of other peoples" (Deut. 4:6). Long before the age of King James, Maimonides noted: "The world has become filled with speech about the messiah, with the words of the Torah, and with talk of mitzvot. They have spread to remote islands and to many nations with insensitive hearts, who now discuss these matters...."[21]

This influence spread primarily westward, to Europe and then America. There are many nations in the Far East and Africa that have not yet been exposed to the Torah. Nevertheless, they, too, have moral rules. It is clear that the search for moral values is a feature of the human race.

Although the Torah is the guide to the straight path to God, Maimonides, nevertheless, characteristically asserts that even one who was not privileged to receive the Torah, but still elevated himself to a lofty moral plane, is "the holiest of the holy," though this is not a common phenomenon. In his words:

---

20. [Editor's note: This is the prevailing view regarding the development of the Cyrillic alphabet in the tenth century. See *Encyclopedia Britannica*, s.v. "Cyrillic alphabet."]
21. *Hilkhot Melakhim* 11:4.

...any individual in the world whose spirit moves him and whose own intellect gives him the understanding to set himself apart in order to stand before God, to serve Him and worship Him, to know God; who walks upright, as God created him to do; and who has cast away the burden of the many calculations that people pursue – is sanctified with the utmost holiness. God will be his portion and his inheritance forever and ever.[22]

Natural Morality and the Morality of the Torah

It is clear that the Torah's aim is to raise the moral level of man, individually and collectively. From the words of our patriarch Abraham, "Shall not the Judge of all the earth deal justly?!" (Gen. 18:25), it emerges that as a matter of principle, Divine morality must comport with human morality. However, there are occasionally exceptional cases where there seems to be a gap between morality and the path of the Torah. We will consider two such examples from which we can abstract principles for understanding the Torah's commandments.

Amalek

The Torah obviously opposes bloodshed, for "God made man in His image" (Gen. 9:6). Woe to the murderer, who has ruined the Divine image within him. This is a fundamental principle of the entire Torah, the guiding rule to which the mitzva to eradicate Amalek is an exception. Nevertheless, according to the moral sense that we have developed and that guides us to this day, the commandment to "blot out the memory of Amalek from under the heavens" (Deut. 25:19) seems immoral.

At first glance, the commandment is clear and straightforward: the nation of Amalek must be wiped out unconditionally. In truth, however, it is not quite so simple. First, we must address the fact that when waging war on Amalek, as in any other war, there is a commandment to offer peace.[23] They are attacked only if they refuse to accept the terms of peace.[24]

---

22. *Hilkhot Shemita VeYovel* 13:13.
23. *Hilkhot Melakhim* 6:1.
24. Ibid. 6:4.

Moreover, descendants of Amalek may be accepted as converts to Judaism. They may even become *"gerei toshav"* – "resident foreigners" of the Jewish commonwealth – a quasi-conversion which entails the acceptance of the seven Noahide laws. An Amalekite who accepts these laws becomes a *ger toshav* and is considered to have made peace with Israel.

Haman was called an "Agagite" because he descended from the Amalekite king, Agag. Astonishingly, the Sages say in several places that: "Descendants of Haman taught Torah in Bnei Brak."[25] They further state: "Beware of the children of the peoples of the earth [*amei ha'aretz*], for Torah will go forth from them."[26] Rashi explains: "'Beware of the children of the peoples of the earth' – who have become Torah scholars; show them honor, for Torah will go forth from them to Israel, as Shemaya and Avtalyon descended from Sennacherib, and descendants of Haman taught Torah in Bnei Brak."[27] This applies to all the peoples of the earth, including Amalek. Indeed, the Book of Samuel refers to "the son of a foreigner (*ger*), an Amalekite" (II Sam. 1:13), which Radak interprets to mean an Amalekite convert.[28]

It is worth citing Maimonides' words about those who think that the Torah's stories are useless: "Know that all the stories that you will find mentioned in the Torah are there for a necessary utility for the Law."[29] As an example, Maimonides addresses why the Torah describes the lineage of the Seirite tribes at such great length, explaining that all of these tribes "were called after the predominant tribe…particularly the descendants of Amalek, for they were the bravest among them."[30] The Torah therefore devotes much space to identifying all of them, including those whose mothers alone were

---

25. Gittin 57b; Sanhedrin 96b.
26. Sanhedrin 96a.
27. Ibid.
28. See *Hilkhot Sanhedrin* 18:7: "That David killed…an Amalekite convert…." Later commentaries note that Maimonides' ruling runs counter to *Mekhilta DeRabbi Yishmael, Masekhta DeAmalek* 2 (Horowitz-Rabin edition, Jerusalem: Wahrman, 1970), pp. 186–87.
29. *Moreh Nevukhim* III:50; p. 613.
30. Ibid., p. 614.

descended from Amalek, to tell us that "those whom you see today in Seir and the kingdom of Amalek are not all children of Amalek," and the commandment to eradicate Amalek does not apply to them. These words teach us that even in war, once must be cautious about who is harmed and who is spared.

However, we must note a fundamental distinction that pertains to the classification of mitzvot. The Torah addresses problems that confront both individuals and society at different historical periods. There is a major difference in how to deal with the Torah's practical obligations – mitzvot and *dinim*[31] that must be performed, and regarding which we must reach a clear decision – and theoretical matters that can sustain different interpretations. This problem is especially acute with respect to matters addressed in Scripture that are no longer practically relevant and that applied under conditions about which we do not have enough information. The Torah clearly viewed Amalek as an embodiment of evil. However, we must acknowledge that we do not adequately understand the commandment to eradicate Amalek, because we are not sufficiently familiar with the conditions that then prevailed.

It is important to emphasize that neither the mitzva to eliminate the seven indigenous tribes of Eretz Yisrael nor the mitzva to eradicate Amalek are applicable today.[32] The Sages have already said: "King Sennacherib of Assyria arose and mixed up all the nations."[33] Maimonides likewise ruled: "When King Sennacherib of Assyria arose, he mixed up all the nations, intermingled them, and exiled them from their locales. The Egyptians who are presently in Egypt are different peoples, as are the Edomites on the plains of Edom."[34] Over the years, the remnants of the seven nations and Amalek assimilated into other nations, and they no longer exist.

---

31. See above, the chapter titled "The Role of the Commandments," in the section on "The Beautiful Captive Woman."
32. See my explanation in *Melumdei Milḥama* §3 and *Yad Peshuta* to *Hilkhot Melakhim* 5:4–5.
33. Mishna Yadayim 4:4.
34. *Hilkhot Issurei Biah* 12:25.

Another basic point must be emphasized. When there is a discrepancy between moral principles and a commandment that is not actually practiced, one must not alter his moral principles just because of a commandment that was practiced in the past but which no longer applies in any way. Rather, he should maintain his moral judgment and may leave the mitzva as an unresolved question, acknowledging that there are certain things that we do not understand.

Some have cited one of the great sages of the last generation as saying that anyone who rises up against Israel has the status of Amalek; similar ideas have been expressed in the past. However, this was intended homiletically. Occasionally it is necessary to lift the spirit of our fellow Jews suffering torments and persecutions by telling them to trust God's promise that He will ultimately vanquish our enemies and mete out justice to our foes. Indeed, when these words were spoken in earlier generations, their audiences understood that these were not intended as normative statements, but figuratively and homiletically; we must not confuse these distinct genres.

Capital Punishment

Some have claimed that the Torah's justice system metes out cruel and excessive punishment. After all, there are thirty-six[35] capital offenses for which one is put to death by the court!

The issue of punishing offenders must be addressed at the fundamental level. Although a healthy person has a moral sense, that is only one of many feelings that arise within man's soul, and sometimes these conflict with one another. Even when one knows what moral response is required of him, he may still be plagued by other thoughts – even thoughts that he would be ashamed to ever translate into action. It stands to reason that man is graced with a certain basic moral awareness, but this awareness is not enough to dictate his behavior, since ultimately he has free choice.

There needs to be a system in place that will challenge and encourage the public to do good and to love and help one another. It also must devise ways to deter and prevent injustice. Maimonides explains that

---

35. *Hilkhot Sanhedrin* 15:13.

one of the central principles of tort law, in addition to the obligation to compensate for damage, is the prevention of damage: "Know that the more frequent the kind of crime is and the easier it is to commit, the greater the penalty for it must be, so that one should refrain from it."[36]

Deterrence requires the threat of punishment, even if those punishments are only carried out under extraordinary circumstances, because the very fact that there are such punishments has an effect. For instance, the death penalty seems excessive for the "wayward and rebellious son"; why does he deserve to die? The truth is that the law of the "wayward and rebellious son" was never meant to be applied. Rather, it was meant to intimidate and deter; it was a way of guiding and educating the community. The Sages said: "There never was and never will be a wayward and rebellious son. Why was it written? To study it and receive reward."[37] So too, the purpose of most of the Torah's punishments is deterrence.

This is the nature of all of the Torah's capital and corporal punishments.[38] R. Tarfon and R. Akiva stated: "Had we been in the Sanhedrin, it never would have put anyone to death."[39] The laws that limit the types of admissible evidence and testimony are so complex that it is always possible to find a way to disqualify the witnesses and thus acquit the accused. However, R. Shimon b. Gamliel responds to the statement of R. Akiva and R. Tarfon: "They would increase bloodshed in Israel." That is, if the death penalty is completely eliminated, it will empower murderers, since there will be no credible deterrent against them.

Still, not every threat is intended to be carried out. All of the Torah's statements about punishments are threats, but the practical implementation of those threats must be kept to a necessary minimum. This is the meaning of the mishna's statement: "A Sanhedrin that killed once in seven years is called 'destructive.' R. Elazar b. Azariah says: Once in seventy years." The laws of court procedure and testimony

---

36. *Moreh Nevukhim* III:41; p. 559.
37. Sanhedrin 71a. See above, the chapter titled, "The Role of the Commandments."
38. See below, the chapter titled, "The Authority of Rabbinical Courts and the Torah View of Punishment."
39. Mishna Makkot 1:10.

are constructed in a way that makes it all but impossible to condemn a person to death, even for murder, God forbid. Nevertheless, the very presence of the threat has an educational value. It is likely that R. Elazar b. Azariah does not disagree with the mishna's initial opinion; rather, they address different periods. Without a doubt, the prevalence of delinquency fluctuates over time, due to various reasons and factors. Perhaps during the time of certain *tanna'im*, one instance of capital punishment in seventy years or more was enough to deter transgressors, but at other times, it was not.

We have already noted[40] that the Torah has a dual purpose. On one hand, it is necessary to set up a legal system for all of society, with basic laws that ensure good governance, for the benefit of the entire population. The Torah's system of capital and corporal punishments exists for this purpose. The Torah even allowed the Sages to reset punitive policy as generations change. With respect to mitzvot of this type, though they are considered "mitzvot for all times," our aim is to advance beyond them, to the point where the violations do not take place and therefore the punishments no longer have to be carried out. Accordingly, as the generations change and progress, the Sages saw fit to enact laws that accord with the Torah's aims, to the point where these punishments would no longer need to be implemented at all; in their stead would be an alternative system of punishments, appropriate for the time. Of such mitzvot which no longer apply in practice it is said: "Study and receive reward."

On the other hand, the Torah has an even higher purpose: fashioning a society that is worthy of being imbued with the Divine Presence. To achieve this purpose, the Torah sets lofty goals for us, challenging and spurring us over the course of many generations. Even the noblest spirits do not achieve these goals fully. It is for this purpose that we were given mitzvot whose goals are the same across all generations, directing man's path and guiding his moral development toward ever-greater refinement. Thus, as one progresses morally and intellectually, he gains access to deeper understandings of the moral content of these mitzvot and broader horizons for their practical fulfillment. In line with these

---

40. Above, at the beginning of the chapter titled "The Role of the Commandments."

goals, we must create an educational system that will cultivate a generation characterized by its knowledge of God.

Commandments of Conscience and Commandments of the Torah

If there is conflict between halakha and one's moral sense, then there is
a flaw in his moral sense, his understanding of halakha, or both, because
as a matter of principle there should be no discrepancy between them.
Unfortunately, many people have a warped moral sense, and sometimes
their understanding of halakha is likewise skewed. Neither one's natural moral sense nor one's comprehension of the Torah's instruction is
immune from error and misunderstanding, whether due to our mental
limitations or due to the distorting effect of the evil inclination.

However, there is a more fundamental question: reality is always
variegated, and so every practical decision involves moral complexity.
The Talmud tells of the profundity of R. Meir's thinking: "his colleagues
could not fathom the depths of his thinking. He would say of something
impure that it is pure, and show evidence; of something pure that it is
impure, and show evidence."[41] Neither intuition nor intellectual analysis
in light of the Torah – nor, in fact, both of them together – can always
provide clear and unequivocal rulings on the proper course of action in
cases of extreme duress, for in every situation there are reasons to incline
one way and the other way.

There are rare cases in which neither the Torah from heaven nor
natural morality instructs a person what to do, practically. In such cases,
the decision is left to man's choice. Such cases express the depth of free
choice; with it, at times, man can "earn eternal life in a mere moment."

The Sages view reality in terms of polarities. Thus, they understand
the universe itself as the product of the interaction of forces and as the
arena for creative interplay between opposing principles. In the Sages'
terms, *raḥamim* (mercy) and *din* (justice) are the poles around which all
existence crystallizes, and the very act of creation *ex nihilo* is the concrete
expression of the tension between *raḥamim* and *din*. A midrashic parable illustrates this idea, which appears frequently in rabbinic literature:

---

41. Eiruvin 13b.

"The Lord God (*Hashem Elokim*)" (Gen. 2:4) – [this can be explained by parable:] A king had empty cups. Said the king: "If I put hot water into them, they will burst. If cold, they will crack." What did the king do? He mixed hot water with cold, filled them, and they endured. So said the Holy One: "If I create the world with the attribute of *raḥamim*, its sins will be numerous. If with the attribute of *din*, how can the world endure? I shall therefore create it with the attributes of *din* and *raḥamim*. Would that it endure!"[42]

In different contexts, the terminology varies. Thus, *din* is sometimes called *gevura* (might) and *raḥamim* is sometimes called *ḥesed* (kindness). Moreover, the dialectics of *din* and *raḥamim* were conceived as being of such all-embracing character that every fundamental antithesis was seen as but another manifestation of the counterpoint between *din* and *raḥamim*. Under the influence of Aristotelian usage,[43] *gevura* and *ḥesed* became identified with matter and form: *gevura* is the power of continuity, the principle of being, the substratum of existence, the matter that is ever-present through all change, yet is itself unchanging. In other words, it is the passive or "female" element (matter) – passivity that in its constancy contains all things within itself. In contrast, *ḥesed* is the principle of action, the "male" element (form), forever sacrificing itself, seemingly of no substance, yet imparting substance to all things and realization to every potential, endowing matter with meaning and significance. It is the power of love, which, in self-effacement, merges itself into the object of its love, impregnating it with the spark of Divine life.

The Torah is the model and blueprint of the world. The Sages taught:

> The Torah is likened to two paths: one through fire and one through snow. If one turns toward this one he dies by fire; if one turns toward the other he dies by snow. What shall one do? Let him go in the middle.[44]

42. Genesis Rabba 12:15.
43. Aristotle, *Physics* I:9. See *Moreh Nevukhim* I:17, p. 43: "Plato and his predecessors designated Matter as the female and Form as the male." See also Plato, *Timaeus*, 50d.
44. Y. Ḥagiga 2:1.

Based on this, Maimonides explains that the Torah's code of behavior represents the middle way, which will bring neither burn nor frostbite to one who follows it.[45] Yet the "mean" may be a tenuous one, for by its very nature, it must in many circumstances represent a compromise between the demands of *ḥesed* and *din*. Under more trying conditions, it may require a choice between alternatives all of which are guilt laden. Clearly if *ḥesed* bids one to act one way and justice another, even where the choice between them or a third alternative is prescribed by halakha, it is only on the level of behavior that the dilemma is resolved. As far as motivation is concerned, there is no escape from the paradox. Yet the motives for our actions are inevitably involved in determining their ethical character.[46]

Interestingly enough, Maimonides singles out David and Elijah as examples of men who exhibited harshness and anger, albeit in righteous causes, to show how lack of love results in the loss of virtue even though, in practice, the exigencies of justice leave no room for choice.[47] It is not surprising, therefore, that halakha itself recognizes the need to suspend the usual halakhic criteria in those instances where conflict on the motivational level is acute.

The archetype is our father Abraham. So boundless is his love for man that he rebels against accepting the divine decree against the wicked city of Sodom and its allies. Scripture states: "Abraham approached" (Gen. 18:23), on which the Midrash comments: "R. Elazar explained thus: If for war – I come; for conciliation – I come; for prayer – I come."[48] Abraham does not shrink from war, as it were, against the Almighty, and driven by love, he hurls an accusation against "the Judge of all earth."

---

45. See *Shemonah Perakim*, chapter 4.
46. As a matter of practical law, it is evident that Maimonides' opinion is that mitzvot do not require intention (*"mitzvot ein tzerikhot kavana"*), and one who performs the required act, even without intention to fulfill his obligation, has nevertheless fulfilled it. However, there is a distinction between intention to discharge an obligation and intention to perform the act. See my explanation in *Yad Peshuta* to *Hilkhot Keriat Shema* 2:1.
47. See *Shemonah Perakim*, chapter 7.
48. Genesis Rabba 49:8.

This question reappears in various guises. In order to save lives, is every action justified? Based on the Talmud's remarks about Esther,[49] Rabbi Yosef Colon saw it as permissible for a woman to surrender to or even arouse the adulterous lust of bandits in order to save the lives of their captives.[50] Rabbi Yeḥezkel Landau demurred.[51] The same question was addressed closer to our own time by Rabbi Yeḥiel Yaakov Weinberg.[52] All the authorities agree that in extreme cases one should not issue unequivocal rulings; the woman's own conscience must be her guide, for only she can determine what her true motives are.

Not only can an overwhelming challenge of *ḥesed* suspend the usual norms. The same applies to the stern demands of *din*. "R. Elazar b. Yaakov said: I have heard that the court may inflict lashes and penalties that are not prescribed by the Torah."[53] After expanding upon this rule, Maimonides adds an admonishment: "All these things are based on what the judge deems appropriate and required by circumstances. In everything, his actions shall be for the sake of heaven, and let not the dignity of men be light in his eyes."[54] Lest one allow himself excessive leeway in deviating from established judicial procedure, Maimonides concludes: "It is the glory of the Torah to act in accordance with its statutes and ordinances."[55]

God's Torah, Man's Torah

It is only in cases of exceptional urgency that the individual is given the liberty to probe his own motives and act as he sees fit regardless of the usual rules. Nevertheless, even when the stakes are not nearly so high, the Sages recognized, at least ex post facto, the justification for unlawful deeds that stemmed from pure motives:

---

49. See Sanhedrin 74b.
50. See *Responsa Maharik* §137.
51. *Responsa Noda BiYehuda, Yoreh De'ah* 2:161.
52. *Responsa Seridei Esh*, (A. Weingort ed., HaVaad Lehotza'at Kitvei Harav: Jerusalem, 1999), 2:37 (3:107 in the four-volume Mosad Harav Kook edition).
53. Sanhedrin 46a; Y. Ḥagiga 2:2. See below, in the chapter titled: "The Authority of Rabbinical Courts and the Torah View of Punishment."
54. *Hilkhot Sanhedrin* 24:10.
55. Ibid.

What [is the meaning of] that which is written, "The paths of
the Lord are straight – the righteous walk on them, and sinners
stumble upon them" (Hos. 14:10)?.... It is analogous to Lot and
his daughters. They, whose intention was for a mitzva – "the righteous walk on them." He, whose intention was to sin – "sinners
stumble upon them."[56]

The general conclusion of this talmudic passage is: "Great is a transgression for the sake of [God]." In fact, the point of dispute is whether
a transgression for God's sake is greater than a mitzva that is performed
for reasons other than for God's sake, or is merely equal; all agree that
intention is no less significant than action.[57]

Halakha posits a hierarchy of norms that enables decisions in certain cases of conflict between specific laws. However, as we have seen,
this is not a complete ordering in the sense that some pairs of conflicting values are equally weighted, and consequently, the rules of halakhic
decision-making are not applicable. Moreover, even where there is a
relative preference that indicates a specific course of action, the scale is
not univalent, since intention and motivation can at least cancel out the
priority of one value over another.

This assertion is true not only if we consider "actions" as units
comprised of acts and intent. Even if we relate to the acts alone – that is,
to behaviors unrelated to intent – we will see that there are situations in
which the clash between mitzvot remains unresolved, allowing the individual to apply extra-halakhic considerations in rendering his decision.

There is a considerable body of halakhic opinion that the impera-
tive "You shall not stand idly by the blood of your fellow" (Lev. 19:16) is
accorded equal status with that of self-preservation. Accordingly, one is
free to choose to sacrifice his own life to save the life of another, though
halakha does not require it.[58] Here, then, is a case where one's personal

---

56. Horayot 10b.
57. See Rav Kook's *Responsa Mishpat Kohen* §143 (at the end).
58. See the dispute between R. Akiva and Ben Petora in Bava Metzia 62a; *Responsa
    Mishpat Kohen* §143 and §144, sections 14–15; Malbim on Leviticus 19:18; *Pitḥei
    Teshuva* on *Yoreh De'ah* 252:6.

prioritization of values produces a subjective hierarchy that halakha then recognizes for that individual, but not generally or unequivocally for others. This demands a great deal of personal responsibility. Only one who has internalized the Torah's values and fashioned his lifestyle in accordance with halakha is capable of properly navigating between these two paths.

However, society needs a legal system that is characterized both by continuity in time and universality in scope. This, in turn, requires standardization and uniformity of practice in most areas. Maimonides articulates this as follows:

> Governance of the Law ought to be absolute and universal, including everyone, even if it is suitable only for certain individuals and not suitable for others; for if it were made to fit individuals, the whole would be corrupted and "you would make out of it something that varies."[59] For this reason, matters that are primarily intended in the Law ought not to be dependent on time or place; but the decree ought to be absolute and universal, according to what He, may He be exalted, says: "As for the congregation, there shall be one statute for you" (Num. 15:15). However, only the universal interests, those of the majority, are considered in them.[60]

Still, we have seen that there are exceptions to this rule, wherein the individual is expected to determine his own hierarchy of values. This is not possible unless his thought patterns and spiritual qualities fit with Torah values. Yet even with regard to the universally-applied halakhic system, the individual, as an individual, still plays a primary role.

Every Jew must challenge himself to study halakha, to know and understand it, to acquire its modes of thought, to sensitize himself to its values, and to become capable of rendering his own decisions. Thus:

---

59. *"Natata devarekha leshi'urim"*; Shabbat 35b.
60. *Moreh Nevukhim* III:34, p. 335.

Mar Zutra explained in the name of R. Ḥisda: Whosoever studies Scripture and Mishna, diagnoses a *terefa*[61] for himself, and apprentices under Torah scholars, of him Scripture states: "When you enjoy the labor of your hands, you shall be happy, and it shall be well with you" (Ps. 128:2).... "You shall be happy" in this world, "and it shall be well with you" in the next world.[62]

Maharsha there explains this interpretation of the verse:

"Happy is one who fears God..." (Ps. 128:1) – that is, one who is presented with what may be a *terefa*, and he fears God and is therefore strict with himself and refrains from eating it, shall be happy in the next world, for he has avoided a possible *terefa*. However, "when you enjoy the labor of your hands," a higher level is attained. That is, one who exerts himself to resolve the doubt, finds it permissible, and then eats it, has gained in both worlds. It says of him: "You shall be happy" in this world, for he eats of it, "and it shall be well with you" in the next world, for he has exerted himself in Torah.

The crucial point is that though no one is born with the right to render his own halakhic decisions, everyone has the obligation to acquire this right by means of diligent and painstaking Torah study. Halakhic ruling as a dialectical process is not one that necessarily takes place always at a particular level of authority. There is ample room for individual judgment, rather than mere obedience.

In this connection, the following statement of Maharal, though not formulated as a halakhic ruling, gives us insight into what I am trying to convey:

It is more fitting and more correct that one should determine the law for himself directly on the basis of the Talmud, even though

---

61. [An animal with an illness or defect that renders it unkosher even when slaughtered properly.]
62. Ḥullin 44b.

there is a danger that he will not follow the true path and not decide the law as it should be in truth. Notwithstanding, the sage has only to consider what his intellect apprehends and understands from the Talmud, and if his understanding and wisdom mislead him, he is nevertheless beloved by the Lord when he decides in accordance with his mind's dictates…. He is superior to one who rules from a code without knowing the reasons which are the grounds of the decision – for such a person walks along like a blind man.[63]

To my knowledge, nobody puts it quite as sharply, nor that strongly, but it is not really a unique view that each person ought to study the sources, consult with scholars, analyze the various opinions, and reach his own conclusions instead of merely submitting to authority. The halakhic decision-making process is not meant to release us from the struggles of conscience and rigorous intellectual inquiry involved in any decision. Rather, it is these elements that transform the process into a worthwhile spiritual experience. If every act of choice is to be laden with meaning, it must be the outcome of a process which involves all the faculties of the soul, not only the overcoming of temptation, important though that is.

Obviously, in many cases there are purely technical procedures for resolving legal issues, and these leave little room for individual variation. That is essential for the orderly development of society. But even with all that, there are still situations, such as those we have noted above, in which the final decision remains with the individual, taken in the privacy and loneliness of one's own conscience, where the immediacy and ethical awareness of the demands of *hesed* and *din* are such that only the individual himself can confront the storms within his heart and determine which demand shall prevail.

We learn in a mishna: "Against your will you are created, and against your will you are born."[64] The Almighty ensconces man in the world without asking him, "man has no choice with respect to it."[65] Man

63. Maharal, *Netivot Olam, Netiv HaTorah* ch. 15.
64. Mishna Avot 4:24.
65. Maimonides, *Commentary on the Mishna*, Avot 4:24.

moves through a world that it not his own. Though he considers himself a "resident," he is actually a mere "foreigner."[66] It would seem that the Torah likewise is God's. He imposed it upon us against our will! "Rava said…The world is His and the Torah is His; does the Torah belong to [the Torah scholar]? Rava subsequently said: Indeed, the Torah belongs to [the Torah scholar], as it is written: 'he shall meditate upon his Torah day and night' (Ps. 1:2)."[67] Rashi explains: "'For God's Torah is his delight, and he shall meditate upon his Torah' – initially it is called 'God's Torah,' but once he studies it and masters it, it is called his Torah."

For one who has studied Torah, it nourishes his soul. "For as the rain or snow drops from heaven and returns not there, but soaks the earth and makes it bring forth vegetation … so is My word that issues from My mouth" (Is. 55:10–11). The soul that is nourished by Torah grows and flourishes, for the Torah becomes "his." Just as when vegetation absorbs water it transforms it into part and parcel of the plant, so too the soul that absorbs God's word makes it into part of its essence and vitality.

One who has studied Torah is no longer subject to external commandments. On the contrary, the power of Torah bursts forth from within him, like a flowing spring. Like a plant sprouts from the soil and turns toward the sun, so too the human soul erupts in yearning for the Creator.

Furthermore, as a sapling that grows and sends forth roots, stabilizing it in the ground and fixing it in place, so too one who has made the Torah his own and who draws his vitality from it; he finds his place in God's world and becomes a "resident." He is the fulfillment of "I shall reside in the house of the Lord" (Ps. 23:6) – "this is the true human perfection."[68]

---

66. Cf. Leviticus 25:23.
67. Kiddushin 32a–b.
68. *Moreh Nevukhim* III:54, p. 635.

Chapter 5

What Is "*Emunat Ḥakhamim*"?

Introduction

The term *Emunat Ḥakhamim* appears in the *baraita* known as *Kinyan Torah*, which was appended to *Avot*:

> Torah is greater than priesthood and royalty, for royalty is acquired by thirty distinctions, and priesthood by twenty-four, whereas the Torah is acquired by forty-eight distinctions.[1]

Among the forty-eight distinctions that man needs in order to acquire Torah, "*emunat ḥakhamim*" is listed twenty-third. *Maḥzor Vitry* explains in brief: "trust [the Sages'] words, unlike the Sadducees and Boethusians."[2] Others explain similarly: "*emunat ḥakhamim*" refers to acceptance of the Oral Torah and trust in its chain of transmission.

---

1. Mishna Avot 6:5. Avot has five chapters; "*Kinyan Torah*," which is chapter 6 in our editions, is not actually part of the tractate.
2. Since this *baraita* is not part of the Mishna, there are few commentaries on it from the medieval rabbis.

There is no doubt that faith in the Oral Torah and in the authority of the Sages, whom Maimonides calls "the transmitters of the teaching" (*ma'atikei hashemu'a*),[3] is mandatory. Without faith in them, it would be impossible to acquire Torah. This is emphasized by R. Yehuda HaNasi at the very beginning of *Avot*, where he presents the chain of transmission: "Moses received the Torah at Sinai; he passed it on to Joshua, and Joshua to the Elders...." Maimonides opens his *Commentary on the Mishna* with a lengthy description of the transmission process and its significance. Yet this is precisely why it is difficult to accept *Mahzor Vitry*'s explanation of the term: Had this been the *baraita*'s intent, why isn't it at the top of the list, instead of in the middle of the list: "less sleep, less chatter, less pleasure, less merriment, less sexual intercourse, patience, a good heart, *emunat hakhamim*, acceptance of suffering..."?

A different explanation appears in *Tiferet Yisrael*:

> He does not believe everything he hears, for that is the trait of a "dupe [who] believes anything" (Prov. 14:15). Rather, he should believe the wise in wisdom of the Torah, even if he cannot understand [their logic] on his own.

It seems that the author of *Tiferet Yisrael* bases his comment on the second half of the cited verse as well: "A clever person discerns the correct path." That is, one needs *emunat hakhamim* in order to reach the level where he "discerns the correct path." Thus, even when he does not fully comprehend their words, he does not, God forbid, ridicule the words of the Sages. On the contrary, he trusts that they have a deeper meaning, and as a result of this trust, works hard, enduring "less sleep, less chatter, etc.," until he successfully understands them at full depth and "discerns the correct path."

Attitudes toward the Sages

A proper attitude toward the Sages is critical; without it, there is no way to achieve the correct understanding of their words. Only one who is willing to invest considerable effort into probing their words, certain that

---

3. Introduction to *Mishneh Torah*, §24; *Hilkhot Talmud Torah* 1:9.

they are important and meaningful, will be able to uncover their truth. "A dupe believes anything" and cannot distinguish between someone who deserves to be taken seriously and a mere prattler. More importantly, he is not willing to probe in order to understand the truth. In contrast, one who craves Torah knowledge must understand that its words are not easy or superficial. Rather, they were "all given by a single Shepherd"[4] and through them the wisdom of the Creator is revealed. Just as the secrets of the universe are not easily disclosed, so too, understanding the words and mysteries of the Sages requires great effort.

Every Torah student can attest that a difficult passage of Talmud cannot be mastered with a casual reading. Only one who delves deeply into the words of the Sages, certain that he will find truthful and logical reasoning in them, can expect to discover their intent. Even a Torah scholar of stature is occasionally stumped by a difficult challenge to a statement of the Talmud, a *Rishon*, or a prominent *Aharon*. It can seem to him that every path he pursues leads to a dead end. Yet he, with his steadfast trust in the Sages, burns the midnight oil until, with assistance from above, the correct answer and proper understanding flash through his mind. Then he may discover that an eminent sage has preceded him in offering this solution, or that the author of the original troublesome passage offered this very solution elsewhere. Indeed, truth has a particular ring.[5]

Emunat ḥakhamim is thus grounded in wisdom. Since the Sages are wise, a wise person can plumb the depth of their words and extract their true meaning. Concerning this, the Talmud (Bava Batra 12a–b) states, "A wise person is greater than a prophet.... Rav Ashi says, this is demonstrated when a great person issues a ruling, and it accords with the halakha to Moses from Sinai." Rabbi Yosef ibn Migash explains:

---

4. Ḥagiga 3b.
5. For example, R. Naftali Tzvi Yehuda Berlin ("Netziv") writes at the beginning of *Ha'amek She'ela* that many unsourced rulings of Rif and Maimonides, which perplexed the leading Torah scholars of subsequent generations, can be deciphered in light of Geonic writings that were unknown in rabbinic study halls for centuries until they were discovered in ancient libraries. Yet even though the sources of their rulings were not known, and even as the rulings were subject to intense questioning and puzzlement, there was never any doubt that they issued from a sacred source.

Even though that person never heard this ruling before, a wise person is greater than a prophet, for a prophet can only say what he has heard and what has been placed in his mouth to say, whereas a wise person states what was said to Moses at Sinai even though he never heard it.[6]

The Talmud then challenges Rav Ashi: "Perhaps he is like a blind person [who finds his way] through a skylight?" That is, perhaps this happened by chance. The Talmud answers: "Did he not give a reason?" Since he gave a logical rationale and explanation, he is not like the lucky blind man. Rather, he applied his intelligence and thus corroborated the law given to Moses at Sinai.

Emunat ḥakhamim thus operates on two parallel planes. On one hand, it is the faith that the words of our Sages contain profound meaning and truth that are worth seeking. On the other hand, it is the Torah student's self-reliance and self-confidence that he has the ability to grasp the hidden wisdom of the Sages by means of his God-given intelligence. This was expounded by Rabbi Yeḥiel Yaakov Weinberg:

I regularly offer an explanation of the Sages' enumeration, among the forty-eight distinctions through which Torah is acquired, of *"pilpul hatalmidim"* (argumentation among students) and *"emunat ḥakhamim"*: These traits seem to contradict each other! Moreover, what does *emunat ḥakhamim* have to do with acquiring Torah?

This is precisely the point: If one does not trust the Sages, he tends to skim over their words casually and arrogantly, smugly saying, "They did not understand." As a result, such a person makes no effort to delve into their words to fully understand them. Ultimately, it becomes clear that it was he who erred, not they. Thus, one of the paths of wisdom is trust that they did not err, God forbid. Rather, we are short-sighted and of limited intelligence. However, simple trust, with no mental effort to study and contemplate intensively, and to say simply instead, "They

---

6. *Shita Mekubetzet* ad loc.

knew, so we may trust them without thinking," is likewise wrong. Rather, one must analyze [their words] and the contradictions and uncertainties [therein], as if they were among us. Through this we arrive at a more profound and penetrating understanding. These two traits, *emunat ḥakhamim* combined with unrestricted argumentation, lead to the acquisition of Torah."[7]

Striving to Ascertain the Truth

In the introduction to his *Commentary on the Mishna*, Maimonides explains at length the difference between a sage and a prophet. He concludes unambiguously that the authority of an established prophet comes from the mitzva: "You shall listen to him" (Deut. 18:15). We do not ask him for reasons or explanations. The main function of a prophet is to guide those to whom he was sent regarding matters that are subject to choice (*devar reshut*). However, with regard to the Torah and its laws, with the exception of temporary measures, a prophet has no special authority by virtue of his prophecy. On the contrary, if he were to claim that Heaven revealed to him how to rule on a particular halakhic matter, it would constitute evidence that he is a false prophet, for we have already received the Torah at Sinai, and no prophet may add anything new to it.

The sage has a different status. Although we are commanded to honor and revere him, it is on account of his Torah knowledge, which can be assessed by the yardstick of logical reasoning. Unlike a prophet, a sage must explain what he says. Even when the Sanhedrin was active, which, in the words of Maimonides, is "the root of the Oral Torah and the pillar of instruction, from which law and justice go forth to all Israel,"[8] its decisions could only be reached after rational deliberation. If all members agreed with one rationale, then there was consensus. But if there was disagreement about how to understand the law, as is often the case, they voted and ruled according to the majority.

---

7. *Responsa Seridei Esh* (A. Weingort ed., Jerusalem: 1999), 1:213 (3:9 in the four-volume Mosad Harav Kook edition).
8. *Hilkhot Mamrim* 1:1.

Nahmanides wrote:

> Everyone who studies our Talmud knows that in disputes among
> commentators there are no absolute proofs nor definitive solu-
> tions for most problems, for this branch of wisdom is not subject
> to logical proofs like geometry or the observations of astronomy.
> Rather, we make our best effort, and it is sufficient that in every
> dispute we dismiss one of the opinions using decisive reasoning
> and showing its incompatibility with talmudic passages. We favor
> an opinion that fits better with the straightforward meaning of
> the text and the reasoning of the talmudic passages, provided
> that it is in agreement with logical thinking. This is the most
> we can do, and it is the aim of every God-fearing scholar when
> studying Talmud.[9]

Since the wisdom of Torah is not like the discipline of mathematics,
there is room for opposing opinions. One sage is convinced of a particular view, and another sage is convinced of its opposite. Both views are
based on arguments and explanations that everyone agrees have merit.
Nevertheless, one disputant considers a particular factor decisive, while
his colleague's decision is based on a different evaluation of the various
factors. Therefore, even one who disagrees with a certain sage still exhibits *emunat ḥakhamim* – that is, he trusts that the words of this sage are
meaningful, and he attempts to understand his motives and reasoning.
This applies to scholars sitting together and debating in a study hall,
and most certainly to the sages of earlier generations, whose reputa-
tions have already been established. This idea is articulated explicitly in
Minḥa Ḥadasha, a commentary on Avot anthologized by Rabbi Yeḥiel
Mikhel Muravsky from ten earlier commentaries:

> *Emunat ḥakhamim* – he trusts the words of the sages, from least
> to greatest…. He does not dispute their statements and rulings
> in order to antagonize, but for the sake of truth, integrity, and
> [according to his understanding] in his particular time and place.

---

9. Introduction to *Milḥamot Hashem* (glosses on Rif).

[He argues] privately, not publicly, never seeking aggrandizement by his fellow's shame, even if he knows he is right and his friend is mistaken – except where there is a desecration of God's name or an urgent need, in which case: "I will speak of Your testimonies in the presence of kings, and I will not be abashed" (Psalms 119:46).[10]

Emunat hakhamim is not supposed to prevent disagreements that stem from alternative viewpoints, divergent assessments, and varying explanations. *Emunat hakhamim* demands that we take the words of every sage seriously and make an honest attempt to understand them. This requires a great deal of work and the cultivation of sophisticated halakhic thinking skills. If, at the end of this process, one must decide between differing opinions, *emunat hakhamim* grants the arbiter the awesome responsibility of acting according to the truth as he perceives it. This principle guided the great *posekim* throughout the ages. Maimonides formulates this idea thus: "If one of the *Geonim* ruled a certain way on a matter of law, and it is clear to a later rabbinical court that the ruling does not comport with the text of the Talmud, we do not heed the first authority, but rather, follow whichever ruling appears most correct, whether the authority is earlier or later."[11]

It is precisely because one who studies Torah for its own sake has such great *emunat hakhamim* that he is given the responsibility of deciding. It is worth citing a responsum from the thirteenth century sage Rabbi Yeshaya di Trani the Elder (also known as "Rid"):

First, I would like to reply to Your Honor concerning what you wrote to me that I should not dispute the great rabbi, Rabbenu Yitzḥak [of Dampierre]: Heaven forbid that I would do such a thing! It never occurred to me that I dispute him. To what am I compared? "A flea" (I Sam. 24:15), as rendered by the Targum,[12] even with respect to his disciple, and certainly when compared to the king himself! Yet

---

10. Photo offset edition (Bnei Brak: 1970). The author does not list the source of each comment.
11. Introduction to *Mishneh Torah*, §32.
12. Targum Yonatan translates "flea" as "ignoramus."

I maintain that I may not heed a statement that I cannot accept, even if it was uttered by Yehoshua b. Nun.[13] I do not hesitate to say what I, with my limited intelligence, think about such matters, thus fulfilling the verse: "I will speak of Your testimonies in the presence of kings, and I will not be abashed." Yet, with Heaven as my witness, even when I think that my view is better than that of all of the earlier *Rishonim*, Heaven forbid that I should arrogantly think that "my wisdom has stood by me" (Eccl. 2:9). Rather, I apply to myself a parable of the philosophers. I heard from the philosophers that they asked the greatest of them: "We concede that our predecessors were wiser and more intelligent than we, yet we readily acknowledge that on many points we speak of them and reject their statements, and we are right. How can this be?" He answered: "Who sees farther, a dwarf or a giant? Surely the giant, whose eyes are much higher up than those of the dwarf. Yet if the dwarf rides on the shoulders of the giant, then surely the dwarf [sees farther], for his eyes are now higher up than those of the giant. So are we dwarves riding on the shoulders of giants, for we have seen their wisdom, so we can ascend higher. It is by virtue of their wisdom that we have become wise, not because we are greater than they."

Even so, we wish to state that we do not evaluate the statements of earlier rabbis except when we see that they dispute one another – when one forbids and one permits. Upon who shall we rely? Can we weigh mountains in scales or hills in a balance[14] in order to determine which is greater and thereby discount the words of the other? We have no choice but to study their words, for "both are the words of the living God,"[15] debating and delving into their words to determine the law.... Wisdom is greater than the wise man, and no sage is free of errors, for there is no perfect wisdom except for God's.[16]

---

13. Based on Ḥullin 124a.
14. Based on Yeshayahu 40:12.
15. Based on Eiruvin 13b.
16. *Responsa Rid* (Jerusalem: Machon HaTalmud HaYisraeli HaShalem, 1967), §62.

Likewise, Rosh wrote in a responsum:

> Who among us is greater than Rashi, who illuminated the dias-
> pora with his commentaries? Yet his own descendants, Rabbenu
> Tam and R. Yitzḥak, disagreed with him on many points and
> rebutted his words. For it is a Torah of truth, and special treat-
> ment is accorded to no man.[17]

This is how Torah luminaries conducted themselves throughout
history.

This duty to ascertain the truth is not limited to arbiters and halakhists exclusively. The Torah was given to all Israel, and every Jew is
obligated to study Torah so that he conducts all of his actions lawfully.
To that end, he must understand the reasons for the laws. As R. Shneur
Zalman of Liadi, the author of *Tanya*, wrote:

> If one does not know the reasons behind the halakha, he does
> not understand the halakhot themselves adequately or properly.
> He is an ignoramus. For this reason, some forbid the issuing of
> halakhic rulings, even for oneself, from halakhic codes, without
> studying the reasons. Therefore, one may not delay the study of
> the reasons...."[18]

Until one has studied sufficiently and become capable of issuing halakhic rulings, he has no choice but to choose a rabbi to ask what to do
and what path to take. Even one who has studied and understands, if he
is truly wise, he will not rely solely on his own judgment but will turn
to other sages for their opinion and advice. Of course, one who has
insufficient knowledge, yet fails to turn to a sage for instruction, relying
instead on his own minimal understanding, is nothing but an egotist
who does not revere God.

Yet even one who asked a rabbi for instruction and was given a
ruling is not absolved of his duty to try to understand the reasons for

---

17. *Responsa Rosh* 55:9.
18. *Shulḥan Arukh HaRav, Hilkhot Talmud Torah* 2:1.

the ruling. The *Rishonim* addressed this very issue, and Rabbi Zeraḥya Halevi's words on it are instructive:

> If you pose a question: Since we maintain that cases of indirect damages (*garmei*) are adjudicated, why do we say[19] that if [a judge] errs on a matter of settled law (*devar mishna*), he may reverse his ruling, but he is exempt from indemnification even if the verdict is irreversible....This implies that he has done nothing even according to one who adjudicates cases of indirect damages...!
>
> The answer is: The reason for this ruling is that...the litigant was negligent. Since the error was in a matter of settled law, the error is well-known, and the litigant should not have relied upon it and acted accordingly, for he should have inquired and revealed the error, for it was as evident as an explicit mishna. Therefore, the litigant was negligent, and the judge has done nothing...
>
> Certainly, however, if the litigant was coerced...then if it is impossible to reverse the verdict, [the judge] is judged as a thief and must indemnify like any other thief.[20]

Thus, one who consults even an outstanding rabbi can be considered negligent if he does not ascertain that the ruling he received is correct. This is the extent to which each individual is responsible for his actions; this is the degree to which one must determine for himself what the law requires and what God demands from him in every scenario!

Of course, in order not to be considered negligent, the litigant must possess a certain amount of knowledge; he must be able to inquire, study, understand, and probe. If one is incapable of understanding the rabbi's ruling, then he is certainly incapable of assessing whether it is correct or not. However, one must not say that since a great rabbi gave him a ruling, he must therefore follow it blindly.

---

19. Sanhedrin 33a.
20. *Hamaor* on Sanhedrin 12a in the Alfasi pages.

True, halakha states explicitly that one may not disagree with his rabbi, but what is the meaning of this halakha? If the rabbi says something, and there are grounds to challenge it, is it forbidden to ask questions? Not only is it permissible, but it is also obligatory! And what if one has attained the qualifications and authorization to issue rulings, and he has examined a law about which his rabbi issued a specific ruling and reached a different conclusion? In many cases, Maimonides cites the rulings of his rabbis and disagrees with them.[21] The law that forbids disagreement with one's rabbi means that one may not establish himself as an arbiter of halakha without his rabbi's authorization. He must obtain his rabbi's license to issue rulings. It does not, however, mean that one must render decisions in accordance with his rabbi on every matter, even if he deems his rabbi's ruling incorrect.

Conclusion

It thus emerges that the trait of *emunat ḥakhamim* is indeed great, but very difficult to achieve. It is not found among the lazy, who wish to spare themselves the burden of study. True *emunat ḥakhamim* obliges one to delve deeply in search of the reasoning behind the words of the Sages, while simultaneously requiring the student or questioner to critically and rigorously investigate, in order to verify that there is no room to differ. Certainly, there is reason in the words of every sage, but we still must determine how to conduct ourselves in practice.

On one hand, one may not rely on his own knowledge to issue rulings – even for himself, and certainly for others – without consulting and asking the sages. As Maimonides wrote:

> Any student who has not yet attained the qualifications to issue rulings but does so is a fool, an evildoer, and an egotist.... Junior

---

21. Editor's note: See, for example, *Hilkhot Ishut* 5:15; *Hilkhot Sheḥita* 11:10; *Hilkhot To'en VeNit'an* 3:2; *Teshuvot HaRambam* §310, 317. See also Rabbi Avraham, the son of Maimonides, *Hamaspik Le'ovdei Hashem* (Dana edition, pp. 70–71): "Had my father and master heard this, he would have conceded, as he instructed me: 'concede to the truth.' Indeed, we always saw clearly that he would agree with the least of his disciples with respect to the truth."

students who have not learned Torah adequately but wish to appear great to ignoramuses and among the people of their towns, who leap to the front so they may judge and issue rulings in Israel – it is they who cause the proliferation of disputes, who destroy the world, who extinguish the light of Torah, and who destroy the vineyard of the Lord of Hosts.[22]

On the other hand, even one who asks for instruction and seeks guidance is not absolved of his personal responsibility to understand halakha and refrain from blindly following one teacher or another. Obviously, if one does not know, he has no choice but to follow his rabbi. However, he still must learn, so that he can understand his rabbi's instruction.

Recently,[23] some have begun applying a completely different meaning – one that the Sages never considered – to the term "*emunat ḥakhamim.*" They take it to mean that sages possess halakhic or prophetic authority even with regard to non-halakhic matters. There is no question that one may consult those who are proficient in the Torah and its wisdom and who, by virtue of their righteousness, Torah knowledge, and intelligence, provide good guidance and sound advice. Indeed, the opportunity to benefit from those greater and better than oneself is surely a boon for anyone. However, there is a difference between asking advice while taking personal responsibility for one's actions and becoming dependent on others while relinquishing any independence of thought. Rabbi Shneur Zalman of Liadi commented on this latter phenomenon: "Has there ever been such a thing in all of history? Where have you found, in any book by a Jewish sage, whether *Rishon* or *Aḥaron*, that it is a good practice to ask for instruction on mundane matters?"[24]

There are those who label such childish behavior as "*emunat ḥakhamim*"; this is nothing but a distortion. Those who adhere to the

---

22. *Hilkhot Talmud Torah* 5:4.
23. See below, the chapter titled, "Halakhic Decision-Making and Rabbinic Leadership," p. 121.
24. *Iggerot Kodesh*, Shalom Dovber Levin, ed., Brooklyn: Kehot, 1980, §24, p. 56. My colleague Rabbi Eli Reif alerted me to this source.

distorted version of "*emunat ḥakhamim*" instead of acquiring true Torah knowledge distance themselves from the light of the Torah and are ultimately incapable of distinguishing their right from their left.

The distinction between the authority of a prophet and the authority of a sage is clear. If a prophet instructs us to do something that is otherwise voluntary, we are commanded to obey,[25] and, moreover, "it is forbidden to second guess his prophecy or doubt that it is true, and it is forbidden to challenge him excessively."[26] This is not so with regard to a sage. *Emunat ḥakhamim* requires us to clarify and elucidate their words to the extent possible; one who does not do so is simply a "dupe [who] believes anything." If this is true of Torah matters, then it is certainly true of all personal decisions. "He who trusts his own heart is a fool, but he who walks in wisdom shall be delivered" (Prov. 28:26).

---

25. *Hilkhot Yesodei HaTorah* 9:2.
26. Ibid. 10:6.

Chapter 6

Halakhic Decision-Making and Rabbinic Leadership

The Purpose of the Mitzvot

Without a legal system to regulate individual and collective needs, no society can endure. Maimonides explains that the various legal systems can be sorted on the basis of their purposes. He writes:

> When you find a Law the whole end of which... [is] directed exclusively toward the ordering of the polis and of its circumstances...not at all directed toward speculative matters...the whole purpose of that Law being, on the contrary, the arrangement, in whatever way this may be brought about, of the circumstances of people...you must know that that Law was promulgated by a [human] legislator.[1]

The main purpose of man-made laws is to address society's worldly needs. The Torah is different in that it is built on the premise that man is not merely flesh and blood; he has a soul as well, and he can achieve eternal life. Therefore, the Torah contains commandments whose main

---

1. *Moreh Nevukhim* II:40, pp. 383–84.

purpose is to improve society and arrange the affairs of individuals therein, as well as mitzvot whose main purpose is to realize man's spiritual potential.

> The Law of Moses our Master has come to bring us both perfections, I mean the welfare of the states of people in their relations with one another through the abolition of reciprocal wrongdoing and through the acquisition of a noble and excellent character. I also mean the soundness of the beliefs and the giving of correct opinions through which ultimate perfection is achieved.[2]

Among the sages of Israel, there is almost no disputing this distinction between man-made legal systems and the Torah's legal system, though there are different approaches to the reasons for the mitzvot. Some maintain that one who believes in the divinity of the Torah must assume that the reasons for every mitzva are beyond human comprehension. They do not seek reasons for the mitzvot, and, moreover, some of them even maintain that the mitzvot do not have reasons that can be grasped by human intelligence. Maimonides vehemently opposed this approach.[3] According to him, it is possible and even necessary to understand the reasons for the mitzvot. He explains:

> The whole purpose consist[s] in what is useful for us, as we have explained[4] on the basis of its dictum: "for our good always, that He might preserve us alive, as it is at this day" (Deut. 6:24).... Every commandment from among these six hundred and thirteen commandments exists either with a view to communicating a correct opinion, or to putting an end to an unhealthy opinion, or to communicating a rule of justice, or to warding off an injustice, or to endowing men with a noble moral quality, or to warning them against an evil moral quality.[5]

---

2. Ibid. III:27; p. 511.
3. See ibid. 26 and 31.
4. Ibid. 27, pp. 511–12.
5. Ibid. 31, p. 514.

It should be noted that Maimonides demonstrates that his approach is rooted in the Torah itself: "for our good always, that He might preserve us alive, as it is at this day." The purpose of all the mitzvot is to benefit mankind and fashion a society in which every individual attempts to reach his potential and realize the Divine image within him.

The idea that the purpose of the Torah and mitzvot is to benefit us in this world as well is expressed in Maimonides' explanation for the very first commandments given to Israel, even before Mt. Sinai, which express the Torah's intended goals. Maimonides explains,[6] based on the Sages' interpretation, that the first mitzvot commanded to Israel in Mara, right after they left Egypt (Ex. 15:25), were Shabbat and civil law. Civil laws (*dinim*), the laws that govern interpersonal relationships, are clearly for the benefit of society. As Maimonides says, they are "the abolition of mutual wrongdoing."[7] But Maimonides explains that the mitzva of Shabbat has a similar purpose.

The Torah gives two reasons for the mitzva of Shabbat. The first is: "For in six days the Lord made heaven and earth…. Therefore the Lord blessed the day of Shabbat and hallowed it" (Ex. 20:10). The second is: "Remember that you were a slave in the land of Egypt…. Therefore the Lord your God has commanded you to observe the day of Shabbat" (Deut. 5:14). Maimonides explains the relationship between these two reasons:

> For the effect, according to the first statement, is to regard the day as noble and exalted. As it says: "Therefore the Lord blessed the day of Shabbat and hallowed it." …. However, the order given us by the Law with regard to it and the commandment ordaining us in particular to keep it are an effect consequent upon the cause that we had been slaves in Egypt where we did not work according to our free choice and when we wished and where we had not the power to refrain from working. Therefore we have been commanded inactivity and rest[8] so that we should conjoin the

---

6. Ibid. 32, p. 531.
7. Ibid.
8. See also ibid. III:43.

two things: the belief in a true opinion – namely, the creation of the world in time, which at the first go and with the slightest of speculations, shows us that the deity exists – and the memory of the benefit God bestowed upon us by giving us rest "from under the burdens of the Egyptians" (Ex. 6:7). Accordingly the Sabbath is, as it were, of universal benefit, both with reference to a true speculative opinion and to the well-being of the state of the body.[9]

There is nothing that works "for our good always" more than providing each individual with a day of rest, even slaves and servants. By means of this day, everyone gets a respite from subservience to his worldly needs, can become more receptive to spirituality, and is able to connect to eternal values. There is no doubt that Shabbat's twin purposes, each in its own way, has contributed to the influence that the idea of the sabbath has had on the world.[10]

The process of shaping the nation of Israel was defined by the mitzvot commanded at Mara. Mara thus charted a course for the covenant at Sinai, where Israel received the Torah which expanded upon the goals of the mitzvot given at Mara, and paved the way to achieving those goals.

This basic premise, that the Torah's goal is to "preserve us alive, as it is at this day," was established as a matter of law, as Maimonides emphasizes in a particularly sharp formulation at the beginning of *Hilkhot Shabbat*, which opens the Book of *Zemanim* (Seasons):

9. Ibid. II:31, pp. 359–60.
10. Amazingly, even though the Romans of antiquity disparaged the Jews for observing Shabbat, accusing them of laziness, nevertheless, long before the development of rapid communication, the idea of the sabbath penetrated every corner of the globe. Derivatives of the Hebrew term "Shabbat" have even been absorbed into many different languages. Most of the world has adopted the seven-day week, even though it has no obvious basis in physical reality, and even though it originated with a small, persecuted people. Indeed, there have been attempts to change the number of days in the week. After the French Revolution, there was an attempt to institute a ten-day week, and the Soviet communists likewise decreed the abolition of the biblical week. Yet all these attempts failed.

It is forbidden to delay the desecration of Shabbat on behalf of one who is dangerously ill, for it is stated: "which if a man shall do them, he shall live by them" (Lev. 18:5) – and not die by them. You have thus learned that the Torah's laws are not vengeance against the world, but rather bring mercy, kindness, and peace to the world. Of those heretics who say that this constitutes forbidden desecration of Shabbat, Scripture states: "Moreover, I gave them laws that were not good and rules by which they could not live"[11] (Ezek. 20:25).[12]

Maimonides was not content with the general assertion: "live by them." Rather, he broadens the issue and specifies the Torah's societal aims: bringing "mercy, kindness, and peace to the world." He thus teaches us what to strive for.

He ends the Book of *Zemanim* in the same way that he began it:

Great is peace, for the entire Torah was given to make peace in the world, as it is said: "Its ways are ways of pleasantness, and all its paths are peace" (Prov. 3:17).[13]

What are the ways and paths of peace? There is peace built on the ethic that "what's mine is mine and what's yours is yours,"[14] in other words: "I have nothing to do with you, positive or negative." It is not for naught that some call this trait "the ethic of Sodom."[15] This type of peace has value if it prevents people from harming one another, but the Torah was not given merely to produce a peace of this sort. There is a greater peace, whose aim is to benefit all, in which each individual has an immediate goal of benefitting others, and in which everyone contributes to the collective good. This is the peace that the Torah intends. Such peace can

---

11. In explaining the plain meaning of the verse, *Targum Yonatan* states: "So I, when they rebelled against my words…distanced them…and they followed their foolish impulses and made decrees that are not good and rules by which they cannot live."
12. *Hilkhot Shabbat* 2:3.
13. *Hilkhot Megilla VeḤanukka* 4:14.
14. Mishna Avot 5:10.
15. Ibid.

be called "productive peace," that is, peace that produces good results in the interpersonal sphere.

Each person must place the goals of the Torah and mitzvot before himself and strive to fulfill the mitzvot with the aim of furthering these goals. All the more so, therefore, must religious leaders seek to guide society forward, toward the realization of the Torah's goals.

There is a difference between a good that is done on behalf of an individual or individuals, and social regulations and actions that benefit society as a whole. The Sages provided an example of this distinction. Anyone who teaches Torah to his friend's child is certainly meritorious, but there is an immeasurably greater merit for one who institutes such a benefit for the public as a whole, as they said: "That man, whose name was Yehoshua b. Gamla, is remembered for the good.... He instituted that schoolteachers would be settled in every region and every city.[16] This social institution is what preserved Jewish identity within larger societies throughout the long exile. It was centuries before civilized nations instituted public education, yet today public education is mandatory in every civilized state. There is nothing that creates peace among all segments of society more than universal education. Here, then, is an example of creative Torah thinking on the part of religious leadership, which worked for the betterment of society as a whole and has continued bringing benefit through the centuries.

The Role of the *Posek* and the Art of Halakhic Decision-Making

Almost every mitzva in the Torah is formulated in a particularized manner, and the reasons for mitzvot are not usually made explicit in Scripture. However, the Sages, and the greatest *posekim* (halakhic decisors) in their wake, taught us how to abstract generalized principles and halakhic rules which enable us to address the varying circumstances of life and the changing times. The Sages also taught us – through their midrashic exegesis of verses and the details of their halakhic instruction – how to understand the purpose of the mitzvot as a whole as well as of individual mitzvot.

---

16. Bava Batra 21a.

The role of the *posek* is to apply the halakhic principles to particular cases that emerge and to formulate practical directives for specific situations. In every generation, Torah scholars have filled this role: they studied and taught how to apply the Torah's commandments to changing times and circumstances. The *posek* must become familiar with the precedents set by earlier authorities and understand accordingly how to pave the way to a practical decision for his time and place.

In his decision, he must consider not only precedents, but also the possible future ramifications of his rulings. He must especially take the Torah's overarching goals into consideration. It is virtually impossible to render halakhic rulings in any area without attempting to understand the goal of the mitzvot and their impact on the behavior of individuals and of society as a whole. The *posek* must not look at each individual ruling in isolation, but as something that fits with the Torah's overarching goals and as a part of realizing the purpose of "for our good always, that He might preserve us alive, as it is at this day," for both individuals and society.

The motivation for rendering halakhic rulings must be concern for people's welfare. The Sages taught us this as well: "R. Simlai expounded: The Torah begins and ends with acts of kindness."[17] One who causes pain to a human being harms the Divine image. Everyone must be careful in this respect, but especially rabbis and communal leaders.

The *posek*'s duty is not just to issue rulings that will be beneficial for people, but to make sure that his ruling will lead everyone to understand that holiness can only be attained by benefiting others. If one isolates himself in his worship of God and does not participate in communal life, his worship is not acceptable. One who separates himself from the community and burdens himself with excessive stringencies[18] is not bringing himself closer to God's service. Maimonides wrote:

---

17. Sota 14a.
18. See *Shemonah Perakim*, chapter 4, p. 63:

    The perfect law which leads us to perfection … aims at man's following the path of moderation, in accordance with the dictates of nature, eating, drinking, enjoying legitimate sexual intercourse, all in moderation, and living among people in honesty and uprightness, but not … afflicting the body…. If one who deprives himself merely of wine must bring an atonement, how much more incumbent is it upon

In this connection, I have never heard a more remarkable saying than that of the Rabbis…. They greatly blame those who bind themselves by oaths and vows, in consequence of which they are fettered like prisoners. The words they use[19] are: "Said R. Iddai, in the name of R. Yitzḥak: Is what the Torah prohibits insufficient for you that you must take upon yourself additional prohibitions?"[20]

It is certainly, then, forbidden for a *posek* to burden others with excessive stringencies. In this context, it is worth citing the words of Rabbi Avraham Yitzḥak Kook:

> There is nothing pious about the inclination toward excessive stringency on matters for which the lenient path has been paved in accordance with the Torah…. In truth, the path of my eminent and righteous masters, whom I was privileged to serve, may their merit protect us and all Israel, was against the inclination toward stringency if there was room to be lenient, and especially with regard to matters that have no strong foundation in the words of the Sages in the Talmudim.[21]

The Sages even established a rule for halakhic decisors: "R. Lazar said: Just as it is forbidden to render the impure pure, so it is forbidden to render the pure impure."[22] They also declared that one who forbids things that are permitted will ultimately permit that which is forbidden: "I do not deem it wicked that you said that the pure is impure, but that

---

one who denies himself every enjoyment…. He enjoined upon them justice and virtue alone, and not fasting…. "Love truth and peace" (Zech. 7:3). Know that by "truth" the intellectual virtues are meant…and that by "peace" the moral virtues are designated, for upon them depends the peace of the world.

19. Y. Nedarim 9:1.
20. *Shemonah Perakim*, chapter 4, p. 66.
21. Rav Kook, *Responsa Oraḥ Mishpat* §112. This source was brought to my attention by my colleague Rabbi Eli Reif.
22. Y. Terumot, end of chapter 5.

you will ultimately say that the impure is pure."[23] It is forbidden to be stringent about things that, as a matter of law, are not forbidden. On the contrary, as Maimonides wrote: "It is proper to permit everything that it is possible to permit to people, so as not to burden them."[24] Reform means the creation of new standards, and thus reform does not only mean permitting the forbidden, but also the invention of stringencies with no source in the Torah and that our ancestors never observed.

Clearly, one who rules leniently must demonstrate that the law accords with him. The Talmud states in several places that "the strength of a permissive ruling is greater,"[25] which Rashi explains to mean: "It is better to inform us of the strength of the opinion of the permissive disputant, for he relies on his learning and is not afraid to permit; however, the strength of the opinion of those who prohibit does not prove anything, for anyone can be stringent, even with respect to something that is permitted."[26] One who permits relies on his learning – that is, he must base his opinion on clear proofs. When a Torah scholar clarifies halakhic truth, the Sages say of him: "the strength of a permissive ruling is greater."[27]

23. Y. Avoda Zara 2:9. See also *Shakh* at the end of §242 (*"Hanhagat Horaot Issur Veheter"*), no. 9; *Pithei Teshuva, Yoreh De'ah* 1:7; *Responsa Teshuva Me'ahava* I:181.
24. *Iggerot HaRambam*, p. 393 (and see also p. 279).
25. See, for example, Beitza 2b.
26. Rashi ad loc., s.v. *"Deheteira adif lei."*
27. On this issue, I heard a clever homily on the *baraita* in Eiruvin 6b from my teacher, the eminent sage R. Pinhas Hirschprung:
    The law always accords with Beit Hillel.... One who wishes to act in accordance with the words of Beit Shammai may do so, in accordance with the words of Beit Hillel may do so... in accordance with the stringencies of Beit Shammai and Beit Hillel – of him Scripture states: "the fool walks in darkness" (Eccl. 2:14).
    The question arises: Why does it make sense to say that one who does so walks in darkness? What is bad about a person who protects himself against any possible mistake by practicing the stringency of every opinion? R. Hirschprung answered based on a dispute the Talmud (Shabbat 18a-b): Beit Shammai maintains that one is obligated to make sure that his tools are not used for forbidden activities on Shabbat, even if the owner himself does not use them. Only if he declares them ownerless (*hefker*) is he exempt, for then the tool is no longer his. Among the objects that the Talmud applies to this is the Shabbat candle. But what Jewish woman would declare her Shabbat candlesticks ownerless? Yet for Beit Shammai this is not a problem,

The role of the rabbi as *posek* is to guide the community to the realization of the Torah's "ways of pleasantness." Indeed, the Yerushalmi states regarding the duty to save lives and engage in rescue efforts on Shabbat: "One who acts quickly is praised; one who is asked is condemned; one who asks sheds blood."[28] One who is asked is condemned because he should have expounded and taught this basic principle publicly, so that people would not have to ask and thereby endanger lives. This illustrates the great responsibility of the *posek* to rule for the public in a way that brings benefit to people.

Halakha itself instructs a *posek* to be cautious in his rulings, both in cases of stringency and leniency. There are things about which the Sages said: "This is the halakha, but we do not rule accordingly (*halakha ve'ein morin ken*)." In other instances, the halakha is taught but only to an individual, not to the public. There are issues about which the *posek* must remain silent, and there are even matters about which it is said: "It is better that people transgress unwittingly and not transgress knowingly."[29] That is, the *posek* must use common sense and assess what the consequences of his ruling will be, especially when it is liable to cause human tragedy, God forbid; sometimes silence is the best course.

Human dignity, love for humanity, and harmony among human beings are the foundations of the entire Torah.

Furthermore, the prevailing notion that for every question there is an unequivocal answer in the books is not only untrue, but also very

---

because according to them, one may declare something ownerless only for specific people, as we learn in a mishna (Pe'ah 6:1): "Beit Shammai says: declaring something ownerless for paupers renders it ownerless [for paupers]; Beit Hillel says: it is not ownerless until it is rendered ownerless for wealthy people as well, as in [the case of] the Sabbatical year." Thus, according to Beit Shammai, one can declare his candlesticks ownerless for his relatives, and they will certainly not come and take the candlesticks for themselves. However, one who practices the stringencies of both Beit Hillel and Beit Shammai is unable to light Shabbat candles, since according to Beit Shammai, a candle that remains lit on Shabbat renders its owner culpable, as his objects must not be used for activities forbidden on Shabbat. Yet he cannot declare them ownerless for his household and relatives, since according to Beit Hillel this does not render them ownerless. Thus, this fool will have to sit in the dark on Shabbat.

28. Y. Yoma 8:5.
29. See Shabbat 148b; *Hilkhot Shevitat Asor* 1:7.

dangerous. The Talmud[30] recounts that during the episode of Phinehas and Zimri, Moses did not want to give any instruction at all to Phinehas. Moreover, with regard to actions like those of Phinehas, Maimonides rules: "If the zealot approaches to kill the fornicator, and the fornicator escapes and kills the zealot to save himself, he is not put to death on account [of killing the zealot]."[31] We are thus faced with a situation: on one hand, Phinehas is praised for killing Zimri, but on the other hand, had Zimri killed Phinehas, he would not have been put to death as a murderer. Here, then, is an example of an action whose outcome can vary from one extreme to the other. It is unthinkable to offer an ab initio practical ruling in such a case!

There are things about which it is said explicitly "*halakha ve'ein morin ken*," but even where this was not said explicitly, that does not imply that one must issue a ruling. Sometimes one does not know what is best for the person asking the question, and in such cases, it is possible that one must refrain from making a ruling. We find, for example, that it is forbidden to disclose that a woman is married to a man that one knows is a *mamzer*.[32] But if one is asked to find a match for the son of a *mamzer*, even though it is forbidden for him to publicize that this man is a *mamzer*, he must avoid making the match since, after all, he knows that the man is a *mamzer*.[33] There are issues that touch upon one's essence, and one must exercise great caution in such cases.

Halakha is a legal system with clear guidelines, parameters, and principles. It also contains instructions on how to act in cases where the facts are uncertain. For instance, the principles established by the Sages: *safek de'oraita lehumra* ("we are stringent with respect to uncertainties in matters of Torah law") and *safek derabbanan lekula* ("we are lenient with respect to uncertainties in matters of rabbinic law"). Halakha also leaves room for discretion, such as when to rely on a minority opinion, etc.

---

30. Sanhedrin 82a.
31. *Hilkhot Issurei Biah* 12:5.
32. Rema, *Even Ha'ezer* 2:5.
33. On determining *mamzerut* by means of genetic testing, see my article, "*Ha'arakha Mada'it Keyesod Lefsikat Halakha*" ("Scientific Assessment as a Basis for Halakhic Rulings"), in *Studies in the Thought of Maimonides*, (Jerusalem: Yeshivat Birkat Moshe, 2010), 169–71.

Nevertheless, the usage of such principles depends on understanding reality and sensitivity to its many layers. Many issues hinge on human behavior, and it is impossible to set clear parameters for such cases. Reality is complex, and consequently, so is the task of issuing practical instruction, since it depends on variable conditions. The *posek* must use logical reasoning combined with sensitivity to the human element and a thorough examination of actual circumstances, since even a minute change in circumstance can lead to a completely different ruling.

Everyone faces dilemmas with pros and cons on each side, and it is impossible to define parameters for every possible scenario. The *posek* must know how to assess the situation correctly. This requires an abundance of divine assistance, but without logical reasoning, he will have no divine assistance.

When one is confined within the "four ells of halakha," he develops his intellect, but that is only part of the *posek's* task. The *posek* must be familiar with human nature and character. He must understand how every individual represents a different world and experiences a different reality, even if it seems superficially that they are all facing the same difficulty.

Where there is concern that a ruling will cause serious pain or cost to human dignity, or if it will be a stumbling block for the public, the *posek* must apply careful discretion and be willing to take responsibility. Of course, not everyone can rely on his own opinion, and a *posek* may need to consult with those greater than him, but ultimately he is obligated to render a decision; one who does not make a decision will ultimately be held accountable.

There are indeed cases where we have no authority and seemingly no way out. There are even rare cases[34] where "no wisdom, no prudence, and no counsel can prevail against the Lord" (Prov. 21:30). However, one who expends effort to find a solution sanctifies God's name and demonstrates to all that "the Torah's laws are not vengeance against the world, but rather bring mercy, kindness, and peace unto the world." This is the task of the *posek*.

---

34. See Berakhot 19b; *Shulḥan Arukh, Yoreh De'ah* 303:1.

Halakha: The Torah of Life

Halakha is the Torah of life; all of its wellsprings originate in the real world, and all of its values are based on the nature of man and society. There is, however, an approach that imagines a *posek* as someone who has constructed a purely theoretical-categorical universe and knows how to fit the case at hand into his conceptual structure. This approach compares halakhic thinking and the task of the halakhist to logical-mathematical thinking with its own autonomous rules.

This approach is difficult, because halakhic rules themselves are based on specific cases that appear in the Talmud. Moreover, in contrast to logic and mathematics, which are governed solely by the laws of logic, the Torah addresses human beings, with all their moral and intellectual weaknesses, and with their free will, with the goal of guiding them to discover the Divine image within. The behavior of a free human being cannot be squeezed into the constraints of a purely conceptual legal system.

Furthermore, an approach that transforms the world of halakha into a world of theory disconnects halakha from the real world and makes it more difficult to implement. The mitzvot and *dinim* are instructions for how to live in the real world, not a completely abstract world. It is theoretically possible to present all sorts of models and let the questions, answers, and outlandish hypotheticals proliferate, because in an autonomous, theoretical world, every perspective is a possibility. But can one decide halakha this way? Halakha is supposed to be translated into action in this world. Only with extensive experience confronting the complexities of real life and human behavior can one come to understand how to act in a way that is both effective and responsive to the human soul's strengths and weaknesses, each of which is different from all others.

Thus, there are concepts and principles that the Sages established based on their view of the human condition in their day. Take, for example, the presumption that "it is better to live with [any] companionship than to live alone."[35] In all likelihood, the Sages knew that even in their day there were individual women to whom this presumption did not apply, but that they were a small minority. Even today, this presumption remains valid in the vast majority of cases; but is this minority negligible

---

35. See, for example, Yevamot 118b; Ketubot 75a.

today? Great caution is necessary when examining which of the Sages' assertions stem from the reality of their time, and which are implanted deeply within human nature.

Halakha is a system constructed from the smallest details; these details can be generalized into principles but that generalization can take different forms – some limited, and some more expansive. For example, legal thinking oscillates between two different conceptions. One approach looks at the written word as it is, according to its narrowest meaning.[36] Other approaches contemplate the context in addition to the text – the way in which the specific laws are integrated into the broader fabric and spirit of the law – not only the local expression of the concept. Some issues are simple, and in such cases the law can be formulated clearly and unambiguously. However, there are also issues that are rooted in competing values, and in such cases it is necessary to achieve balance between them in order to arrive at the truth.

Maimonides shows us an example of the more expansive view when he innovates a new halakha based solely on his own logic. Although he maintains that the Sages decreed that we are stringent with respect to uncertainties in matters of Torah law, there are cases when this decree cannot be applied. As he explains:

> Why do I say that a child of unknown paternity and a foundling are not forbidden to marry any woman who might be an *erva* (i.e., a woman with whom relations might be incestuous)? Because the acceptable child of a mother who was examined [to confirm that the father was not forbidden to her] is not forbidden to any woman who might be an *erva*. It is stated in the Torah: "Do not degrade your daughter and make her a harlot" (Lev. 19:29), on which the Sages comment: "In such a case, a father would marry his daughter and a brother his sister." Had the law been that anyone who is not certain of his paternity may not marry any woman because she might be an *erva*, we would never face this situation, and the land would not be filled with promiscuity. From this we learn that we do not prohibit a woman on the basis

---

36. Nowadays, this approach is called "legal formalism."

that she might be an *erva* unless it is known for certain that she is an *erva* to him. For if this were the case [that we would prohibit because we do not know], then every orphan in the world who does not know his paternity would be forbidden to marry anyone, lest they violate an *erva*."[37]

Note that Maimonides begins with the words, "I say," and later adds, "from this we learn." In a well-known letter that Maimonides wrote to R. Pinḥas HaDayan,[38] he informs him how to identify the source of his rulings in *Mishneh Torah*: "When something is of my own derivation, I will explicitly state: 'It seems to me that the matter is thus' [or: 'I say that the matter is thus'],[39] or I say: 'From here you learn that the matter is thus.'" This is the reason why Maimonides troubled himself to explain the reason for his ruling: "For if this were the case ..." it would be cruel to orphans who never knew their fathers, and it is inconceivable that the Sages would apply their decree to such a case.

The *posek* must learn when to apply the narrow approach and when to apply the broader approach. The *posek* must know the purpose of halakhic ruling, and he must make sure to apply it in a way that enables the fullest realization of that purpose, while aiming to further the truth of the Torah.

Halakhic Rulings in a Changing Reality

As halakhic literature developed over time, different genres of halakhic works came into being: commentaries on earlier literature, codes, comprehensive works on specific topics that one may "study and receive reward,"[40] and collections of responsa to halakhic questions that arose from actual cases. Although some responsa address hypothetical questions, these are a small minority; true responsa, constituting almost all of the responsa literature, deal with problems that have arisen in practice. There is a major difference between responsa and halakhic

---

37. *Hilkhot Issurei Biah* 15:29. But see *Arukh Hashulḥan, Even Ha'ezer* 4:58.
38. *Iggerot HaRambam*, p. 443.
39. This version appears in several variants. See n. 58.
40. See the chapter titled "The Role of the Commandments," at n. 55.

monographs: the halakhic monograph mainly deals with theoretical questions, and therefore it can address a discrete, well-defined issue without getting caught up in tangential factors that "distract" from the discussion. Responsa, on the other hand, contain long, complex discussions, because they relate to specific cases that occurred within a given set of circumstances, with all their human complexity. A *posek* must relate to the existing conditions of how we live now; one who has only book knowledge is akin to a "donkey laden with books."

Thus, for example, because of changing conditions, questions arise today that could never have been asked before. Some of these questions address major societal needs – medical questions, for instance. Some even touch upon the very foundations of morality and the Torah's principles: organ transplantation (in context of which the moment of death must be determined),[41] surrogate motherhood, and the like. At the same time, there are halakhot and past rulings that are no longer applicable because they address scenarios that no longer exist. On one hand, the *posek* must relate to these rulings as well, since they too may contain latent implications for various contemporary cases; on the other hand, the *posek* must discern the changes in reality and the resulting differences in applied halakha. Unfortunately, there are those who focus only on written halakhic texts without attending to the proper application for our times. They have one answer for every question: "What is new is forbidden" ("*Ḥadash asur min haTorah*").

Halakhic discourse is constructed by comparing and distinguishing between cases. Almost every halakhic question hinges on the unique background conditions of the case. It has some similarities to other cases, but it is also somewhat distinct, and the *posek* must decide which factors prevail. However, if one has no idea of the prevailing conditions which must be assessed, how can he compare or draw distinctions? Without the conceptual tools to render judgment, it is very difficult to deliberate, and impossible to apply the halakha. Thus, leading Torah scholars

---

41. See my essay, "Scientific Evaluation as a Basis for Halakhic Rulings" (Heb.), in my *Studies in the Thought of Maimonides*, Jerusalem: 2010, pp. 152–76; and my *Responsa Si'aḥ Naḥum* §79 (Maaleh Adumim: Me'aliot, 2008).

are generally hesitant to issue halakhic rulings on purely theoretical or hypothetical matters.

Nevertheless, faced with modern technological and cultural changes, the *posek* must address issues that are just now on the brink of applicability. Yet he must exercise great caution when ruling on such matters, because it is impossible to predict how they will develop. He certainly must address issues that are already fully applicable.

Almost two thousand years of exile rendered entire sections of the Torah moot – for instance, mitzvot that pertain to the land of Israel. The miraculous establishment of the State of Israel posed a challenge that our forebears of many generations never faced: how to build a state in accordance with the Torah.

Maimonides, it is true, codified not only matters that are practical in exile, but also the laws of kings and other areas of the Torah that were purely theoretical until very recently. Nevertheless, we must distinguish between theoretical issues and the functioning of society in actuality. We may be able to derive concepts and values from different aspects of the codified law, but extreme caution is necessary when dealing with such subjects, and certainly when attempting to reach definitive practical conclusions, since with respect to these issues we do not have a tradition for applying the halakha in practice within an independent state. (Even when diaspora Jewish communities enjoyed the support of the government and a significant degree of self-rule, a community within a foreign regime cannot be compared to a sovereign state.) This is all the more true of matters pertaining to saving lives, waging war, and governing a state.

Halakha is a way of life, and it is the *posek*'s job to reach a decision. He must examine halakhic sources and the responsa literature, but ultimately he is responsible to render instruction based on discretion, fear of God, love of humanity, and striving for truth.

On a Single Binding Halakhic Authority for All of Israel

The age-old discussion about the power of halakhic authority is vast and complex, and our goal here is only to highlight and illuminate certain aspects of it. In ancient times there was a high court – the Sanhedrin – in Jerusalem, and there was a systematic procedure for determining binding halakha. The process is described in the Tosefta:[42] When a halakhic question arose, a local scholar or court was consulted. If the question was not a new one, they would issue a ruling, and that was the end of the matter. However, for unprecedented questions, although the local judges ruled as they saw fit, the process did not end here. The local response was not binding on all Israel, because it was possible that elsewhere another sage would rule differently; after all, in matters of discretion, there can be differences of opinion and disputes. Moreover, the questioner might suspect that the court caused him unjustified monetary loss. He might accept the verdict of the local judges, but only on condition that they rule in accordance with halakha. However, if the questioner or litigant thought that the ruling was not in accordance with halakha, he would want to appeal. In addition, the judges themselves may not be certain about their verdict. To prevent dispute, and to ensure that justice is properly served, they would turn to higher judicial authorities. As long as the matter was not settled with finality, the case would rise through the legal system until it arrived at the highest authority: the high court, which sat in the Chamber of Hewn Stone on the Temple Mount in Jerusalem. On matters pertaining to the public at large, the judges would vote, and halakha would be determined by the majority. Such a ruling would have binding force over all Israel, as it is written: "In accordance with the instruction that they instruct to you, you shall do" (Deut. 17:11).

This prevented prolonged disputes, with one group practicing one way and another group another way, and kept the Torah from becoming, God forbid, like two Torahs.

Yet even while the Sanhedrin functioned, it did not vote on every issue. There were disputes that lasted for several generations.[43] It stands to reason that these were not the types of disputes that could have caused schism within the nation, and the judges certainly had good reasons not to reach a decision immediately. Sometimes the demand for complete unity causes excessive frustration. There are also relatively rare questions

---

42. Tosefta Ḥagiga 2:4 (2:9 in the Lieberman edition). The *baraita* is likewise cited in Sanhedrin 88b.
43. See Mishna Ḥagiga 2:2.

that are not easy to decide, and as long as it will not lead to social divisions and factionalism, it is better to defer a final resolution, since it is possible that new factors will emerge, which must be taken into consideration in order to determine the truth of the law.

During periods when all of the Sages operated with a sense of unity, the Sanhedrin was effective at preventing divisions among the people. However, there were times of intense divisiveness. Maimonides, in his introduction to the Mishna, explains that it was not only the loss of the Sanhedrin that caused the proliferation of disputes, but also a decrease in inquiries by disciples. It is likely that there were also decrees by the foreign rulers of Eretz Yisrael preventing the Sages from gathering.

Later, the Sanhedrin migrated away from its initial location in Jerusalem, and eventually ceased to exist. The convening of the Sages likewise ended. In the times of the Talmud, there was still a gathering of Sages representing the majority of Israel, and the Jewish population was still concentrated in a few places. The decisions of the Sages of the Babylonian academies were accepted by all of Israel, and therefore, the rulings and decisions of the Talmud have the force of a ruling by the Sanhedrin – not because the Sanhedrin still existed then, but because the Talmud was accepted by all of Israel.[44]

After the Talmud was concluded, the population was scattered, and Jews reached faraway places. Over time, the glory of the Babylonian *yeshivot* faded, and new centers of learning emerged in various places, making it impossible to convene all the Sages to decide matters of dispute. In every locale, disputes about new and unprecedented halakhic issues arose. There were even new disputes about how to interpret the Talmud – disputes that resulted in conflicting halakhic rulings. In addition to halakhic disputes, different customs emerged in different

---

44. See the introduction to *Mishneh Torah* (§§28–34):

> Ravina and R. Ashi and their colleagues were thus the last of the great Sages of Israel who transmitted the Oral Torah…. Their decrees, enactments, and customs spread through all of Israel, wherever they lived…. Whatever is in the Babylonian Talmud is binding on all of Israel…for all those matters in the Talmud were agreed upon by all of Israel, and those Sages who enacted, decreed, instituted, made rulings, and taught the law constitute all or most of the Sages of Israel.

communities. The greatest *posekim* of each generation attempted to decide various questions, but naturally there were differences of opinion and different rulings. These rulings did not have the power to obligate all of Israel, as Maimonides summarizes:

> After the court of R. Ashi... Israel was scattered to all the lands....
> The acts of the courts that arose in every place after [the closing
> of] the Talmud, which decreed or enacted or established practice
> for the people of that place, did not spread to all of Israel due to
> the remoteness of their residences and the difficulty of travel, and
> because the court of that place was comprised of individuals....
> Therefore, the people of one place are not forced to act in accor-
> dance with the practices of a different place, nor is one court told
> to issue a decree that was enacted by a different court in its place.
> So too, if an eminent sage taught that the path of justice is such-
> and-such, and a later court determines that this is not the path of
> justice written in the Talmud – we do not heed the earlier one,
> but the one that makes the most sense, whether it is the earlier
> one or the later one.[45]

Technically, since the Talmud was closed, there is no authority that can be binding on all of Israel, the primary reason being, as Maimonides emphasizes, the lack of consensus of all Israel. Nevertheless, over time, there were authorities who were accepted by very large parts of the public. At a certain point, mainly after the appearance of *Shulḥan Arukh*, they began to accept the authority of the *posekim* who lived before the *Shulḥan Arukh* – the *Rishonim* – though no one *Rishon* was accepted as an exclusive authority. Rather, all of the *Rishonim*, with all of their differences of opinion, were accepted collectively as being authoritative, although certain *Rishonim* were accepted as more authoritative than others. Accordingly, a *posek* may dispute a *Rishon* as long as his opinion is supported by other *Rishonim*. That is, the collective authority of the *Rishonim* was accepted, but not the individual authority of any one *Rishon*.

---

45. Ibid. §§29–32.

The appearance of *Shulḥan Arukh* effected another change as well. Rabbi Yosef Karo, the author of *Shulḥan Arukh*, created an artificial procedure for deciding amongst the *Rishonim*. He chose three *posekim* whose authority was widely accepted – Rif, Maimonides, and Rosh – and generally ruled in accordance with them. In cases where there was no unanimity between these three, he ruled in accordance with two against the third. To be sure, the Torah's statement, "incline after the majority" (Ex. 23:2), does not apply to disputes between *posekim*. Majority rule applies when all disputants are sitting together and debating the issue, trying to make their case and persuade their colleagues. It does not apply in a case where the disputing *posekim* lived in different places and eras. Nevertheless, *Shulḥan Arukh* generally follows the majority of these three *posekim*.

The rulings of *Shulḥan Arukh* were generally accepted in many communities,[46] especially Sephardic communities and the communities of North Africa and the Middle East – communities for whom Maimonides had long been accepted as the foremost *posek*. Maimonides' halakhic system is essentially the same as Rif's, so when there is a dispute among the three *posekim* that determine the rulings of *Shulḥan Arukh*, Rif and Maimonides are almost always in agreement against Rosh, who followed the path of the *Rishonim* of Germany and Northern France. Thus, in effect, *Shulḥan Arukh* almost always ruled in accordance with Maimonides. *Shulḥan Arukh* is essentially a mosaic of Maimonides' rulings; the order of the rulings follows *Tur*, but the content of each law mainly follows Maimonides.

When *Shulḥan Arukh* was published, it could not be accepted by Ashkenazic communities, where there was a long tradition of following

---

46. Editor's note: For a discussion of the spread of *Beit Yosef* and *Shulḥan Arukh*, the reactions against them, and the relationship between these works and Maimonides, see, for example: Menaḥem Elon, *Jewish Law*, vol. 2 (Philadelphia: JPS, 1994), 1309–1422; Meir Benayahu, *Yosef Beḥiri* (Joseph My Chosen One) (Jerusalem: Yad HaRav Nissim, 1991), 335–51; Yitzḥak (Isadore) Twersky, "*Harav R. Yosef Karo Ba'al HaShulḥan Arukh*" ("Rabbi Yosef Karo, Author of Shulḥan Arukh"), *Asufot: Sefer Shana Lemada'ei HaYahadut* 3, M. Benayahu, ed. (Jerusalem: Yad HaRav Nissim), 1989, 245–62; Eliav Shochetman, "*Al Hastirot BeShulḥan Arukh ve'al Mahuto shel Haḥibur Umatarotav*" ("On Contradictions within Shulḥan Arukh and on the Substance and Purpose of the Work"), ibid., pp. 323–30.

the halakhic path of Rashi and the Tosafists. To be sure, Maimonides' *Mishneh Torah* was accepted in Ashkenazic lands as a halakhic code,[47] and for a long time it was used much as *Shulḥan Arukh* was used later, but since they had an ancient halakhic tradition based on the teachings of the Tosafists, even where they used *Mishneh Torah*, they did not wish to stray from Ashkenazic tradition. When *Shulḥan Arukh* was published, the sages of Ashkenaz saw that there was indeed a need for such a code, which was briefer and more concentrated than *Mishneh Torah* and *Tur* with their commentaries. Yet they could not accept its halakhic rulings, which was counter to their tradition. Thus, Rema added his glosses, based on the teachings and halakhic tradition of the Ashkenazic sages, to the text of *Shulḥan Arukh*.

Even after Rema added his glosses, *Shulḥan Arukh* was still not accepted as a sole authority, though it was very useful. It made knowing halakha much easier, even for rabbis, who could now find clear, organized, and easily accessible halakhic rulings without having to search, consider, and ultimately render a decision.

The innovation wrought by *Shulḥan Arukh* sparked a wave of opposition. Most prominent among its opponents was Maharal (a contemporary of Rabbi Karo), who took an extreme position against *Shulḥan Arukh*. He wrote that God finds it more pleasing when one studies on his own and tries to clarify the law from its sources, even if he makes a mistake as a result, than if he studies a compendium of halakhic rulings and acts accordingly (Maharal does not mention *Shulḥan Arukh* by name, but it is his target).

It is more proper and more correct to render rulings from the Talmud. Even though there is concern that one will not follow the path of truth and not rule in accordance with the law, which would render his ruling truthful, nevertheless, a sage has nothing but what his intellect enables him to understand of the Talmud. When his insight and wisdom mislead him, he is still beloved by God when he teaches according to the dictates of his intellect.... He is better

---

47. Editor's note: With the additional comments of *Hagahot Maimuniyot*, noting the rulings of the Ashkenazic authorities.

than one who issues rulings from one work, without knowing the reason for it, for he walks like a blind man on the path.[48]

Another opponent of the approach of *Shulḥan Arukh* was Rabbi Yehoshua ben Yosef of Krakow, the author of *Meginei Shlomo*, who wrote: "Anyone with clear evidence may disagree, even with statements of *Rishonim*."[49]

Maharal's formulation is indeed quite extreme, but the principle is correct. The ideal is certainly that everyone study and acquire the skill of rendering halakhic rulings, and then make his own decision from the sources whenever a question comes up. In fact, there were always sages who did so, though it is clear that they also accepted, to one degree or another, the authority of earlier sages.

Over time, the redeemers of *Shulḥan Arukh* arose: its commentaries, such as *Magen Avraham*, *Ḥelkat Meḥokek*, *Siftei Kohen* (*Shakh*), and others. They provided the background for each halakha and reopened every question. Typical of sages who discuss halakhic questions, they disagree in many instances–with Rabbi Karo, Rema, and amongst themselves.

This seems paradoxical. On one hand, it was the addition of these commentaries that made *Shulḥan Arukh* authoritative and led to its acceptance in most Jewish communities, but since those same commentaries argue with it and Rema in many instances, there is once again a situation (like at the close of the period of the *Rishonim*) in which *Shulḥan Arukh* together with its commentaries became a virtually unchallenged authority collectively, even as no one element attained such authority.[50]

---

48. Maharal, *Netivot Olam*, *Netiv HaTorah* 15.

49. *Responsa Penei Yehoshua*, *Yoreh De'ah* 34; see also *Responsa Maharam Lublin* §135.

50. Editor's note: see Rabbi Ḥayim of Volozhin's *Responsa Ḥut Hameshulash* 1:9: "I was cautioned by my sainted master, the great rabbi, the eminent and pious Rabbi Eliyahu of Vilna, may his soul rest in paradise, not to show favoritism in halakha [even to the rulings of the authors of *Shulḥan Arukh*]." The bracketed statement was omitted from the printed versions and replaced with "etc." See Rabbi Yehoshua Heschel Halevi (Levin)'s *Aliyot Eliyahu* (Jerusalem: 1989), pp. 90-91, n. 62, which cites the full text. R. Shlomo Yosef Zevin noted this in *Ishim Veshitot* (Jerusalem: Kol Mevaser, 2007), p. 8, n.5.

Since then, additional halakhic codes have been composed, and the responsa literature has grown immeasurably. As a general rule, after the Sanhedrin ceased to function, and since the Jewish people have not accepted a specific, uniform authority, there is technically no uniform ruling that is binding on everyone. Yet *Aharonim* rarely dispute *Rishonim* unless they find support in the opinion of another *Rishon*. *Posekim* typically relate to their predecessors, and especially to those specific *posekim* whose works and rulings were accepted as being more authoritative, with respect and reverence.

But there are other *Aharonim* who attained a special stature. Rabbi Akiva Eger, for example, who lived less than 200 years ago, attained a stature that virtually places him on par with the *Rishonim*.[51] It is worth citing a letter that Rabbi Akiva Eger wrote to his son. Rabbi Akiva Eger did not publish his own responsa, but his son collected them and sent his father a request for his consent to publish the volume. The son asks, in the letter, whether the book can be called "Rulings and Writings" ("*Pesakim Ukhtavim*"). His father responded:

> Regarding what you asked, my beloved son, whether I would like to call these *pesakim* and those *ketavim* …. The name "*pesakim*" is unbecoming, for it looks as though I decide halakha definitively. This is not what I had in mind when I agreed to publish them …. I relied on the fact that the questioner would study and examine my words and choose …. I have difficulty with the practice I hear about, namely, that some decisors rule in accordance with new books whenever they come out. What they do is not good. Rather, they should delve to the best of their ability, and if, after studying it thoroughly, they agree with the words of the author, they should follow it. But to believe everything they read – this is not the path of wisdom.[52]

In the time since the reception of *Shulhan Arukh* and its commentaries, there has once again been a proliferation of opinions and a diffusion of

---

51. See R. Ḥayim Berlin's words at the beginning of his father's (Netziv) work, *Meromei Sadeh* (Jerusalem: Defus Hatechiya, 1955).
52. *Responsa Rabbi Akiva Eger*, p. 1.

halakha. Therefore, there have been several attempts in recent centuries to produce halakhic codes that summarize all of these developments. For instance, on matters pertaining to everyday life (*Oraḥ Ḥayim*), there are *Ḥayei Adam*,[53] *Mishna Berura*, and *Ben Ish Ḥai*. The *magnum opus* of Rabbi Yeḥiel Mikhel Halevi Epstein, *Arukh Hashulḥan*, deserves special mention, as it was the first attempt in many generations to write a comprehensive halakhic code on all areas of the Torah, based on the precedent set by Maimonides' *Mishneh Torah*. It is worth noting that since he saw and took into consideration all previous works, including *Mishna Berura*, which he mentions in several places, *Arukh Hashulḥan* was considered the most authoritative halakhic work in Greater Lithuania before World War II.[54] Nevertheless, it is impossible to say that any one of these works was accepted as the exclusive authority, the sole basis for issuing rulings.

Consequently, as I wrote elsewhere,[55] the prevailing view that Jews of Sephardic, North African, and Middle Eastern origin always follow Rabbi Yosef Karo while Ashkenazim always follow Rema is nothing but a myth. *Shulḥan Arukh* spread and was accepted throughout

---

53. Editor's note: See R. Avraham Danzig's (author of *Ḥayei Adam*) introduction to his *Ḥokhmat Adam*:

> You will not find in this work any words from my relative by marriage, the master of the entire Diaspora community, the pious R. Eliyahu (=the Vilna Gaon), and that is because I heard the slander of many people who are angry at me for objecting to his rulings in a few places in my work *Ḥayei Adam*. Without a doubt, the angry people do not know the manner of *posekim*, for the way of our holy Torah is that one builds and another demolishes, and that the disciple disputes the master, as written in *Shulḥan Arukh* .... The Vilna Gaon certainly has more satisfaction from my engagement with his statements than from one who says, "He spoke well".... I therefore opted to remain silent, so they will not complain about me. They will be held accountable for withholding from the Vilna Gaon the satisfaction he has when one engages with his words.

   This appears in several copies of the first edition of this work [Vilna: 1825], but was omitted from later editions. See Haim Liberman, *Ba'al Ḥayei Adam VehaGra MiVilna* ("The Author of *Ḥayei Adam* and the Vilna Gaon"), *Kiryat Sefer* 37 (1962), p. 413; reprinted in idem, *Ohel Raḥel*, vol. 1 (New York: Empire Press, 1980), pp. 471–72.

54. I heard this from Rabbi Yosef Eliyahu Henkin, who would refer to the author of *Arukh Hashulḥan* as "the last *posek*."

55. *Responsa Si'aḥ Naḥum* §86, and see also §§87–88.

Israel not as the rulings of an individual *posek*, but as a *posek* along with commentaries. It is well known that on many issues, the commentaries settle disputes between Rabbi Karo and Rema, and they sometimes rule against both. The job of the halakhist is to ascertain and clarify the law, and to rule according to the logic that seems true to him.

Additionally, questions that are not addressed in halakhic compendia arise in every generation, and they must be addressed by contemporary rabbis. In recent times especially, technological and cultural developments, the ingathering of the exiles, and the return to Eretz Yisrael have given rise to questions that our forebears never considered. There will always be those who ask questions and those who provide answers, and there will always be multiple ways of looking at things. Ideally, each person will make the effort to acquire the knowledge and skills that enable him to decide the halakhic questions he confronts. However, until he has reached that level, he must use the accepted works of halakha. Of such situations it is written: "One who wishes to act in accordance with the words of Beit Shammai may do so, in accordance with the words of Beit Hillel may do so."[56] However, he must know not to practice two contradictory leniencies or stringencies, and that there are rules for deciding uncertain cases, like "*safek deOraita leḥumra.*"

If one studies an issue in depth and reaches a view which reflects that of one of the major *posekim* of the past, he can rely upon this view, even if it is a minority opinion. Nevertheless, such a ruling must be undertaken cautiously and level-headedly, especially if it goes against a halakhic ruling that is already widely accepted. A halakhist must work hard to clarify and elucidate the law from its sources, with intellectual integrity and fear of God, free of external interests, while giving due consideration to the tradition of previous generations, in accordance with what he understands and decides using his intellect and judgment, for the truth of the Torah and the sake of heaven.

Any Torah scholar who clarifies a halakhic issue that pertains to his community or audience must do what he deems correct after having determined the law. However, if the issue also pertains to others,

---

56. Eiruvin 6b.

and all the more so if it pertains to the public at large, wisdom dictates that he listen as well to the opinions of other *posekim*. Who can say: "I am, and there is no one besides me" (Is. 47:8)? Even if he thinks that he has accurately determined the halakha, he should clarify it with great *posekim* and listen to their views. In earlier generations, the sages of the Sanhedrin would consult with one another; we, too, hope and pray that we may merit the fulfillment of the verse: "I will restore your judges as at the first" (Is. 1:26).

Beliefs and Opinions

I.

The fundamental concepts of Jewish belief – the unity of God, the election of Israel, etc. – are based on Scripture; matters of belief and doctrine have occupied us since ancient times. The Talmud speaks of "four who entered the orchard," clearly referring to matters that we would call "Jewish thought" nowadays – the in-depth study of the fundamentals of faith.

In contrast to halakhic decision-making, which is clearly the provenance of rabbis, the realm of beliefs and opinions is not only for rabbis. In reality, though, only a select few engaged in abstract religious thought – in contrast to practical halakhic thought – and the broader community, even most of its sages, refrained from delving into this area.

Jewish thought was influenced in part by general philosophical currents. Thus we find that medieval Jewish thinkers borrowed from Muslim philosophers ideas which originated in ancient Greece. Obviously, the Jewish thinkers only espoused ideas that were compatible, in their view, with Jewish tradition, and which could be supported by Jewish sources as well. In addition, there is also a Jewish esoteric tradition with ancient roots, but it is hard to know how complete and continuous this tradition has been, since its contents were accessible to very few.

It is worth considering the main difference between the realm of thought and the realm of practice, which is the realm of halakha. In the practical realm, there are authority, obligation, and rulings. For instance, with all the various disputes, the laws of keeping kosher are fundamentally the same laws in all observant communities. Even if there are certain differences, they are not large, and so any observant Jew may eat the food of any other observant Jew. However, with respect to Jewish thought, there were always major differences between various Jewish thinkers. There is fundamentally no such thing as a "ruling" on matters of belief and opinion, with the exception of the principles of faith articulated by Maimonides; and there are *Rishonim* who disagreed with him even about those.

Maimonides emphasizes that man's freedom of choice is the basis for the entire Torah; the arena of man's freedom has few limitations. Had man not had the freedom to choose, what would be the point of all the Torah's commandments?

In addition to this principle, Maimonides clearly articulated another thirteen principles of faith. There were others (most notably Rabbi Yosef Albo in his *Sefer Ha'ikarim*) who grouped them into just three principles: God's existence, the giving of the Torah, and reward and punishment. Another fundamental principle of faith is the election of Israel. With regard to all other matters of doctrine and philosophy, Maimonides states explicitly that if something has no practical ramifications, it is not subject to rulings or binding authority:

> I have already told you more than once that if the Sages disagree about some idea or opinion that has no practical ramification, there is no saying "the law accords with so-and-so."[57]

There were those who disagreed on this point, but the halakhists, following Maimonides, always emphasized that there should be no set obligations on matters of thought and belief, beyond the fourteen principles (free choice plus the other thirteen principles).

This view has roots in the Geonic era, in a responsum of Rav Hai Gaon, for instance:

---

57. *Commentary on the Mishna* on Sota 3:3 and likewise on Sanhedrin 10:3 and Shevuot 1:4; see also *Sefer Hamitzvot*, negative commandment 133.

> Words of *aggada* are not like [halakhic] traditions; rather, every-
> one preached that which he thought of, but as a possibility and
> an alternative, not as a settled matter. Therefore, we do not rely
> on them.[58]

Does the fact that there is so much leeway on matters of doctrine and
opinion mean that Judaism has no ideological message? Of course not!
Scripture and the works of the Sages contain many fundamental ideological points which have greatly influenced and impacted the trajectory
of the entire world. The ideas of monotheism, free choice, and personal
responsibility for one's actions have influenced most of the world, as have
the Torah's ideas about slavery, how to treat the downtrodden, resting
every seventh day, etc., etc.

However, we must understand that the ideas themselves are
not formulated as binding commandments because philosophy, by
its very nature, evolves and develops as man learns more and understands the universe better. Man was created with the intelligence to
penetrate the mysteries of creation. The urge to understand reality
and nature is the driving force for man's quest to delve deeper. The
process is ongoing and never-ending.

Mankind continuously discovers the degree to which God's creation contains mysteries that the ancients could not have imagined, and
the conditions by which man can probe creation's wonders well beyond
what previous generations could fathom are also continuously devel-
oping. Setting boundaries on free inquiry – as certain religions did – is
an incomparable tragedy, for it sentences the human spirit to a sort of
imprisonment in bygone eras and does not allow man to advance beyond
the notions of those earlier generations. This is in no way the Torah's goal.

There is no doubt that those who believe in the progress of the
world are correct. Although this progress also means that the forces of
evil accumulate new powers, the world nevertheless advances morally

---

58. *Otzar HaGe'onim, Ḥagiga,* commentaries, pp. 59–60. See also the introduction of
Rabbenu Baḥya to his *Ḥovot Halevavot,* which states that Deuteronomy 17:8–11
(which describes the process of appealing to the Sanhedrin) does not apply to
philosophical matters.

and ethically. In the modern era, man's abilities and capacities have expanded greatly. The possibility of doing good and, God forbid, perpetrating evil has grown to unprecedented magnitude. With the touch of a button, man can destroy a world and its inhabitants, or, on the other hand, improve life for the masses. This fact constitutes an unprecedented challenge and imposes great responsibility upon each individual.

The purpose of the Torah is to open before man the endless possibilities contained in creation, and to that end, freedom of thought is necessary. It is through the differing approaches of different individuals that development in the realm of ideas takes place. In addition, man's freedom of choice in the realm of action is what enables him to improve and develop, and that freedom is based in the freedom of thought.

Still, the practical realm differs from the world of ideas. In the practical realm, commandments are necessary, because erroneous choices and injurious acts can bring destruction not only upon the individual, but upon the entire world.

II.

Judaism has bequeathed many concepts to the world; there are also many concepts which originated with the sages of other nations. As Maimonides has taught us: "Accept the truth from whatever source it proceeds."[59] For instance, a major principle of the Torah and of halakha is that any social structure, like the leadership of a city or region, must be designed so that it reflects public will and opinion. But the practical implementation of this principle is not defined anywhere. Through the generations, the Jews had various systems for electing communal leaders, and they were not always the best possible systems. The entire civilized world faces the same problem: deciding which form of government will best achieve equality and effective governance in a way that addresses the needs of the entire public, without discrimination. Thinkers have grappled with these questions for centuries, both in the abstract as well as on the practical level, in

59. *Shemonah Perakim*, Introduction, pp. 35–36.

the quest to find a system of government that best produces these two results. There is no doubt that we can learn from the approaches which have arisen in the developed world. Studying forms of governance and their implementation is not just a technical exercise; it bears implications for moral values.

The history of ideas and actions demonstrates that when new ideas come into being, it takes time for them to penetrate society and impact living conditions. As long as practical boundaries are maintained and things proceed cautiously and gradually, such changes can be for the better, and they are usually a source of blessing.

III.

Over time, the study of Jewish thought declined for various reasons. Paradoxically, even though the lack of formal rulings on matters of doctrine and opinion was supposed to stimulate engagement with this aspect of Torah study, in fact it was marginalized, perhaps precisely because there is no binding tradition on such matters. The situation deteriorated to the point that when the Haskalah (Jewish Enlightenment) movement and the crisis of secularism appeared in recent centuries, works of Jewish thought were all but neglected, even in yeshivot and even among Torah scholars. This situation must be fixed, and, thank God, it is in fact steadily improving.

Now that we have won our independence, we must make room for the study of Jewish thought. It is clear that comprehensive, in-depth study of Jewish thought requires time and openness to ideas that originate outside the Jewish world. At the same time, one of the primary goals of yeshivot is to cultivate Torah scholars and men of action who have spiritual stature. The amount of time usually spent in yeshiva is not very long, and it must provide the foundation of Torah observance and familiarity with methods for reaching halakhic conclusions. Such a task demands a great deal of time, leaving little opportunity to study other subjects. In a few short years, it is impossible to develop an entire generation that is proficient in multiple subjects. It is therefore difficult to provide a definitive outline for how time should be distributed, but clearly there should be training that enables students to progress independently later on, and everyone must plan to continue growing in knowledge and understanding throughout life.

The popular trend in contemporary religious society is to emphasize thinkers who are less than rational or who base their thought on esoteric doctrine. The neglect of rationalist thinkers in general, and Maimonides' thought in particular, is a terrible mistake. We would not be exaggerating if we said that Maimonides was the greatest Jewish thinker of all time. It is not for naught that he was called the Moses of his generation.[60] They also said of him: "From Moses to Moses, none arose like Moses." Concealing Maimonides' thought from the next generation is a terrible injustice – not for Maimonides, but for the next generation. The youth must understand that Torah thought must be not only attractive and enlightening, but also clear and, more than anything else, intelligible through rational thought and not obscured by undecipherable secrets. If the very discourse is unintelligible, how can the idea be comprehended?!

There are things that we cannot understand, but we should not pretend that we understand them. Maimonides teaches us that we must be as rational as possible. Rationality has its limits, of course, because human beings, like all creatures, have limits. The Holy One created His world with limits. The attraction to non-rational thought today stems from various sources – it is less difficult and is part of a postmodernist *zeitgeist*. Yet this sort of thought is deeply problematic, as it leads man to flee from social responsibility and focus on his personal dreams and imaginings.

In our generation, we are privileged to witness impressive growth in the number of Torah scholars in many communities. Let us hope that, together with the increased engagement in halakha, there will also be increased interest in matters of faith, the roads that lead to love and reverence for God.

---

60. Editor's note: See S. D. Goitein, *Auotograph shel HaRambam Umikhtav elav me'et Ahoto Miriam* ("A Maimonides Autograph and a Letter to him from his Sister Miriam"; Heb.), *Tarbiz* 32 (Winter 1962–3), p. 187. Maimonides was also called "the Moses of the age"; see *Iggerot HaRambam*, p. 264.

Halakhic Decision-Making and Rabbinic Leadership

One of the main roles of a rabbi is to lead the community, and as a leader it is the rabbi's job to improve society. He must not settle for the way things are but be driven to improve the members of his community. The spiritual elevation achieved through growth in Torah and fear of God is necessary in order to build an ideal society for the nation as a whole. Naturally, this requires people whose job is to advance this goal.

A spiritual leadership that views its role as merely maintaining the status quo, and is content with the community not veering to the right or left, is guilty of perpetuating present social ills and keeping those at the margins of society where they are, and also fails to understand reality. Life is not static, and every individual and community faces new challenges. Leaders must know how to address constantly changing conditions and how to guide the community in the face of new developments.

There have always been spiritual leaders who succeeded in elevating their communities and making broad improvements. Two prominent examples from recent centuries are the yeshiva movement, which began primarily with the yeshiva of Rabbi Ḥayim of Volozhin, and the movement started by Rav Kook which inspired the religious community to recognize the revolution taking place in the status of the Jewish people and that Israel was undergoing a period of awakening as a nation.

The role of rabbinic leadership is not only to help people recognize what is taking place, but also to guide developments in a positive direction, by the light of the Torah, and to anticipate the future. Rabbinic leadership must develop creative plans – solutions that promote both material and spiritual growth.

If the rabbi himself rests on his laurels, is content with what he has, and does not yearn to achieve more, he will certainly not be able to influence his community to improve. However, if the rabbi himself strives to grow in Torah and wisdom, and to blaze new paths of spiritual and communal advancement, he will influence the entire community as well.

The rabbi's role as a communal leader raises a serious question about the degree to which the rabbi should seek to influence the decisions of elected officials and in political matters, and the manner in which he should do so. On one hand, the rabbi must eschew political involvement to the degree possible, because these pursuits, by their very nature, provoke disputes and divisions, which are ruinous to the rabbinate as well as to the community and society, and cause a desecration of God's name. (It goes without saying that a rabbi may not participate in political rivalries, scheming, etc.) On the other hand, public issues are not just "politics." They are also moral, ethical, halakhic, and pertinent to the very survival of the community or nation. There are also instances where, in the rabbi's assessment, he can identify blatant mistakes that might lead to terrible results. In such cases, there is room for him to intervene, but he must be careful to speak only about the moral aspects of the issue and not about the political aspects of it; politics have the power to bring destruction, God forbid, as well as the power to facilitate social and spiritual improvement, but extreme caution and moral discretion are needed to formulate the proper response. There are times to shout and times to remain silent. Since reality is complicated, it is likely that rabbinic involvement in certain issues will be met with understanding and even admiration within some circles, while others will turn their backs on the rabbi as a result. Thus, the rabbi must be very cautious and use common sense when deciding whether and how to get involved; he must weigh potential benefits against expected costs.

Recently, a new catchphrase has appeared. It refers to a doctrine that grants rabbis authority in realms that have nothing to do with halakha. This new slogan is "Da'as Torah." The Da'as Torah doctrine began in the late nineteenth century, and it expands the authority of Torah sages to non-halakhic matters, demanding obedience on matters that are neither mitzvot nor transgressions, that lie outside the realm of permitted or forbidden. It is applied to private matters, and especially to public issues. However, the fact that one is a rabbi does not grant him expertise in disciplines that are not his occupation. A rabbi is not a doctor and not an expert on national defense. Consequently, it makes no sense for a rabbi to meddle in the considerations of true experts.

On the other hand, when there is mutual trust between a rabbi and an expert in a given field, there are certainly issues that invite cooperation and productive dialogue in which each party benefits from the contributions of the other party. A rabbi can offer a moral, ethical, or spiritual perspective on the issue.

Although there is a halakha that a king may not commit the nation to an elective war without the consent of the 71-member high court, this is a unique law that pertains only to warfare and pertains to the relationship between the two centers of governing power in Israel: the king and the Sanhedrin. It is likely that the requirement to consult the Sanhedrin stems both from the fact that its sages represent the people and from the fact that they can examine the king's decisions and the purity of his intentions: is this war really necessary? Does it seem like it will help the Jewish people? Or is it, perhaps, being waged only for the king's own glory? In the latter case, they certainly must stop him from launching the war. Thus, no inferences can be made from consultation about discretionary wars to other issues.

Some subjects demand expertise, understanding of the situation, and broad-minded judgment. Occasionally, one who is not proficient in a particular subject will have a hard time properly understanding the breadth of the perspectives and considerations it involves. One capable of making fine halakhic distinctions cannot necessarily forecast where historical processes lead; historical discernment requires a completely different way of looking at things. Some issues, like defense and foreign policy, require practical knowledge as well. From this perspective, it is quite likely that even if a rabbi is wise, ethically conscientious, and sound of judgment, he will still lack the practical expertise necessary to understand the circumstances properly. The fact that a rabbi spends his days and nights engaged in Torah and halakha does not automatically grant him the practical wisdom or skills to judge such matters.

There may be issues on which hearing the rabbi's opinion is worthwhile, because of his Torah knowledge or his sound judgment, with the understanding that he limit himself to considerations of values without deciding the issue from standpoints on which he has no special knowledge. Knowledge of the Torah should imbue man with integrity and the fear of God and lead him to moral and ethical understanding, though this too is not guaranteed, as there are people with Torah knowledge who unfortunately do not fear God, thus turning the Torah into a stumbling block. However, from this perspective, the proper address for consultation is not necessarily a rabbi, but anyone whose moral judgment and integrity are respected. One turns to a rabbi for such issues to receive advice, not because he possesses any oracular authority.

Conclusion

In addition to observance of the mitzvot and Torah study, which are obligatory for all of Israel, we have seen that Torah scholars should function in several capacities: rendering halakhic decisions, clarifying matters of belief and opinion, and providing moral and ethical guidance to the public. The return of Israel to its homeland and the ingathering of the exiles that is being realized before our eyes pose new challenges to the people of the Torah. We have firm faith that the Almighty will help guide those who are worthy of His assistance to respond to the needs of the public and fill all these roles with wisdom, understanding, and sensitivity. May God grant them success.

Chapter 7

The Natural Sciences and the Reasons for the Mitzvot

Introduction

Throughout his writings, Maimonides ascribes great importance to the natural sciences. In various places,[1] Maimonides emphasizes that knowledge of the natural sciences is an essential prerequisite for the most fundamental mitzvot, namely, loving and revering God. Accordingly, he asserts:

> When one contemplates these matters and becomes familiar with all creations...and sees the wisdom of the Holy One, blessed be He, in every creature, his love for the Omnipresent will increase, and his soul will thirst and his flesh will yearn to love the Omnipresent. He will fear and dread his own lowliness, impoverishment, and insignificance.[2]

---

1. See, for example, *Sefer Hamitzvot*, positive commandment 3; *Commentary on the Mishna* on Ḥagiga 2:1; *Moreh Nevukhim* III:28; *Responsa Maimonides* §150.
2. *Hilkhot Yesodei HaTorah* 4:12. In these laws, Maimonides' goal is to inspire the student who is ignorant of the natural sciences to lift his eyes heavenward, as it is

Maimonides therefore considered it necessary to give a basic outline of
the natural sciences, primarily astronomy, at the beginning of his halakhic work, *Mishneh Torah*. Furthermore, he included the obligation to
study natural science in the mitzva of Torah study: "The subjects called
'*pardes*' are included in '*talmud*.'"[3]

However, in addition to emphasizing the importance of the natural sciences for recognizing the Creator, Maimonides undertook an
additional task in *Moreh Nevukhim*: training man to properly understand
the reasons for the mitzvot. To that end, he considered it necessary to
sketch the basic outline of the correct approach for studying "the work
of creation," the wisdom that encompasses all of the natural sciences.
According to Maimonides, this wisdom serves as the framework and
model for addressing the reasons for the mitzvot.

The Parallel between Scientific Inquiry and the Investigation of the Reasons for the Mitzvot

In order to understand the fundamental connection that exists, in
Maimonides' view, between natural science and the reasons for the
mitzvot, we must first consider three basic principles that characterize
the natural sciences according to Maimonides. These principles are part
of the heritage of Greek philosophy in general, though Maimonides
places singular emphasis on some of them. We will also see that in his

written: "Lift your eyes heavenward and see Who created these?" (Is. 40:26), and
as Maimonides wrote (*Hilkhot Yesodei HaTorah* 2:2): "so that they serve to initiate
the intelligent individual to the love of God," for contemplation of "His great and
wondrous works and creatures" (ibid. 1) automatically leads man to love and revere
God. He therefore briefly surveys the theory of epicycles as though it is clear cut,
without going into various difficulties and uncertainties. However, for one who has
already studied *Mishneh Torah* and advanced in the natural sciences to the point that
he understands astronomy, Maimonides reveals the contradictions and problems
of the science of astronomy (see *Moreh Nevukhim* II:24; and see Maimonides' introductory letter to *Moreh Nevukhim*, addressed to his student for whom he wrote
that work, along with others like him [p. 1]: "You read under my guidance texts
dealing with the science of astronomy"). For such students, he developed his own
methods of understanding the basic problems of science.

3. *Hilkhot Talmud Torah* 1:11. See also *Hilkhot Yesodei HaTorah* 4:13.

investigation of the reasons for the mitzvot, Maimonides builds his theory on the same principles.

1. In scientific investigation, more is unknown than is known.

Maimonides points out that a great deal of progress was made with regard to the collection of data on planetary motion from the age of Aristotle to the time of Ptolemy, and likewise from the time of Ptolemy to Maimonides' own time, which undermined basic premises of Aristotelian physics. Nevertheless, this progress did not lead to further clarity or the discovery of all the laws governing celestial bodies; on the contrary, the accumulation of observed data only deepened the perplexity. As Maimonides concludes:

> The extreme predilection that I have for investigating the truth is evidenced by the fact that I have explicitly stated and reported my perplexity regarding these matters as well as by the fact that I have not heard nor do I know a demonstration as to anything concerning them.[4]

Yet this is the case not only with respect to certain astronomical matters. At the beginning of his work he declares, as his opening position:

> Know that with regard to natural matters as well, it is impossible to give a clear exposition when teaching some of their principles as they are.... You should not think that these great secrets are fully and completely known to anyone among us.[5]

Even so, the human mind can penetrate the fog and glean ever-deepening knowledge and understanding of the universe.

2. Natural laws are statistical.

Aristotle asserted that natural laws are true only "for the most part." There are always exceptions that cannot be integrated into the framework

---

4. *Moreh Nevukhim* II:24, p. 327.
5. *Moreh Nevukhim*, Introduction, p. 7.

of fixed regularities. Nevertheless, I have explained elsewhere[6] that Maimonides' approach is that even possibility can be quantified, and the degree of possibility should be measured:

> Some things that are possible are very probable, some are very improbable, and some are right between these two; the possible is a very broad realm.[7]

This premise can be expressed a bit differently in contemporary terms: the laws of nature are statistical. That is, the likelihood of events occurring as predicted by the laws is relatively high, but there are outliers, and the likelihood of deviation can itself be calculated and measured.

3. The nature of existence can be learned by means of observation.

Maimonides emphasized the empirical approach,[8] and it is possible that his medical vocation influenced his theory of science. Medieval physicians were aware of the need to observe phenomena and even to experiment with various treatments. It is interesting that with regard to biology, the field in which Aristotle did most of his practical scientific work, he himself appears to have preferred the path of the observer and collector of empirical data to that of the practitioner of pure science, which he defined as the knowledge of universals that cannot be acquired by means of sensory perception.[9]

These guidelines for scientific investigation remain valid in the investigation of the reasons for the mitzvot. Maimonides explicitly asserts

---

6. See my essay, "The Concept of 'Possibility' in Halakhic and Scientific Thinking," in *Studies in the Thought of Maimonides* (Jerusalem: 2010), pp. 177–93.
7. *Sefer Hamitzvot*, negative commandment 290.
8. See, for example, *Moreh Nevukhim* I:71, p. 179, where he quotes Themistius: "that which exists does not conform to the various opinions, but rather the correct opinions conform to that which exists"; "Letter Concerning Astrology," *Iggerot HaRambam*, p. 479: "Nothing is worthy of believing unless it is one of three things.... The second is something that man perceives with one of the five senses"; *Commentary on the Mishna* on Eduyot 1:2: "I measured as precisely as I could and found...." See also *Commentary on the Mishna* on Bekhorot 8:2.
9. Aristotle, *Posterior Analytics* I:31.

the parallel guidelines. We will first present them and then attempt to analyze their implications.

1. *In the investigation of the reasons for the mitzvot, more is unknown than is known.*

Toward the end of his discussion of the reasons of the mitzvot, Maimonides wrote:

> Marvel exceedingly at the wisdom of His commandments, may He be exalted, just as you should marvel at the wisdom manifested in the things He has made. It says: "The Rock, His work is perfect; for all His ways are justice" (Deut. 32:4). It says that just as the things made by Him are consummately perfect, so are His commandments consummately just. However, our intellects are incapable of apprehending the perfection of everything that He has made and the justice of everything He has commanded. We only apprehend the justice of some of His commandments just as we only apprehend some of the marvels in the things He has made, in the parts of the body of animals and in the motions of the spheres. What is hidden from us in both these classes of things is much more considerable than what is manifest.[10]

However, we can expand our knowledge of both natural science and the reasons for the mitzvot by means of piercing investigation, and inscrutable secrets will slowly be revealed.

With these words, Maimonides indicates that all he writes in *Moreh Nevukhim* about the reasons for the commandments is no more than general guidelines that he proposes in order to aid one who is investigating the reasons for the mitzvot. The bulk of the work remains to be done.

---

10. *Moreh Nevukhim* III:49, pp. 605–6. Note that this conclusion does not contradict what Maimonides wrote at the end of that chapter (p. 613): "I have now dealt one by one with all the commandments included in these classes, and we have drawn attention to the reasons for them. There are only a few and some slight details for which I have not given reasons, even though in truth we have virtually given reasons also for these to him who is attentive and understanding."

2. *Mitzvot and moral laws are statistical.*

Maimonides devotes an entire chapter of *Moreh Nevukhim* to explaining the parallel between mitzvot and the natural order with respect to this principle. He writes:

> The Law does not pay attention to the isolated. The Law was not given with a view to things that are rare. For in everything that it wishes to bring about, be it an opinion or a moral habit or a useful work, it is directed only toward the things that occur in the majority of cases and pays no attention to what happens rarely or to the damage occurring to the unique human being because of this way of determination and because of the legal character of the governance. For the Law is a divine thing; and it is your business to reflect on the natural things in which the general utility, which is included in them, nonetheless necessarily produces damage to individuals...
>
> In view of this consideration also, you will not wonder at the fact that the purpose of the Law is not perfectly achieved in every individual and that, on the contrary, it necessarily follows that there should exist individuals whom this governance of the Law does not make perfect. For not everything that derives necessarily from the natural specific forms is actualized in every individual. Indeed, all things proceed from one deity and one agent, and "have been given from one shepherd" (Eccl. 12:11). The contrary of this is impossible.... Only the universal interests, those of the majority, are considered in them.[11]

Based on this principle, on the words of the Sages, and on close familiarity with the life of several communities in his day, Maimonides asserted what today we would call a law of sociology: "At no time is there ever a community that has no licentious individuals or forbidden sexual unions."[12]

---

11. Ibid. 34, pp. 534–35.
12. *Hilkhot Issurei Biah* 22:19.

3. *The reasons for the mitzvot can be learned by means of observation.*

In contrast to the first two rules, the third rule offers practical guidance for furthering study and scholarship, toward uncovering the wisdom of the Creator embedded both within the universe and within the Torah. According to this rule, the impact of Torah obedience is tangible, and consequently, through observation over the short- and long-term and tracking the effect and impact of the mitzvot on the individual and society alike, one can gain insight into the reasons for the mitzvot. To that end, it is necessary to look upon the individual and society through a critical lens, accumulating data about human behavior in different situations and under various conditions. Another tool for measuring the impact of the mitzvot is the comparative study of different societies and legal systems, "so that you should have a criterion by means of which you will be able to distinguish between the regimens of *nomoi* (human legislation) that have been laid down and the regimens of the divine Law."[13]

Since man, by nature, must live in a society with other human beings, legal orders and social hierarchies were already developed in ancient times to meet society's needs and to further goals that seemed desirable to those who developed said legal systems. These systems included, "the ordering of the polis and of its circumstances and the abolition in it of injustice and oppression … for their obtaining, in accordance with the opinion of that chief, a certain something deemed to be happiness."[14]

Many mitzvot of the Torah are oriented toward a similar end, and their effectiveness in achieving those ends can be assessed, since "every commandment from among these six hundred and thirteen commandments exists … [either] to communicate a rule of justice, or to ward off an injustice, or to endow men with a noble moral quality, or to warn them against an evil moral quality."[15] Mitzvot of this sort, "whose utility is clear to the multitude, are called *mishpatim*."[16] About

---

13. *Moreh Nevukhim* II:40, p. 383.
14. Ibid.
15. Ibid. III:31, p. 524.
16. Ibid. 26, p. 507.

them Maimonides wrote in *Mishneh Torah*: "The *mishpatim* are mitzvot whose reasons are revealed, and the benefits of performing them in this world are known."[17] God's Torah stands apart from man-made *nomoi* in that, unlike them, the Torah's goal is to educate man and guide him toward correct opinions. Thus:

> All [the commandments] are bound up with three things: opinions, moral qualities, and political civic actions.[18]

Therefore, the good that is achieved through the performance of mitzvot in this world is the true good, not the happiness imagined by a lawmaker based on his worldview.

However, there are mitzvot that do not lend themselves readily to rational explanations nor do they clearly lead to a desirable end. Such are the prohibitions on wearing *sha'atnez* (an admixture of wool and linen), cooking or eating milk and meat together, the Yom Kippur scapegoat, and the like – mitzvot that the Sages termed "*ḥukim*" (statutes). With regard to *ḥukim* as well, "there indubitably is a cause for them – I mean to say a useful end – but that it is hidden from us either because of the incapacity of our intellects or the deficiency of our knowledge."[19] Indeed, this is an explicit verse: "For it is no vain thing for you" (Deut. 32:47), on which the Sages comment: "If it is vain – it is because of you."[20] Maimonides elaborates:

> This legislation is not a vain matter without a useful end.... If it seems to you that this is the case with regard to some of the commandments, the deficiency resides in your apprehension.... One should seek in all the Laws an end that is useful in regard to being: For it is no vain thing.[21]

---

17. *Hilkhot Me'ila* 8:8.
18. *Moreh Nevukhim* III:31, p. 524.
19. Ibid. 26, p. 507. Cf. ibid. 49, p. 612: "most of the *ḥukim* whose reason is hidden," and note that he writes "most."
20. Y. Shevi'it 1:5; Genesis Rabba 1:14.
21. *Moreh Nevukhim* III:26, pp. 507–8.

With regard to the definition of a "useful end," Maimonides emphasizes that this end must be discernible in this world and capable of being revealed to all, for Scripture attests: "on hearing all of these statutes [other peoples] will say: 'Surely that great nation is a wise and discerning people'" (Deut. 4:6). Maimonides infers:

> Thus it states explicitly that even all the statutes [*ḥukim*] will show to all the nations that they [Israel] have been given with wisdom and understanding. Now if there is a thing for which no reason is known and that does not either procure something useful or ward off something harmful, why should one say of one who believes in it or practices it that he is wise and understanding and of great worth? And why should the religious communities think it a wonder?[22]

Why would it be said of someone who believes or practices something whose reason is unknown and which does not bring benefit or prevent damage that he is wise and understanding?

It follows that we are enjoined to seek reasons accessible to human intelligence for the mitzvot. As long as their benefits have not been discovered, the *ḥukim* seem to be impenetrable secrets. But just as we firmly believe that the human mind can reveal at least some of the secrets and mysteries of creation, we are likewise certain that careful investigation will yield fruit and disclose some of the secrets of the mitzvot. "The Law, although it is not natural, enters into what is natural."[23]

Understanding the Purpose of the Mitzvot from their Results

The notion that the reasons for the mitzvot are to be sought in their practical effects is not new. Indeed, it was already proclaimed by the Psalmist: "O taste and see that the Lord is good" (Ps. 34:9).[24] However, Maimonides developed this idea to unprecedented lengths.

---

22. Ibid. 31, p. 524.
23. Ibid. II:40, p. 382.
24. See *Pesikta Zutreta*, Ecclesiastes, Introduction; Exodus Rabba 17:2.

As an example of how to seek the purpose of the mitzvot, he cites the natural science of biology as an analogy. Specifically, within the field of anatomy, programmatic guidelines can be identified. The bodily structure of an animal all but declares that it was designed for a proximate or distant purpose. Maimonides cites extensively from Galen's *On the Utilities of the Parts of the Body*, concluding with a single detail, on which he builds his entire system:

> Similarly the deity made a wily and gracious arrangement with regard to all the individual mammals. For when born, such individuals are extremely soft and cannot feed on dry food. Accordingly, breasts were prepared for them so that they should produce milk with a view to their receiving liquid food, which is similar to the composition of their bodies, until their limbs gradually and little by little become dry and solid.[25]

In the physical realm, it is understood that large, qualitative changes do not occur suddenly, but through a step-by-step process of development.

If this is true of the human body, then it is certainly true of the human soul, spirit, and behavior. To shape one's personality, one must work in ways that parallel physical development, "for a sudden transition from one opposite to another is impossible. And therefore man, according to his nature, is not capable of abandoning suddenly all to which he was accustomed."[26] This principle, which governs all aspects of biology, is also true of human psychology.

Since Maimonides was a physician, he brought examples from the world of medicine. The goal of medicine is to improve health, whether by treating illness or preventing it. To that end, the field of medicine actively engages in scientific research. The scientific method is based on various techniques, most fundamentally those of observation, formulation of hypotheses, and experimentation. Medical researchers try to predict which treatments can bring about the desired effects. They test

---

25. *Moreh Nevukhim* III:32, p. 525.
26. Ibid., p. 526.

and experiment with various treatments and remedies, assessing their effectiveness on the basis of the results.

Maimonides refers to sages as "physicians of the soul":

> Just as when people, unacquainted with the science of medicine, realize that they are sick, and consult a physician, who tells them what they must do...so those whose souls become ill should consult the sages, the physicians of the soul.[27]

Maimonides traces the idea that sages are moral healers to the Torah. The wisest of all men wrote of the Torah: "It will be a cure for your body, a tonic for your bones" (Prov. 3:8). Seen in this light, the Torah and its commandments constitute a plan to mold a nation, over the span of many generations, to become "a kingdom of priests and a holy nation" (Ex. 19:6). This is how Rabbi Avraham, the son of Maimonides, interprets this verse in his father's name:

> The priest of the flock is the leader that is most eminent and is its role model, whom members of the flock follow and thereby find the straight path. Thus, it says: You shall be, through observance of My Torah, leaders of the world. You will be to them as the priest to his flock. The world will follow after you, imitating your actions and walking in your path. This is the explanation of the verse that I received from my father and master, of blessed memory....
>
> He promised the future fulfillment of this in His word to Isaiah (2:3): "And the many peoples shall go and say, 'Come let us ascend the Mount of the Lord, to the House of the God of Jacob, so that He may instruct us in His ways, and so that we may walk in His path.' For instruction [Torah] shall go forth from Zion, and the word of the Lord from Jerusalem."[28]

---

27. *Shemonah Perakim*, chapter 3, pp. 51–52. [Gorfinkle has "moral physicians."]
28. *Perush HaTorah LeRabbi Avraham ben HaRambam*, ed. E. Weisenberg (London: Solomon David Sassoon, 1959), 302.

This is the general purpose of the Torah; to understand the role of specific mitzvot within this system, we must apply the norms and procedures which ought to be applied to the exploration of reality in all its aspects.

Just as a healer of the body must be aware of man's physical needs, a healer of the soul must understand man's psychological and spiritual needs, which, if man is to function properly, must be fulfilled. By looking at patterns of human behavior, one can gain insight into the motivations of the human psyche, which find expression in man's speech and action.

A typical example of this approach is Maimonides' explanation of the mitzvot of the holidays:

> The festivals are for rejoicings and pleasurable gatherings, which in most cases are *indispensable for man*; they are also useful in the establishment of friendship, which *must exist* among people living in political societies.[29]

Here Maimonides mentions two types of necessity. The latter is straightforward and well-known: in order for civilized society to be maintained, there must be friendship and cooperation. The first one is entirely different, though, and Maimonides speaks of it as he speaks of natural laws: "Rejoicings and pleasurable gatherings" are "indispensable for man"; not *sought after* or *desired*, but *indispensable*. This is some kind of deep-seated psychological need which characterizes man qua man.

To reinforce this principle, Maimonides sees fit to enlist Aristotle's support, quoting him to explain the timing of the festival of Sukkot. Had Maimonides' intention been only to explain why there should be a festival after the autumn gathering, he would not have had to refer to Aristotle's writings. Maimonides' intention, then, is to point out an objective psychological need, which, if completely unsatisfied, results in a fragile psyche. In this state, man is at risk of being unable to continue coping with life and its challenges. Just as the belly craves food, so the heart craves joy.

Not only joy needs to find external expression. The same is true of sorrow:

---

29. *Moreh Nevukhim* III:43, p. 570.

For those who grieve find solace in weeping and in arousing their sorrow until their bodily forces are too tired to bear this affection of the soul; just as those who rejoice find solace in all kinds of play.[30]

Appropriate outlets for the heart's anguish and sorrow are indispensable if one is to overcome his pain and not buckle under the crushing weight of grief.

How can one recognize needs which stem from basic human drives and distinguish such universal needs from those which are merely characteristic of people in specific societies in particular periods of history?

Maimonides states[31] that he took pains to read all existing works by the Sabians,[32] an ancient pagan sect, explaining that, "the meaning of many of the laws became clear to me and their causes became known to me through my study of the doctrines, opinions, practices, and cult of the Sabians,"[33] and emphasizing that "this was a religious community that extended over the whole earth."[34] In several contexts, Maimonides mentions things that were "the general practice of the religious communities in ancient times."[35] It is evident from *Moreh Nevukhim* that Maimonides sought out information about many different peoples and religions, both contemporary and from earlier eras – Zoroastrians, Turks, Hindus, Chaldeans, and Babylonians in addition to Greeks, Muslims, Christians, and others. Clearly, by comparing the rituals of various cultures, he sought to uncover the fact that they fulfill basic needs of the human psyche, needs which the Torah too must necessarily address. Once we recognize these universalities, we can understand the purpose of many mitzvot.

30. Ibid. 41, p. 567.
31. See "Letter Concerning Astrology," *Iggerot HaRambam*, p. 481.
32. On the "Sabians," see I:63, n. 3, in Michael Schwarz's edition of *Moreh Nevukhim* (Tel Aviv: Tel Aviv University Press, 2002).
33. *Moreh Nevukhim* III:29, p. 518.
34. Ibid., p. 515.
35. E.g., ibid. 43, p. 572.

In modern times, comparative studies of cultures and religions have come into vogue. A modern psychoanalyst defines "ritual" as "an avenue of expression for deep-lying psychological impulses."[36]

It is worth noting that Maimonides found evidence for the divinity of the Torah by comparing it to the religions purporting to supersede it, namely, Christianity and Islam. He discusses this in *Moreh Nevukhim*,[37] but he addresses it at greater length in a letter:

> A person ignorant of the secret meaning of Scripture and the deeper significance of the Law would be led to believe that our religion has something in common with another if he makes a comparison between the two. For he will note that in the Torah there are prohibitions and commandments, just as in other religions there are permitted and interdicted acts. Both contain a system of religious observances, positive and negative precepts, sanctioned by reward and punishment.
>
> If he could only fathom the inner intent of the law, then he would realize that the essence of the true divine religion lies in the deeper meaning of its positive and negative precepts, every one of which will aid man in his striving after perfection, and remove every impediment to the attainment of excellence. These commands will enable the throng and the elite to acquire moral and intellectual qualities, each according to his ability. Thus the Godly community becomes pre-eminent, reaching a two-fold perfection. By the first perfection I mean, man's spending his life in this world under the most agreeable and congenial conditions. The second perfection would constitute the achievement of intellectual objectives, each in accordance with his native powers. The tenets of the other religions which resemble those of Scripture have no deeper meaning, but are superficial imitations, copied from and patterned after it.[38]

---

36. Theodore Reik, *Ritual* (New York: Grove Press, 1962), p. 17.
37. II:40.
38. *Moses Maimonides' Epistle to Yemen* (Halkin and Cohen ed.), p. iv.

Maimonides had extensive direct knowledge of various aspects of the Muslim world, and he valued its positive manifestations. Moreover, he did not ignore the shortcomings of Jewish society, about which he expressed sharp criticism. Nevertheless, he was convinced that the preeminence of the Torah could be recognized by looking to its effects, which "aid man in his striving after perfection" – aid that is visible to the discerning eye even under the conditions of exile.

Natural science strives to attain true knowledge. True knowledge is knowledge that corresponds to reality, "that what has been represented is outside the mind just as it has been represented in the mind."[39] The mitzvot, likewise, correspond to reality. "Most laws of the Torah are but 'counsel of old' (Is. 25:1), from He Who is 'great in counsel' (Jer. 32:19), to correct moral qualities and make all actions straight."[40] By performing the mitzvot, man can reach the perfection which is the purpose of his creation.

This is comparable to the body of any creature, which requires proper, balanced nutrition. The appropriate food and drink sustain the body and help it grow. Though this nourishment originates outside the body, as long as it is absorbed into the body in the right proportions and through the right processes, it is not treated as foreign to the body and does not cause an immune response or any other rejection by the body. On the contrary, it becomes integrated into the body. However, toxic substances can also be inserted into the body, as can foods that are physically appetizing but which do not fit the body's needs and instead harm it. The goal of the science of nutrition is to determine which substances the body requires and in what quantities, and also which substances must be avoided altogether or used with caution. We are still far from complete knowledge in this area, but if and when we do achieve it, then one who conducts his life according to scientific knowledge can be said to be acting in accordance with the truth. Even today, with our incomplete knowledge that offers likelihood but not certainty, one who uses the truth as a guide must adopt that which has been demonstrated to most likely be correct.

---

39. *Moreh Nevukhim* I:50, p. 111.
40. End of *Hilkhot Temura*, 4:17.

The same applies to the human spirit, soul, and personality. Acting in accordance with the needs of man's spirit and psyche is acting according to the truth; this cannot be considered coercion by an external force. On the contrary, those deeds that properly address the needs of the soul are what nature demands, and they most accurately express man's essence.

Since "He fashions their hearts alike, He understands all their deeds" (Ps. 33:15), it is self-evident that God commanded us to perform the mitzvot only to guide us toward perfection. The mitzvot as a whole satisfy the demands of human nature that are necessary for the full realization of the potential inherent in man. Discovery of the reasons for the mitzvot creates a basis for the scientific study of man, including the healing of his body[41] and the healing of his soul. Investigating the psyche to ascertain its nature is the search for truth. As we discover the reasons for the mitzvot, we disclose additional facets of the human psyche and human nature.

The reverse is true as well: the deeper our understanding of the natural laws that govern the psyche, the more we can comprehend the reasons for the mitzvot, because the mitzvot express truths. It will thus become clear that the mitzvot stem from the nature of man, imbued in him by the Creator, and that observing the mitzvot aids man to achieve perfection.

It follows that the more we understand the reasons for the mitzvot, the more meticulously we can perform them. Knowing the reasons for the mitzvot is thus of great importance, for if knowing the laws of creation impacts how we can use them to our benefit, then certainly awareness of the reasons for the mitzvot leads one to observe them with greater vigor. When one understands the reasons for the mitzvot, then one accepts them willingly due to their natural congruence with man's spiritual needs.

Man is expected to "do that which is true because it is true,"[42] but to achieve this, he must first discover the truth within the mitzvot. Thus, Maimonides ruled:

---

41. See, for example, *Shemonah Perakim*, chapter 4, p. 63: "The perfect Law...aims at man's following...in accordance with the dictates of nature...but not...afflicting the body"; *Hilkhot De'ot*, chapters 3 and 4; *Moreh Nevukhim* II:39.

42. *Hilkhot Teshuva* 10:2.

It is fitting for man to meditate upon the laws of the holy Torah and to comprehend their full meaning in accordance with his ability. Nevertheless, he should not take lightly something for which he finds no reason or knows no cause.... [43]

Instead, he should redouble his efforts to plumb its depths, and he will thus "increase his cleaving to the Torah."[44]

Directing Man's Deepest Impulses

Maimonides describes[45] several elemental factors that led to the rise of idol worship, addressing, in this context, certain basic aspects of human culture and the human psyche. Ritual and ceremony are universal phenomena. In every age and every culture, worship of the supernatural occupies an important place. Likewise, in every culture in every era, social structures require legal and political orders that concentrate the task of governing in the hands of the few. In many cases, these two elements were linked, and the impulse for worship was manipulated to perform a political function, to secure the rulers in their power.[46] Some rulers even declared themselves to be divine. Pharaoh declared: "My Nile is my own; I made it" (Ezek. 29:3).[47] Thus the worship of false gods develops into an elaborate and ramified set of practices.[48]

---

43. *Hilkhot Me'ila* 8:8.
44. Ibid.
45. See *Hilkhot Avoda Zara*, chapter 1; *Moreh Nevukhim* III:29–30.
46. Ibid. 29.
47. See Exodus Rabba 5:14; *Tanḥuma Va'era* §16.
48. Of course, in the medieval period it was impossible to foresee the development of secularism, which emerged in modern times, but it can be considered one of the idolatries and false beliefs that Maimonides addresses, for when the prevailing fashion among those who consider themselves "enlightened" is to cut themselves off from established religious traditions, and when makers of public opinion declare their faith in rationalistic scientism, then the extreme form of secularism that results is itself a false god that enslaves its believers. The atrocities committed by the totalitarian regimes of the past century were the direct result of the deification of the regime, the state, and the laws of materialistic so-called science. Millions of human sacrifices were slaughtered on the altars of these idols. The foolish faith of the masses in perverse slogans of "progress" can be understood only by means of the notion Maimonides developed: Man requires faith, and if one turns away from

Moreover, human beings are attracted to the sweet, the tempting, and the intoxicating; they recoil from pain, fright, and suffering. Pagan priests exploited these human feelings, claiming that the only way to survive the dangers that threaten man is to curry favor with the gods by means of various rites and acts of sorcery. These exercises, they claim, will also bring man different forms of benefit.

Maimonides maintains that the Torah seeks to bar us completely from anything connected to magic and sorcery and negates any attempt to bypass the laws of nature, because these are all based on falsehood. Even if they are not ugly and immoral in the way of certain pagan rituals, they are still nothing but fantasy and delusion:

> In order to keep people away from all magical practices, it has been prohibited to observe any of their usages, even those connected to agricultural and pastoral activities, etc., I mean: all that is said to be useful, but is not required by speculation concerning nature, and takes its course, in their opinion, in accordance with occult properties.[49]

However, with regard to the rituals of worship, the Torah does not command "the rejection, abandonment, and abolition of all these kinds of worship."[50] There is no blanket prohibition on all forms of worship, for they express deep spiritual impulses. Rather, it seeks to adapt them to other, more sublime ends, and thereby to eliminate cruel, repulsive, and undesirable features. All nations had grown accustomed to animal sacrifice and incense-burning as modes of worship; the Torah therefore acknowledges their value as well and adopts sacrificial worship, albeit under specific conditions:

> Therefore He, may He be exalted, suffered the above-mentioned kinds of worship to remain, but transferred them from created or

---

faith in God he will inevitably attach himself to other gods, even if he calls them by different names.

49. *Moreh Nevukhim* III:37, p. 543.
50. Ibid. 32, p. 526.

imaginary and unreal things to His own name…. For one kind of
worship – I mean the offering of sacrifices – even though it was
done in His name, may He be exalted, was not prescribed to us
in the way it existed at first; I mean to say in such a way that sacrifices could be offered in every place and at every time.[51]

Similarly, there is a "generally known" sense of holiness and cleanness
associated with objects or states of veneration. The Torah couples this
idea of holiness with spiritual and physical cleanliness. From within the
state of holiness and cleanliness, the yearning for spiritual heights, which
flows from the deepest recesses of the heart and culminates in love and
reverence for the Almighty, can find expression.

The reverse also holds true. There is an opposing sense of recoil
and disgust, of apprehension and anxiety, of contamination and impurity,
which is likewise linked to specific subjects. Idolaters created rites and
ceremonies to alleviate and ease these fears and to ward off monstrous
forces and abiding hazards. Revulsion, guilt, and fright seem to well up
from the depths of the soul to produce the "fancied notions" that the
Sabian cult ascribed to the forces of uncleanliness. Although these Sabian
notions are certainly fanciful, they are nevertheless responses to genu-
ine stirrings in the human soul. It is impossible to ignore this fact and
to abolish, with a stroke of the pen or a wave of the hand, all the varied
rites that different cultures developed and linked to their false gods and
depraved worship. Indeed, the Torah seeks to "facilitate the actions of
worship and to lighten the burden."[52] Above all, it seeks to uproot false
beliefs and sever all possible connections with idolatry and superstition.
Yet the Torah must also address the underlying impulses that manifest
themselves in what we now designate as taboos and which are well-nigh
universal in one form or another.

The clean/unclean dichotomy is present in the Torah as well, but
in a more refined form, embedded in an exclusively spiritual context, as

---

51. Ibid., pp. 526, 529. On Maimonides' approach to sacrifices and the Temple, see my
essay: "Society and History: The Uniqueness of Maimonides," in my *Studies in the
Thought of Maimonides* (see above, n. 6), pp. 214–27 (Heb.).
52. *Moreh Nevukhim* III:47, p. 592.

Maimonides summarizes in *Mishneh Torah,* at the end of the Book of *Taharah* ("Cleanliness"):

> It is plain and manifest that uncleanness and cleanness are decreed by Scripture and are not among those matters about which the human mind can form judgment. They are among the *ḥukim.* Likewise, immersion [to remove] uncleanness is among the *ḥukim,* for uncleanness is not dirt or excrement that can be removed by water, but is a decree of Scripture, dependent on the heart's intention.... There is an allusion in this: just as one who intends to become clean is rendered clean once he immerses, even though there is nothing new about his body, so too one who intends to cleanse his soul from spiritual uncleanness – wrongful thoughts and false convictions – once he has resolved in his heart to abandon those opinions and has brought his soul into the waters of intelligence, he becomes clean. Scripture states: "I will sprinkle clean water upon you, and you shall be clean; from all your uncleanness and from all your fetishes, I will cleanse you" (Ezek. 36:25). May God, in His abundant mercy, cleanse us of all sin, iniquity, and guilt.[53]

The Attainment of Correct Beliefs

The "ultimate perfection" of man "is to become rational in actuality.... This would consist in his knowing everything concerning all the beings that it is within the capacity of man to know."[54] The unique characteristic of the Torah consists in the fact that in addition to providing for the ends for which every legal system is designed, namely, the proper functioning of society, it also seeks to give some of the intellectual insights "through which ultimate perfection is achieved." Yet due to human limitations these teachings are but few in number, comprising only the most basic truths about existence in general and about man in particular.

In selecting which truths to reveal and which to leave to man's own initiative to discover, and in formulating the method of imparting

---

53. *Hilkhot Mikvaot* 11:12.
54. *Moreh Nevukhim* III:27, p. 511.

the principles taught, the criterion is that of utility—the same standard as applies to the commandments:

> God, may His mention be exalted, wished us to be perfected and the state of our societies to be improved by His laws regarding actions. Now this can come about only after the adoption of intellectual beliefs, the first of which being His apprehension, may He be exalted, according to our capacity.[55]

Likewise, Maimonides explains the absence of direct mention of the Resurrection in the Torah:

> Why is the Resurrection not mentioned in the Torah?... How can someone who has not accepted the truth of prophecy be told something that has no proof but the reliability of the prophet?... The matter continued thus until these tenets were strengthened and became certain over time, and there remained no doubt about the prophecies of the prophets or about the renewal of the miraculous. After that, the prophets told us that which they were told by the Almighty concerning the resurrection of the dead, and it was easy to accept it.[56]

An example of a teaching of the Torah which is of obvious utility is repentance. The Torah emphasizes that man is unique in having been endowed with free will. However, unless man is aware that his will is indeed free, he will not be willing to bear responsibility for his actions, and laws and commandments will thus have no impact on his actions. The principle of free will became especially important in the face of the fatalism that pervades several Islamic movements.[57] On the other hand, the awareness of his freedom and his consequent responsibility may become an intolerable burden to the man who has succumbed to sin and transgressed. Unexpiated guilt can destroy the personality. Thus the

---

55. Ibid., Introduction, pp. 8–9.
56. "Treatise on Resurrection," *Iggerot HaRambam*, pp. 368–69.
57. *Moreh Nevukhim* III:17, the third opinion.

principle that repentance is possible is a truth which is needed urgently by all men, even by those whose intellectual endowments are limited. This belief cannot be left for man to discover on his own, since it is possible that it will only be reached after a long and intensive search, if it is reached at all. In the interim, many generations will be lost to despair. Without belief in the possibility of repentance:

…the existence of individuals cannot be well ordered. For an individual cannot but sin and err, either through ignorance – by professing an opinion or a moral quality that is not preferable in truth – or else because he is overcome by desire or anger. If then the individual believed that this fracture can never be remedied, he would persist in his error and sometimes perhaps disobey even more because of the fact that no stratagem remains at his disposal. If, however, he believes in repentance, he can correct himself and return to a better and more perfect state than the one he was in before he sinned. For this reason, there are many actions that are meant to establish this correct and very beneficial opinion.[58]

The utility of the belief in repentance is evident to anyone who studies man's actions. It is precisely because of its utility that the Torah taught us this concept. The criterion of utility enables us to understand why the Torah teaches some true beliefs to the exclusion of others.

The principle of repentance is predicated on an even more fundamental belief, one that Maimonides calls: "a major principle, the pillar of the Torah and the commandments"[59] – the principle of free will:

Every person is given power over himself: if he wants to steer himself toward the path of goodness and become righteous – he has that power; and if he wants to steer himself toward the path of evil and become wicked – he has that power.[60]

58. Ibid. 36, p. 540.
59. *Hilkhot Teshuva* 5:3.
60. Ibid. 1.

These doctrines – free will and the possibility of repentance – are examples of ideas whose realization in fact is aided by belief in them. To an extent, the fact of free will is the direct result of conscious belief that man's will is indeed free. This is an observable fact: one who is convinced that he is free to make serious decisions in fact does so, thereby creating an arena in which there are real choices for him to make. On the other hand, one who resigns himself to blind fatalism inevitably sinks into utter passivity and apathy, to the extent that his entire life is completely determined by the factors that operate in his environment. One who refuses to believe that there is free will effectively abrogates it, while one who believes in free will and acts according to this belief contributes significantly to the shaping of his own personality and way of life. Likewise, one who accepts the possibility of repentance can make profound changes to his personality. These are the kinds of truths that cannot come into being unless they are believed in, and faith in them is self-justifying.

On a deeper level, effectiveness should be seen as evidence of truth. Of course, false beliefs, too, can produce desirable results, and so there must be clear criteria for determining which empirical data are reliable and which are not. Yet this problem applies to the sciences as well, and especially to medicine. Here, too, there is a parallel between the healing of the body and the healing of the soul.

In antiquity, the practice of medicine was often connected with magic, astrology, and other occult practices that originated with idolatry and its paraphernalia. With very few exceptions, it was not possible to understand how and why various remedies and treatments worked. Indeed, Maimonides, explaining the Talmud's ruling that medicine is excluded from the prohibition on engaging in gentile practices,[61] goes so far as to write: "All that is recommended after speculation into nature is permitted, whereas other practices are forbidden."[62] In other words, any course of treatment which can be rationally accounted for is legitimate. However, the very concept of a "rational explanation," or, in Maimonides' terminology, "speculation into nature," reflects the scientific principles

---

61. Shabbat 67a.
62. *Moreh Nevukhim* III:37, p. 543.

that prevailed at a specific time. Consequently, there are many things that medieval science "required" that have been entirely disproven over time, in light of discoveries in every scientific discipline. Still, it can be said that since the concept of "speculation into nature" has a propensity to change in every era, logic dictates that just as "one cannot but go to the judge of his day,"[63] so too one cannot but go to the physician of his day, who is expert in the current state of scientific knowledge. Yet, that part of medicine which can be described as "rational" was in Maimonides' day, and perhaps even in our own, capable of dealing with only a fraction of our ailments.

There is, however, another class of treatments which, though lacking a foundation in reason, have been shown to work again and again. Therefore, Maimonides adds:

> For it is allowed to use all remedies similar to these that experience has shown to be valid even if reasoning does not require them. For they pertain to medicine and their efficacy may be ranged together with the purgative action of aperient medicines.[64]

Maimonides does not fail to observe that the experience upon which a claim is made for particular remedies may be unreliable and misleading, and criteria are required to determine what is trustworthy experience. Nevertheless, it has been established beyond a doubt that certain substances function as effective cures for specific ailments, such as, for example, the well-known "aperient medicines."

Maimonides had no qualms about using remedies whose efficacy had been proven by careful observation. Moreover, he concludes his exposition of the principle that proven efficacy validates medicine with an enlightening comment in praise of this principle:

> You who are engaged in speculation, grasp fully and remember the marvelous observations contained in my speech. "For they

---

63. Rosh HaShana 25b.
64. *Moreh Nevukhim* III:37, p. 544.

shall be an ornament of grace unto thy head, and chains about thy neck" (Prov. 1:9).[65]

Maimonides' choice of verse is especially significant as it alludes to an exposition of the Sages:

> R. Ḥizkiyah b. Ḥiya taught: The Torah is a crown upon the head, as it says: "For they shall be an ornament of grace for your head, and chains around your neck." It is a cure for the heart, as it says: "rejoicing the heart" (Ps. 19:9); a salve for the eye, as it says: "making the eyes light up" (ibid.); a bandage for a wound, as it says: "it will be healing to your flesh" (Prov. 3:8); a potion of roots for the innards, as it says: "and nourishment to your bones" (ibid.). And whence do we learn that it is absorbed into the 248 limbs? Because it says: "and [it brings] health to his entire body" (ibid. 4:22).[66]

Each of these tried and tested cures for the body parallels the Torah, which heals the soul. As for the "ornament of grace for your head," Maimonides himself explained:

> Moreover, the [Sages'] phrase, "with their crowns upon their heads," means: the *de'ah* that they apprehended, by virtue of which they attained life in the World to Come, remains with them. It is their crown, as King Solomon said: "The crown with which his mother crowned him" (Song. 3:11).... The crown to which the Sages refer here is *de'ah*.[67]

The meaning of this metaphor is clear: the fact that a certain substance has healing properties is not coincidental but is evidence of some fundamental law of nature, i.e., an intellectual truth which we do not yet grasp. It is possible that over time we will discover the basic law and

---

65. Ibid.

66. *Midrash Tehillim* (Buber ed.) 19:15.

67. *Hilkhot Teshuva* 8:2. Regarding "*de'ah*," see above, chapter 1, "Grant Our Portion in Your Torah," in the section "Crown of Torah."

thus understand the medicinal properties of that substance as but one of manifold phenomena. It is true that, at present, a feature may be isolated, but there is no doubt that it is a particular instance of a broader truth. As long as that broader truth is withheld from us, we cannot locate the particularity within a comprehensive framework. Nevertheless, the particular fact is true in its own right.

In exactly the same way, the proven efficacy of the belief in the possibility of repentance in enabling sinners to rise above their moral failings is itself evidence of the validity of this belief, even though we do not possess demonstrative proof. The historical experience of the generations proclaims the power of repentance to heal suffering souls. To ignore the empirical facts in the absence of logical confirmation of the universal principle is to discard genuinely scientific evidence of the only kind available to us. One who negates cumulative empirical knowledge undermines the foundation of all natural science.

Since false beliefs, too, may sometimes produce useful effects, we need precise and practical criteria to determine which observations are acceptable and which are unreliable. Yet the same demand is made of all empirical information, in every discipline.

Additionally, as explained earlier, sometimes the efficacy of rites associated with false beliefs is, in fact, due to some aspect whch indeed satisfies basic needs—an aspect which can and should be isolated from its undesirable and base associations. Even out of the repugnant and corrupt catalogs of idolatry and magic, some kernels of truth can sometimes be distilled. These are what human beings seek, even when they are blind and have lost their way.

The Steadfastness of Israel's Faith

With the election of Israel and the giving of the Torah to them, a prolonged educational process began, whose purpose was the fulfillment of human destiny. The history of the Jewish people, from the moment it became a nation, attests to the power of the Torah to mold the character of the nation destined to be a model for all of humanity. It is possible to measure the success of this "experiment" only over the long term, for each individual in each era must acquire his virtues anew. Yet, although there is no proof that virtue can be acquired through biological heredity, there is nevertheless no doubt that the power of a society to bequeath a "cultural legacy" is very potent, for good or for ill. Habituation and education are a major, if not the decisive, influence on the soul of man. "Man has love for, and the wish to defend, beliefs to which he is habituated and in which he has been brought up, and has a feeling of revulsion for beliefs other than those."[68]

The same applies to interpersonal attitudes, ethics, and behavior. The Sages recognized the characteristic virtues of Israel, and Maimonides elaborates:

> Anyone who possesses brazenness and cruelty, who hates people and is not kind to them, is extremely suspect…for the marks of Israel, the holy people, [is that they are] bashful, merciful, and kind.[69]

He asserts with absolute certainty:

> This is the way of the seed of Israel and their proper mind.[70]

However, these should not be regarded as hereditary traits. Rather, they are the result of the Torah's influence, as Maimonides wrote:

> The children of our patriarch Abraham, that is, Israel, upon whom the Holy One bestowed the Torah's goodness and who He commanded with just laws and statutes, are merciful to all.[71]

The efforts of many generations bore fruit that is clearly seen in the disappearance among Jews of idolatrous beliefs, even though they were exposed to foreign influences at all times, and especially during periods of exile and enslavement, when they were subject to the severe pressures of their powerful persecutors.

---

68. *Moreh Nevukhim* I:31, p. 67.
69. *Hilkhot Issurei Biah* 19:17.
70. *Hilkhot Teshuva* 2:10.
71. *Hilkhot Avadim* 9:8.

Still, even though the purpose of many mitzvot is the elimination of superstitions and foolish customs, Maimonides nevertheless felt it necessary to note that even the cumulative impact of thousands of years of Torah observance has not brought complete success. In describing the horror of Molech worship, Maimonides laments a strange phenomenon:

> Know that traces of this action subsist up to now.... You will see that midwives take small children in their swaddling clothes, throw a fumigant having a disagreeable odor upon the fire, and move the children over this fume above the fire. This is indubitably a sort of passage through the fire.... Its trace was not effaced though the Law has opposed it for thousands of years.[72]

On the other hand, we can attest to Israel's adherence to its spiritual heritage. They have withstood frequent severe trials, sacrificing their lives so as not to reject the Torah or deny its Giver. The memory of the giving of the Torah accompanies this nation through the travails of a bitter exile. This memory is passed from generation to generation:

> We have been given adequate divine assurance that not only did all the persons who were present at the Sinaitic Revelation believe in the prophecy of Moses and in his Law, but that their descendants likewise would do so, until the end of time.... Consequently it is manifest that he who spurns the religion that was revealed at that theophany, is not an offspring of the folk who witnessed it.[73]

The steadfast faith of Israel through the generations is nourished by Torah study, which is the source of vitality and the wellspring of the power of constant renewal. Through Torah study, national memory is invoked and becomes personal memory, strengthening one who studies it and steeling him against any attack: "Put your trust in the true promises of Scripture, brethren, and be not dismayed at the series of persecutions or the enemy's ascendency over us, or the weakness of our

---

72. *Moreh Nevukhim* III:37, p. 546.
73. *Moses Maimonides' Epistle to Yemen* (Halkin and Cohen ed.), p. vi.

people."[74] Maimonides declares that the purpose of the revelation at Sinai was "to confirm us in the faith so that nothing can change it, and to reach a degree of certainty which will sustain us in these trying times."[75]

In every generation, it is possible to invoke the echo of Sinai and draw upon it for the courage to remain steadfast in the face of the waves of hatred and currents of hostility that inundate us and threaten to overcome us: "God revealed Himself to you thus in order to give you strength to withstand all future trials. Now do not slip nor err, be steadfast in your religion and persevere in your faith and its duties."[76]

Here, then, is another example of a belief that verifies itself. Those who do not believe that they can withstand the trials and tribulations of the exile will certainly tire of the struggle, whereas experience has shown, time and again, that from those whose faith is steadfast, a remnant will survive.

The Concealed Outweighs the Revealed

Just as the study of existence advances step by step, thus enabling human intelligence to penetrate the secrets of creation and discover traces of the Creator's hidden wisdom, so can the investigation of the reasons for the mitzvot advance. It grows deeper in every generation, as we broaden our knowledge and understanding of the contours of man's soul and of the wonders of the universe. Still, Maimonides acknowledged that human intelligence has limitations that cannot be overcome; even after the intense intellectual effort of many generations, some secrets of creation will remain indecipherable:

> Know that the human intellect has objects of apprehension that it is within its power and according to its nature to apprehend. On the other hand, in that which exists there are also existents and matters that, according to its nature, it is not capable of apprehending in any way or through any cause; the gates of their apprehension are shut before it.... The fact that [the intellect]

---

74. Ibid.
75. Ibid., p. 7.
76. Ibid.

apprehends does not entail the conclusion that it can apprehend all things – just as the senses have apprehensions but it is not within their power to apprehend at whatever distance the objects of apprehension happen to be. Similarly with regard to all other bodily faculties.... For man's intellect indubitably has a limit at which it stops.[77]

This limit cannot be outlined in advance; nevertheless, there are those who are not content with what can be learned, through hard work of many years. They seek shortcuts to circumvent the barriers that stand in the way of apprehension of existence as a whole. These individuals are attracted to delusions and imaginings, and they disparage the little information that can be acquired through slow, systematic investigation. There is no reason to argue with them, for they have already cast aside knowledge and reason.

Maimonides' view, which he addressed to the intellectually mature, can be summarized in the words of the wisest of men: "It is best that you grasp the one without letting go of the other" (Eccl. 7:18). That is, on one hand, one must marvel at that which is concealed from him, in awe of the exaltedness of the Master of all, but on the other hand, he must not relent in his effort to reveal that small fraction he can of the great mystery by exercising the human intellect to its limit – for this is the sum of man.

By implanting within us the power of the intellect, the Holy One did us a great kindness. Maimonides wrote: "because of the divine intellect conjoined with man ... it is said of the latter that he is in the image of God and in His likeness."[78] He even imbued within us a longing for wisdom: "There are things for the apprehension of which man will find that he has a great longing. The sway of the intellect endeavoring to seek for, and to investigate, their true reality exists at every time and in every group of men engaged in speculation."[79]

---

77. *Moreh Nevukhim* I:31, p. 65.
78. Ibid. 1, p. 23.
79. Ibid. 31, p. 66.

An inner drive inspires man to climb to the highest peaks and descend to the depths of the sea, to set out through space and to fly to the moon – and, at the same time, to search the recesses of the soul and chart the most labyrinthine pathways of the heart. This drive is what advances science; the more knowledge is attained, the more momentum accumulates. All of existence is a single organism, a macro-anthropos, "one individual."[80] The laws fixed by the Creator apply uniformly to heavenly beings and to the human spirit – and the human intellect has access to them.

As man broadens his knowledge and deepens his understanding, to the point that he senses the presence of the "Owner of the castle" concealing Himself behind it, so does his love grow within him:

> When a man contemplates these things and becomes familiar with all creations, such as angels, spheres, man, and the like and sees the wisdom of the Holy One in every creature, his love for the Omnipresent will increase, and his soul will thirst and his flesh will yearn to love the Omnipresent.[81]

Yet recognition of the truth leads to a better evaluation of the relationship between the revealed and the concealed. The further the intellect penetrates, the more rationality is impressed by the power of that which remains hidden and secret. The solution to one riddle challenges the observer with many riddles whose existence he could not even have imagined earlier. The wellspring from which love flows is also the source of awe:

> When he contemplates those same matters, he will immediately recoil in awe and fear, and he will realize that he is a small, lowly, benighted creature of little and weak intelligence standing before Him of perfect intelligence.[82]

---

80. Ibid. 72, p. 184.
81. *Hilkhot Yesodei HaTorah* 4:12.
82. Ibid. 2:1.

Investigation of the reasons for the mitzvot is essentially an attempt to illuminate the secrets of human nature, both on the individual level and as part of a society. This study enables us to understand the truth of the mitzvot commanded by the Creator. Without it, the performance and observance of mitzvot are insufficient:

> And similarly in all cases in which you perform a commandment merely with your limbs – as if you were digging a hole in the ground or hewing wood in the forest – without reflecting either upon the meaning of that action or upon Him from Whom the commandment proceeds or upon the end of the action, you should not think that you have achieved the end. Rather you will then be similar to those of whom it is said: "Thou art near in their mouth, and far from their thoughts" (Jer. 12:2).[83]

Summary

There is no doubt that, despite the yawning gap of 800 years between Maimonides' time and our own, had Maimonides been afforded a glimpse of our generation, he would have noticed familiar principles of natural science – principles to whose establishment and advancement he contributed greatly[84] – which can serve, even today, as a bridge between Torah and science and as a point of departure for knowing God. In our times, the natural sciences have advanced immeasurably, and though they progress gradually, they have managed to alter human life beyond recognition. Yet when it comes to the reasons for the mitzvot, Maimonides' method has been neglected, and it is possible that this is one of the contributing factors to many Jews' estrangement from the Torah and their faith.

---

83. *Moreh Nevukhim* III:51, p. 622.
84. See my book: *Probability and Statistical Inference in Ancient and Medieval Jewish Literature* (Toronto: University of Toronto Press, 1973), 166 ff.; my article, "The Concept of 'Possibility' in Halakhic and Scientific Thinking" (see above, n. 6); my article "The One and the Many: Early Stochastic Reasoning in Philosophy," *Annals of Science* (34), 1977, pp. 331–44; and my article, "Maimonides as a Scientist," in *Encounter*, ed. Schimmel and Carmell (New York: 1989), 244–66.

Maimonides would certainly have taken great interest in the development of psychology and in questions like: what can theories of the subconscious teach us about the role of the mitzvot in the maintenance of mental health and stability? Given his great interest in the structure of society and government, he would have seen ample opportunity to apply the Torah's principles of justice and mercy in new political frameworks.

The establishment of the State of Israel and the return of Jewish sovereignty give us the opportunity, for the first time in 2,000 years, to implement the laws commanded by the Torah in order to found a just society that reflects our eternal values. By tracking social developments, we are likely to discover needs that will shed new light on the reasons for various mitzvot. According to Maimonides, the reasons for the mitzvot are not a closed and completed field of study. On the contrary, we can now study and investigate, with greater vigor, the utility of the mitzvot – how they impact the individual and the community in an era of technological advancement and revolutions in the conditions of human life.

These and similar questions emerge naturally from Maimonides' presentation of the reasons for the mitzvot. In astronomy, for example, the search for new data continues unabated as new vistas constantly open up for investigation. So too, "The judgments of the Lord are true, righteous altogether" (Ps. 19:10), and as we continue to collect data, patient empirical research will be rewarded with the discovery of information which in the long run will reveal the truth. It is with all of this that we face the challenge of clarifying the utility of the mitzvot and thus fulfilling Maimonides' charge:

> Apply to the whole matter the principle to which the Sages, may their memory be blessed, have drawn our attention: "For it is no vain thing from you" (Deut. 32:47). And if it is vain, it is so because of you.[85]

During difficult times of persecution and apostasy, Maimonides pointed out the usefulness of the mitzvot in sustaining Israel. Now that we have

---

85. *Moreh Nevukhim* III:50, p. 617.

been privileged, thanks to His great kindness, to experience the return of Israel to its land and the ingathering of the exiles, perhaps the utility of the mitzvot can be distilled into a single sentence that Maimonides wrote in his "Epistle to Yemen": "The sign that we will never perish is the enduring presence of God's Torah and Word in our midst."[86] The rest is commentary – go and study.

---

86. *Moses Maimonides' Epistle to Yemen* (Halkin and Cohen ed.), p. vii.

Chapter 8

Torah and Science: Conflict or Complement?

Introduction

Conventional wisdom is that the modern era began about 300 years ago. During the eighteenth century, the world underwent three distinct revolutions: scientific, industrial, and political. These revolutions raised a series of acute problems for the Jewish people that have yet to be resolved.

The phenomenon of secularization and the disintegration of religious Judaism in Europe were the direct result of the failure to meet the array of challenges posed by cultural, spiritual, and social forces in the modern era.

One of the questions raised by these revolutions is the conflict between Torah and science. The successes of science and its impressive discoveries made it attractive to many; just as the rays of the rising sun illuminate the east side of a mountain while casting a shadow to the west, so too, the new and ascendant light of science created significant challenges and sparked a crisis of faith. How must one relate to the world of Torah and mitzvot in light of scientific progress?

The most commonly asked questions in this realm deal with particulars – the age of the universe, for example. Geologists speak of millions and billions of years, whereas traditional Jewish chronology seems to posit a much younger universe. These questions about specifics lead to sharper and more all-embracing problems, like that of the theory of evolution versus the biblical account of the creation of the earth and its creatures.[1]

In dealing with these and similar questions, most Jews preferred to embrace one of two extremes. Many tried to isolate completely from the mighty torrent of scientific discovery in modern times. Others, who climbed over the barriers and devoted themselves to scientific endeavor, assumed that the Judaism of their fathers was inconsistent with a disinterested and objective pursuit of Truth. The one severed himself from science, the other from Judaism; both made a terrible mistake.

The economic security of a society – and certainly of a society beset by external threats to its security – is inconceivable without the cultivation of science and technology, which allow people from all walks of life, not just the elite, to escape the shackles of poverty and live comfortable lives. This, in turn, affords opportunities for individuals to broaden their minds and engage in spiritual, moral, and Torah-based pursuits. It goes without saying that abandoning Judaism and breaking the covenant are likewise unconscionable. The House of Judah will never be like all the nations. Can one commit suicide and yet live?

Yet if Torah and science are indeed two separate realms, built on irreconcilable assumptions and foundations, then it is impossible to bridge the gap between them, and all efforts to square the circle are for naught. Certainly there are many on either side who believe this to be the case. If they are correct, God forbid, we would have to admit that Israel's future is in jeopardy, for then there is no hope of building an advanced, productive, and economically robust society that will fulfill and realize the vision of God's kingdom on earth.

---

1. In addition, there are the challenges of harmonizing halakhic assertions with new scientific data and of applying halakha to situations created by advanced technology, such as determining the moment of death for the purpose of organ transplantation, cloning, in-vitro fertilization, and the like. On such topics, see my essay, "Scientific Evaluation as a Basis for Halakhic Rulings" (Heb.), in my *Studies in the Thought of Maimonides* (Jerusalem: 2010), pp. 152–76.

Commonalities between Torah and Science

Scientific Axioms

Are these two realms, Torah and science, indeed in conflict? To answer this question, we must first consider the axioms on which science is based. Every scientific discipline, of course, has its own methods and principles, and each has postulates that have been accepted by all who work in that field. However, it is the merit of the scientific method that these postulates, like the theories built upon them, are subject to constant adjustment and change as research progresses. The concepts of contemporary physics do not resemble the concepts of fifty or a hundred years ago. There are disciplines in which theories are replaced even more quickly. As long as the discussion is about theories which are known to undergo alterations as a matter of course, there is no conflict with faith, for such theories are only temporary.

However, the scientific method itself has its own axioms, which are relatively stable. If these axioms are found to contradict faith, then the problem becomes significant.

The key to science and its advancement is critical reasoning, with freedom of thought and inquiry. Science progresses by discovering the weak points of existing theories. As data that cannot be explained by the current reigning theories is discovered, new theories and methods are proposed. Each scientific hypothesis must pass through the crucible of rationality and experimentation. The detection of previously unknown natural phenomena reinforces existing theories when it can be demonstrated that the theories explain and even predict the newly discovered phenomena, such as in the confirmation of Maxwell's theory of electromagnetic radiation upon the discovery of radio waves. In other cases, the new discoveries disprove the reigning methods, such as when the results expected according to Newton's theories were not borne out by the famed Michelson-Morley experiment. Thus science progresses while discovery of the whole truth remains distant. Science does not have blind faith in any theory, and theories are all just temporary. Nevertheless, the path that leads to truth is built on two basic axioms:

The first axiom is firm belief in the power of the mind to set forth systems of thought that can explain not only past occurrences, but even predict future ones. It is belief in the power of human intelligence to disclose the secrets of nature. The astounding victories over the forces of nature that technology has bequeathed to us attest to the power of critical reasoning and to the veracity of the belief that our intellects can grasp, to a degree, the foundation of all existence.

The second axiom is the assumption that the universe is unified. All of existence in its manifold variety, from the tiniest particles that constitute the building blocks of subatomic existence to the greatest celestial bodies, reflects a fundamental unity: everything is connected by mutual influence and functions according to uniform laws. Science presumes that human intelligence can reveal these laws, or at least some of them.

The Torah's Attitude to Scientific Axioms
What is the Torah's view of all this?

Regarding the world's pervasive unity, there is no need for a lengthy discussion. The first verse that a Jewish schoolchild learns is *"Shema Yisrael"*: "Hear, O Israel: The Lord is our God, the Lord is one" (Deut. 6:4). *The idea of the Creator's oneness is reflected in the idea of the unity of all creation.*

Regarding the Torah's attitude towards the role and possibility of critical reasoning, the prophet states: "Therefore My people will go into exile for lack of knowledge" (Is. 5:13). The knowledge (*da'at*) that the prophet mentions here is much more than the practical instructions detailed in *Shulḥan Arukh*. Fashioning a proper approach, in accordance with Torah values, to basic problems, whether social or cultural, scientific or economic, requires *da'at*. "To increase learning" is the purpose of man, even if so doing "is to increase heartache" (Eccl. 1:18).

The Sages further stated: "The words of Torah grow and multiply."[2] Ever since the Torah was given, the scholars of each generation have tried to encompass all of halakha in a single work but they could not. Each generation continues to add. They hang mountains of laws on a scant few verses. As times changed and circumstances shifted, the Torah's interpreters found solutions to new problems. In each generation, the Jewish scholars were called upon to rule on matters that their forebears could not imagine, and so they issued novel rulings. Where

2. Ḥagiga 3b.

did they get them from? It is not only permitted to ask this question, but required. After all, the reason that we "record the words of those who [vote to] acquit and the words of those who [vote to] convict"[3] is so that we know their reasons and explanations. The Sages said of a ruling with no reason: "These are nothing but words of prophecy,"[4] and the early commentators disagree about whether this is praise or denigration.[5]

How is it possible that calling something "words of prophecy" denigrates it? Is anyone greater than the prophets, who beheld divine visions and were imbued by God with a spirit of holiness? Nevertheless, there is an undisputed halakha: "'These are the mitzvot' – a prophet has no license to institute something new from this point forward."[6] "Therefore, if a man arises ... and performs a sign or wonder and says ... that God instructed him that the law is such-and-such or that the law follows the opinion of so-and-so, he is a false prophet and is put to death by strangulation even if he performs a sign, for he has come to deny the Torah, which states: 'It is not in heaven' (Deut. 30:12)."[7]

Indeed, "a sage is preferable to a prophet."[8] If even a novice student sitting before his master suggests a reasonable explanation, we heed him and even establish halakha in accordance with his opinion. Halakhic decisions are made not on the basis of supernatural signs and wonders, but by the persuasiveness and rationality of scholars' arguments.

Talmudic debate continues to this very day, and every scholar subjects the opinions of his colleagues and even his predecessors to critical analysis. One makes the argument for one position, and another argues to the contrary, and through rational discourse each attempts to reach a final determination. In some cases, there is an unequivocal and undisputed interpretation and resolution of the issue at hand. In other cases, each party to the debate has arguments on which to rely.

3. Sanhedrin 34a.
4. Bava Batra 12a.
5. See *Tosafot* on Bava Batra 12a, s.v. "Amar R."; Eiruvin 60b, s.v. "Ein."
6. Megilla 2b.
7. *Hilkhot Yesodei HaTorah* 9:1–4.
8. Bava Batra 12a. See also the beginning of Maimonides' introduction to his *Commentary on the Mishna* (pp. 29–32), where he explains the fundamental difference between the authority of a prophet and that of a sage.

All of the voluminous literature of Torah is nothing but the processing of Scripture and the traditions received at Sinai – small quantities that hold vast amounts of content – through the vehicle of human intelligence. *The Torah was given prophetically, but once it was given, prophecy no longer plays a role in it.* Halakhic rulings on new questions are rendered solely by means of solid and straightforward logic. Only through critical examination and probing analysis can one truly understand the sources inherited from earlier generations and bequeath them to future generations as part of a rich, living tradition.

"When Rabbi Akiva was compiling halakhot for his disciples, he said: 'Anyone who has heard an explanation from a colleague should come and state it.'"[9] He added that every statement must undergo meticulous critical assessment: "Not all who rush forward [to state a ruling] deserve praise – unless they offer an explanation!" When he saw that R. Shimon's words made more sense, "R. Akiva retracted and taught in accordance with R. Shimon's words."

A critical intellect is the pillar on which science rests as well as the pillar that supports halakha. Were it not possible to rely on human logic and intelligence, most of the Torah would, God forbid, be rendered null.

The Torah was not given to the fearful, the faint of heart, or those who choose to evade responsibility through imagined certainty: "Lest the judge say: 'Why do I need this trouble?' the Torah therefore teaches: '[The Lord] is with you when you pass judgment' (II Chr. 19:6) – the judge has nothing but what his eyes perceive."[10] A Jew who acts "in fear of the Lord, with fidelity, and with whole heart" (ibid. 9) can be certain that He "is with you when you pass judgment,"[11] and he can therefore

---

9. Tosefta Zavim (Zuckermandel ed.) 1:5–6.

10. Sanhedrin 6b.

11. It is worth noting that this approach is characteristic of halakhists in every era. Although later generations have diminished status, we too have only what our eyes perceive. One of the greatest halakhists of the last generation, Rabbi Moshe Feinstein, wrote in the introduction to his collection of responsa, *Iggerot Moshe*: "The truth, for the purpose of rendering a ruling, is what seems to the Torah scholar to be the correct practical decision once he has labored and toiled to clarify the halakha through the Talmud and the codes to the best of his ability, with proper gravity and fear of God. He is obligated to render his decision ... and it is considered true judgment."

rely on his perception – on his intellect and its ability to approach truth in all fields of inquiry. God created man and gave him intelligence not for naught, but so that he can learn and understand.

Science, Morality, and Faith

We now arrive at the crux of the matter. The Torah scholar, like the scientist, uses the tools of logic and critical thinking. But does that suffice? If man could be a soul without a body, like the disembodied intellects of which the medieval philosophers spoke, then intellect alone would suffice, since a disembodied intellect can wait until it attains knowledge. A living human being, however, has no such luxury. Life flows constantly, and each day one must act in one way or another. Even the slightest action has consequences and ramifications for both the one who performs it as well as others. So what is the proper path for mankind to choose before it reaches knowledge? There is an old philosophical debate as to whether it is possible to ascertain moral principles on the basis of humanistic premises alone. Even if we presume that it is possible, the road to such certainty is a long one. What should be done by all the generations before those moral principles are discovered?

There is a fundamental difference between the natural sciences, like physics, chemistry, and biology, on the one hand, and the social sciences and ethics, on the other. For example: we have no idea what might be discovered in the process of experiments to alter the genetic structure of certain cells. Thus, the decision to continue such experimentation entails inevitable risk, even if the risks are unknown. The ethical question of engaging in such experimentation cannot be answered by natural science, yet the question cannot be deferred until we achieve certainty. Moral principles and the acceptance of the yoke of heaven are vitally necessary from the beginning of our path in life.

Who knows if man will ever discover the purpose of life? We must be content with the search for that knowledge, even if it ultimately remains beyond our reach. However, without rock-solid faith that life has a purpose, man is apt to lose his footing in the world. This is the meaning of the psalmist's words: "I have chosen the path of faith; I have set Your laws before me" (Ps. 119:30). Once one has chosen the path of faith and is sure that the Creator and His laws are true, he may rely on his own knowledge to understand and to render decisions concerning His law.

One who is not willing to bear the burden of man's duties in the world until he has scientific proof that they are indeed his duty – "woe unto him and woe unto his neighbor." Practical commitment to ethical behavior is a *sine qua non* of a properly functioning of society. Similarly, the acceptance of certain basic premises – that is, articles of faith – is necessary for anyone who strives to operate in the world of science. The story is told of a Ḥasidic rebbe who was once asked about the hymn *"Ein Kelohenu,"* which is recited at the end of the prayer service: since it begins by unequivocally asserting, "There is none like our God," why do we then ask, "Who is like our God?" He answered that without the faith that "there is none like our God," it would be impossible to endure in a world of toil and distress. One who doubts for a second that the world has a Guide might question the worth of his life. After all, "it is better for man to have never been created" (Eiruvin 13b). One with eyes to see the tears of the oppressed who have no comfort, or ears to hear the sighs of the persecuted who have no succor, may ask: Why do I need to live in a world of such emptiness, where all of man's desires and actions come to naught? Such a person drowns in despair. His thinking becomes confused; he is unable to ask the right questions or find true answers. However, once one asserts with full conviction that "there is none like our God," his thinking achieves clarity and, with it, the freedom to fathom the ultimate questions of existence. One who is convinced that "there is none like our God" is free to ask anything, even "Who is like our God?"

If the meaning of one's life hinges on the results of a particular study, will he be able to consider and exhaust all possibilities, coldly and rationally, and accept the conclusions, whatever they may be, as the truth? Let us take, for example, the revolutionary theories of Sigmund Freud. He trained several disciples who were serious researchers, but his influence went well beyond the narrow academic context, pulling millions into his orbit. How many of them look to his ideas in a quest for truth alone, and how many are driven by desire, disguised in the mantle of science? One who has difficulty restraining his sexual impulses and therefore seeks justification for his behavior in theories of the subconscious cannot act as a dispassionate researcher of the truth. Only one who does not look to such alleged "discoveries" to justify the adoption of new and fashionable ideas can study every phenomenon and its causes, and progressively clarify and refine his findings until he ultimately arrives at the truth.

Maimonides, the great teacher of all generations, taught us:

> I say that it is not fitting to "walk in the orchard" (i.e., study esoteric philosophy) unless one has "filled his belly with bread and meat"; "bread and meat" refers to knowing the explanations of what is forbidden and permitted, and so forth for all mitzvot... for they settle one's mind beforehand.[12]

If one's mind is not settled, how will he ever attain knowledge?

Science and the Thirteen Principles of Faith

Is the conflict between science and Judaism, then, to be so easily dismissed? Even if it is true that both believe in the unity of the universe and in the power of human intelligence to disclose the secrets of creation, even if both the Torah and science demand a critical approach to any question that emerges, is it not possible that free inquiry will pose unanswerable challenges to faith? What if it can be proven that the tenets of faith are false? Such questions are heard occasionally, and, truth be told, there is greater fear of such questions among Jews who observe the Torah and mitzvot. That science and religion share a faith in the unity of all existence is not of primary importance to us as believers. For us, this is merely a consequence of the fact that the universe is the handiwork of the one Creator, Who is Master of all.

Although the greatest thinkers of yore attempted to prove God's existence, no one thought that it would be possible to prove that He does not exist. In truth, God's existence does not require any proof. Those who sought to prove it were motivated mainly by polemical concerns, in particular, to counter the Aristotelian doctrine of the eternity of matter. Moreover, according to modern philosophical thinking, it is impossible

---

12. *Hilkhot Yesodei HaTorah* 4:13.

to prove the existence of the Creator. But, as noted, there is no need for proofs, because a believer knows and senses in his bones that "though I walk through a valley of the deepest darkness, I fear no evil, for You are with me" (Ps. 23:4). When You are with me, who needs proofs?

However, the tenet of God's existence is not sufficient. There are several other principles of faith; what of them?

We must first state that we are only interested in the thirteen principles of faith which Maimonides enumerated (although even regarding these, several were the subject of disagreement by Jewish sages), of which Maimonides states: "When a person has complete faith in all these principles, he enters into the community of Israel."[13]

There are many truths about matters of the utmost importance – about "what is above and what is below; what happened at the beginning and what will happen at the end" (Ḥagiga 2:1) – that were not included in the thirteen principles. Of them it is said: "Happy is one who believes, and even happier is one who knows!" One who is privy to the secrets of wisdom will rejoice in these truths, but one who is not in that category need not become preoccupied with them. If one is attracted to conjecture, whatever its source – whether it stems from scientists or Torah scholars – it is ultimately nothing more than conjecture, and not binding.

Of the thirteen principles, there is only one that overlaps with the realm of scientific inquiry. The rest cannot be challenged on the basis of scientific conclusions. Science does not pretend to go beyond the natural into supernatural realms. The natural sciences have no access to the spiritual, and consequently they have nothing to say about God, the nature of the divine, the relationship between man and his Creator, the reward and punishment in store in the next world, or the promise of a messianic era, may it arrive soon. There is only one principle that addresses an event in the concrete, material world: the giving of the Torah at Sinai.

Indeed, there are those who sought to undermine the eighth principle of faith, namely, that the Torah is from heaven. In truth, though, the natural sciences cannot disprove any one-time historical event, including

13. *Commentary on the Mishna*, Introduction to the Tenth Chapter of Sanhedrin (*Perek Ḥelek*), p. 145.

the giving of the Torah. One can accept or reject the testimony of past generations, but there is no way to scientifically prove what happened at Mt. Sinai. It is not a phenomenon that can be reproduced for examination under laboratory conditions.

When it comes to history, we have nothing to rely upon except testimony from the past and the lasting impression it continues to make on the present. One of the greatest philosophers pointed out that while many nations created books, only one book created a nation.[14] We are the people that was created by the book of the Torah, and while most of the nations that "made many books of no end" (Eccl. 12:12) have ceased to exist, we are alive and well. Just as a tool attests to its maker, so the Jewish people attest to the uniqueness of the Torah. As Maimonides wrote, in explaining God's promise (Isaiah 66:22), "For as the new heavens and the new earth, which I will make, shall remain before me ... so shall your seed and your name remain":

> For it sometimes happens that the seed remains while the name does not. Thus you can find many people that are indubitably the seed of Persia of Greece, but are not known by a special name, being absorbed in another religious community. This, to my mind, is likewise an indication of the eternity of the Law because of which we have a special name.[15]

The heretics, however, take a different approach. They try to cast doubt on the value of the Written Torah by "proving" that it is but a compilation and concoction of fragments from various sources produced over long periods of time.

Bible criticism became a field of interest for many people, including not a few anti-Semites. Despite the pretense of espousing scientific methods, in general, this revolutionary form of criticism is unsupported.

---

14. Blaise Pascal, *Pensées*, §481 (Penguin ed., 1966, p. 181): "What a difference there is between one book and another! I am not astonished that the Greeks made the Iliad, nor the Egyptians and the Chinese their histories ... There is a great difference between a book which an individual writes, and publishes to a nation, and a book which itself creates a nation."

15. *Moreh Nevukhim* II:29, p. 342.

The natural sciences attempt to clarify the inner connections between various phenomena. The scientist is not interested in whether these phenomena have special significance for people. The natural scientist does not seek the purpose of existence, and consequently he does not reach conclusions about what he observes based on some imagined purpose. He sees existence as it is, and he tries to discover which processes remain constant under specific conditions. Since the time that scientists abandoned questions of teleology and restricted themselves to describing that which exists, science has advanced by leaps and bounds. Maimonides too had already espoused an empirical approach.[16] Precisely because the purpose of creation – the intention and goal of the Creator – is beyond human comprehension, we cannot take it into consideration or draw any conclusions from it. This does not mean that creation has no purpose; God's works are certainly not futile! Rather, we are not capable of breaking the constraints of time and space to attain even an inkling of why God created the world. Thus, when studying nature, we must not consider what lies beyond nature, and thus science does not address moral meaning or any other form of meaning.

This all applies to natural phenomena. With regard to Torah, however, the receptacle must be distinguished from the content. If someone sends you a letter, and you discuss it like you would discuss a volcanic rock or a type of plant, testing and examining its physical substance – the paper, the ink, the orthography, etc. – while ignoring the fact that this letter contains statements whose meanings go beyond its material form, then all the trouble of writing the letter was for naught. One only sends a letter in order to transmit a meaningful message, and so if the recipient wishes to extract the meaning of the letter, he must take an entirely different approach. It is not the type of paper or ink that should interest the recipient, but the content of the letter. It is not even enough to understand the language of the letter. It might not be possible to decipher the letter without knowing the identity of the sender, for the same words can have different and even opposite meanings when spoken by different people.

One who refuses *a priori* to accept that this letter has profound meaning will never discover that meaning. One who does not recognize

---

16. See above, "The Natural Sciences and the Reasons for the Mitzvot," p. 157.

that the Creator communicates with human beings will never know how to distinguish between the words of the living God and fairy tales. Unlike the natural scientist who, upon encountering a difficulty, attributes the shortcoming to his own understanding and to the inadequacy of the regnant scientific theories, the Bible critic attributes all difficulties to the ignorance of the author of the text. The questions and difficulties that are seized upon by Bible critics were not discovered by them. They were already long known to Torah scholars, who saw them as an opportunity to plumb the Torah's most profound depths and achieve greater understanding of God's word. The critics, however, dove into the mighty waters but came up empty.

The believing Jew heeds the demand to "turn it over again and again, for everything is in it."[17] To that end, he enlists the tools of logic and scholarship to clarify and explain Scripture. He does not fear "the new interpretations that emerge each day."[18] On the contrary, he views them as a blessing, for it is through them that he reveals the meanings of the "letter" – the perfect Torah.

Yet the prerequisite for deciphering the Torah's message is the presumption that the Torah is not coming to teach us physics, biology, or even history lessons. Its intention is to illuminate roads leading to moral understanding. The Torah places signposts along the path leading to the knowledge of God. Its whole concern is guiding man's free choice. In contrast to the natural sciences, which examine reality as it is and as it can be, the Torah deals with values by which man can choose to change what can be changed.

Furthermore, there is a clear distinction between the halakhic portions of the Torah and its non-halakhic portions. The halakhic portions, though subject to dispute, are acknowledged by all to be obligatory, and there are even rules for settling disputes. The non-halakhic portions, on the other hand, are not binding on a normative level and are subject to many different interpretations, which occasionally are even diametrically opposed to one another.

---

17. Mishna Avot 5:22.
18. Rashbam on Genesis 37:2.

Rabbi Avraham, the son of Maimonides, wrote:

> Do not entertain the view of those who have not reached true
> knowledge who believe that every time a verse is expounded [by
> the Sages], they have a tradition, as is the case with the princi-
> pal parts of the Torah and tradition. This is not so! Instead, you
> should know that the interpretation of verses that do not involve
> a fundamental tenet or a Torah law is not based on received tradi-
> tion. Rather, some of these interpretations are based on their own
> logic…. Thus, I have no doubt that R. Yehoshua's statement on
> the passages about Yitro – "What news did he hear that brought
> him? He heard about the war of Amalek and came"[19] – is his opin-
> ion, not a received tradition. This is evident from the statement:
> "for this [Yitro] immediately follows it [the war of Amalek]";
> had this been a tradition, he would not have needed to prove his
> interpretation. It is also evident from the fact that other Sages
> have different explanations of this verse. Had it been a received
> tradition, it would not have been disputed.[20]

The fact that there is such a broad range of interpretation on these matters indicates that the Torah did not wish for their meaning to be fixed.

Apparent Contradictions between Torah and Scientific Theories

We will briefly illustrate these ideas by means of three contemporary
problems. We will see that if there is conflict between science and religion, it is only at the hypothetical level.

1. The artificial creation of life: is it possible to create life from
   inanimate substances?
2. The theory of evolution: did the world in general, and its animal
   species in particular, gradually evolve from less developed forms
   of existence?
3. The uniqueness of man: are there intelligent beings in outer space?

---

19. *Mekhilta DeRabbi Yishma'el, Yitro, Masekhta DeAmalek* 1.
20. "Essay on the Homilies of the Sages," p. 91.

It should be said at the outset that I am not an expert in these fields and cannot assess whether it is likely that organisms will be created in a test tube. I do not know enough to form an independent opinion about whether the theory of evolution, in one form or another, should be accepted as truth. It is superfluous to add that I do not pretend to know whether there are intelligent creatures or any living organisms somewhere in outer space.

At present, I wish only to deal with the question: if one proposes an affirmative answer to one of these three questions, does he thereby deny Jewish faith? I will not attempt to answer this question with a thorough demonstration of the consonance or dissonance of these ideas with the view of the Torah. In my humble opinion, it is sufficient to show that great Torah scholars of various periods contemplated such possibilities and entertained similar ideas. Indeed, some of those sages cited biblical prooftexts for their opinions, but they never claimed that these proofs are binding. Since we find among great Torah scholars both those who affirm and those who negate these ideas, it is clear that the Torah does not dictate answers to such questions. Consequently, there cannot be conflict between Torah and science with respect to these and similar questions.

Creation of Life from Inanimate Substances
There is a well-known statement of the Sages: "If everyone in the world convened, they would not be able to create a mosquito and inject a soul into it."[21] Nevertheless, the Jewish sages did not refrain from contemplating and conjecturing about such possibilities. During medieval times, there were lively debates among scholars about this question. The matter was summarized succinctly in *Sha'ar Hashamayim* by Rabbi Gershom b. Shlomo, a son-in-law of Nahmanides. Without any reservation, he cites the position of the philosopher Ibn Sina (Avicenna):

> ...it is not impossible that...a mixture will form in the earth, which is suitable to receive the human form.... Man's generation from man is not necessary, but only what is most frequent; it is

---

21. Y. Sanhedrin 7:13.

the most appropriate and the easiest [mode of generation], just as most frequently a mouse is generated from a mouse, a frog from a frog, although occasionally a mouse comes to be from the earth, a frog from rainwater. The same holds of other species, too…. The difference between the mouse, the frog, and others which are born and give birth, and man is only a quantitative difference: this kind of [spontaneous] generation is very rare in man, indeed most infrequent, whereas in the mouse and the frog it is not all that rare, although it is still infrequent.[22]

Indeed, for much of history, it was all but universally accepted that some animal species can spontaneously generate from water, dust, or decay, without being born from another animal. Even the Mishna mentions such a creature, which, during the course of its formation, is "half flesh and half earth."[23] It is worth noting that Maimonides had a deep intuition that such a thing is impossible, but since he could not prove it, he accepted the testimony of those who claimed to have witnessed such phenomena:

The formation of a mouse specifically from dust, so that it is part flesh and part mud, but entirely motile, is a very well-known account; innumerable people have told me that they have personally observed it. Yet the existence of an animal of this kind is astounding to the point that no possible explanation is known for it.[24]

Maimonides' astonishment notwithstanding, the author of *Tosafot Yom Tov* ascribed great significance to the existence of this creature, writing: "This, in my opinion, is a strong claim against believers in the eternity

22. Gershon b. Shlomo, *Sha'ar Hashamayim* (Roedelheim: Heidenheim and Schwartz, 1801), Essay 8, p. 45. [The English translation is excerpted from Gad Freudenthal, "(Al-) Chemical Foundations for Cosmological Ideas: Ibn Sina on the Geology of an Eternal World," in *Physics, Cosmology and Astronomy, 1300–1700: Tension and Accommodation*, S. Unguru, ed. (Boston: Springer Science & Business Media, 2012), p. 65.]
23. Mishna Ḥullin 9:6.
24. *Commentary on the Mishna*, Ḥullin 9:6.

[of the universe]."[25] It is noteworthy that the author of *Tiferet Yisrael* had difficulties with this "strong claim," yet the fact that he was aware of scientific developments in his own day caused him to try to prove that such a strange creature indeed exists.[26]

In this context, we must mention the Talmud's stories about how R. Ḥanina and R. Oshaya studied *Sefer Yetzira* and created a calf, and about how Rava created a man.[27] It is likely that these narratives are allegorical and not to be taken at face value, as is evident from the statement of Abaye deriving from the story of the created calf that certain practices of "sorcery" are permitted ab initio, since they are only sleight of hand and not actual magic.[28] Nevertheless, many in fact took the story at face value, and one of the greatest *Aḥaronim* has a responsum on the halakhic status of such a man-made creature![29]

The Theory of Evolution and the Age of the World

Did the world in general and all the creatures that inhabit it evolve from less-developed forms?

The theory of evolution has ancient roots. In Jewish sources as well, there is an abundance of different ideas and hypotheses on this subject, concerning the world as a whole as well as the evolution of humans specifically. I will cite a few examples.

In medieval times, there was a major dispute between those who believed in creation *ex nihilo* and philosophers who supported the view that the world is eternal. Rabbi Yehuda HaLevi devotes an extensive discussion to this subject, and he concludes:

> The question of eternity and creation is obscure, whilst the arguments are evenly balanced... If, after all, a believer in the Law finds himself compelled to admit an eternal matter and the existence of many worlds prior to this one, this would not impair his belief

---

25. *Tosafot Yom Tov*, Ḥullin 9:6.
26. *Tiferet Yisrael*, Ḥullin 9:6., *Bo'az* §b.
27. See Sanhedrin 65b.
28. Sanhedrin 67b.
29. *Ḥakham Tzvi* §93.

that this world was created at a certain epoch, and that Adam and Eve were the first human beings.[30]

For Rabbi Yehuda HaLevi, the possibility that someone committed to the Torah would be compelled to believe in the existence of multiple worlds due to as yet undiscovered proofs and arguments seemed remote indeed. However, kabbalists found support for the idea of prior worlds in ancient midrashim that speak of worlds that God created and destroyed before creating the present world.[31] Closer to our own time, when the disciplines of geology and paleontology began to develop, the author of *Tiferet Yisrael* addressed the idea:

> From all this it is clear that everything that the kabbalists have told us for hundreds of years, that there was already a world and that it was destroyed and reestablished four times, and that each time the world appeared in a more perfect state than before – now in our time it has been shown to be right and true.... Consider the letter *bet* with which the Torah begins, and reflect on the four crowns on this *bet*: the kabbalists tell us that the four crowns allude to the notion that this is the fourth iteration of the world and all its hosts, and the enlarged *bet* informs us that the greatest creation – the soul of *homo sapiens* – is in its second iteration.[32]

The questions of the age of the universe and reconciling different time-lines did not bother these Torah scholars. Furthermore, there were Jewish sages who divided human history into two distinct stages. The first stage was before man obtained an "intelligent soul," during which he was "merely a beast, without speech, until he was created in [God's] image and likeness."[33] We find something similar in a responsum of Rav Yosef Gaon of Mata Meḥasia:

---

30. *Kuzari* I:67. Translated by Hartwig Hirschfeld (New York, 1905), p. 54.
31. See Rabbi M. M. Kasher, *Torah Shelema, Genesis* 1:29 and 73, and the footnotes ad loc.
32. Part three of "*Derush Or Haḥayim,*" which is appended to *Tiferet Yisrael* on Nezikin.
33. Rabbi Ovadia Sforno on Genesis 2:7.

In the first hour of the day, he arose in [God's] thought; in the second, he was created [it seems that he was created at the end of the second – he was physically complete and had become a *golem*. He had a vital soul like one of the animals, at it is written: "A wild ass's colt is born a man" (Job 11:12). And in the fourth chapter of Sanhedrin we say: "In the second hour, he became a *golem*];[34] in the third, his limbs extended; in the fourth, a soul was injected into him"[35] – perhaps this refers to the intelligent soul, for he had vitality immediately upon becoming a *golem*.[36]

This means that the second period of human history began when he was given a unique soul, thus becoming a "speaking spirit."[37] At this stage, his physical form improved as well, and this may be what the Sages mean when they expounded: "'The man became a living soul' – R. Yehuda says: This teaches that he was made with a tail, like a beast, but [God] later removed it for man's honor."[38]

It is worth noting that it emerges from the statements of one of the *Rishonim*, Rabbi Yehuda b. Barzilai, that there were three stages in man's creation. He explains that when the Mishna (Avot 5:9) states that "script and writing were created at twilight [of the sixth day]," it means that the invention of writing required a unique form of intelligence; even after man gained the power of speech, he had not yet learned written language. It was only at twilight that the Creator endowed him with greater intelligence and brought him to a higher plane. At this third stage, man was elevated to his present state, and his creation was complete.[39]

---

34. Editor's note: See *Ginzei Kedem* 3, Rabbi Binyamin Menashe Levin, ed. (St. Louis: Moinester Printing, 1925), p. 59, in the comment of the editor, R. B. Levin, which states that the bracketed segment was a copyist's addition. See also what Rabbi M. M. Kasher wrote in *Torah Shelema, Genesis*, §738.
35. Sanhedrin 38b.
36. This responsum was published at the end of the *Responsa Rif*, Z. Bendowitz, ed. (Bilgoraj: 1935). It is cited and annotated in *Ginzei Kedem* 3, p. 59.
37. *Targum Onkelos* on Genesis 2:7.
38. Genesis Rabba 14:10.
39. See the commentary of Rabbi Yehuda b. Barzilai to *Sefer Yetzira* (Mekitze Nirdamim: Berlin 1885), p. 139.

Although some say that the descriptions at the beginning of Genesis all refer to Adam, the individual first man, others explain otherwise, and Abarbanel summarizes (and disagrees with) their view in his commentary on the Torah:

> The proper explanation is that the "*adam*" mentioned throughout this section is the name of the species. It is of this that the verses speak, not of the individual first man.[40]

Among those who take this view are Maimonides, Ibn Ezra, and others.

Our concern is not to attempt to decide in favor of one view or another on the basis of exegesis or scientific inquiry, and certainly not to reconcile a particular view of the commentators with a current scientific theory. We are attempting only to discern fundamentals, and fundamentally it makes no difference whether human development occurred over a short or long period. After all, the movement of time is relative, and time is measured by the developments that take place.

Intelligent Extraterrestrial Life

The Sages said: "If a man merits it, he is told: 'You are first in all creation.' If not, he is told: 'The mosquito preceded you; the earthworm preceded you.'"[41] This view would have seemed strange to most of the world. The gentile sages saw man not only as the elect among all creatures, but also as the purpose of all existence. If so, how can one say that even the mosquito and the earthworm precede man? Moreover, in ancient times it was believed that the earth is the center of the universe, and that all the celestial bodies were created to serve it. Thus, when Copernicus and Galileo discovered that the earth is not at the center, and that it revolves around the sun, the entire Christian world was shaken. Christianity, which deifies and worships a man, had good reason to fear these astonishing

---

40. Abarbanel on Genesis chapter 2, s.v. "Vekhol si'ah" (p. 91 in the Arrabal edition). See also Rabbi M. M. Kasher, *Torah Shelema, Bereshit* 1:792: "'He created him in the image of God' – He created specifically him in His image, but the image of his descendants varied...."
41. See Leviticus Rabba 14:1.

discoveries: if the earth is no longer at the center, then man is no longer at the center, and is certainly not a deity.

Judaism, on the other hand, never recoiled from Copernicus' ideas. The question of the earth's motion was already discussed by our scholars in medieval times.[42] They based their judgment on their perception that the earth is stationary. However, they did not reach that conclusion because of dogmatic belief, but because of what they deemed to be purely scientific reasoning. Regarding the view which considers man the apex of all creation, Maimonides teaches:

> Know that the majority of the false imaginings that call forth perplexity in the quest for the end [i.e., purpose] of the existence of the world ... have as their root an error of man about himself and his imagining that all that exists, exists because of himself alone.[43]

Maimonides goes on to explain that this erroneous assessment is rooted in human psychology:

> The reason for this whole mistake lies in the fact that this ignoramus and those like him among the multitude consider that which exists only with reference to a human individual. Every ignoramus imagines that all that exists, exists with a view to his individual sake; it is as if there were nothing that exists except him.... However, if man considered... that which exists, and knew the smallness of his part in it, the truth would become clear and manifest to him.... Now the true way of considering

---

42. Ralbag addresses it at length in his magnum opus, *Milḥamot Hashem*, in the first section of the fifth treatise, chapter 51. The fifth treatise is still in manuscript and has never been printed because it addresses complicated astronomical matters. He writes there: "It is impossible to reconcile the visible motion of the stars with the premise that the earth is in motion while the heavens are at rest. If this were so, all the stars would be in a single relation.... The distance and relation from one to another would not vary, yet this is not what we find. Rather, we find that some of them complete their movement over long periods of time, some in shorter periods. Some are occasionally fast, and some are occasionally slow and sometimes regress. This is all impossible according to that premise...."

43. *Moreh Nevukhim* III:25, pp. 505–6.

this is that all the existent individuals of the human species and, all the more, those of the other species of the animals, are things of no value at all in comparison with the whole that exists and endures. It has made this clear, saying: "Man is like unto vanity" (Ps. 144:4).[44]

The Talmud states that there are 18,000 worlds,[45] and some of the *Rishonim* discuss the meaning of this statement. Rabbi Yehuda b. Barzilai addresses some different questions about this notion, including: Are those worlds like our own, with a heaven and earth? Are the hosts of its heaven as numerous as ours? Is there life on those worlds? If there is life, are there any creatures with free will? And if there are creatures with free will, did the Creator give them Torah?[46]

R. Hasdai Crescas, in his book *Or Hashem*, disagrees with the premise that the world is necessarily finite. He suggests that there may be innumerable universes, each an independent and self-contained entity, like our universe, with a full complement of visible and invisible heavenly hosts. Thus, even under the geocentric premise, the earth is not the center of all the worlds, and certainly we should not attribute absolute uniqueness to the human beings that inhabit our world.[47]

Yet man's primary value and significance do not require his uniqueness and superiority. Indeed, "Man is like unto vanity," and thus the psalmist wonders: "When I behold Your heavens, the work of Your fingers, the moon and stars that You set in place: What is man that You have been mindful of him, the son of man, that You think of him?" (Ps. 8:4–5). Nevertheless, "Wherever you find the power of the Holy One, you also find His humility.... 'Thus says the High and Lofty One, Who lives eternally, Whose name is holy,' followed immediately by, '[Who is] with the contrite and low of spirit' (Is. 57:15)."[48] The Sages

---

44. Ibid. 12, p. 442.
45. See Avoda Zara 3b.
46. See his commentary of *Sefer Yetzira*, pp. 171–72.
47. See *Or Hashem*, fourth treatise, second exposition. He opposes the claims advanced by Ralbag in *Milḥamot Hashem*, sixth treatise, chapter 19.
48. Megilla 31a.

state: "Beloved is man, in that he was created in the Divine image."[49] We must praise and thank the Creator for this closeness to Him – "Yet You have made him just a little less than angels" (Ps. 8:6). Man is given the opportunity to generate sublime spiritual and moral insights. His value lies in his being both a creature and a creator. "If a man merits it, he is told: 'You are first in all creation.'" He is not first in the order of creation; facts remain unchanged. His precedence is not based on chronology, but on virtue and merit. On matters of virtue and vice, science has no say.

We have specified three areas in which there are disputes between religion and science in the Western world. While Christian misgivings are not our concern, their disputes with science have, in fact, influenced us, to the extent that the erroneous notion that science is incompatible with faith – not just Christianity – has taken root. As their religious institutions were weakened and the spirit of heresy grew strong, these clashes invaded our spiritual world as well. Jews who wanted to drink from the wellsprings of scientific knowledge found that they were all under secularist control. Thus, we lost many of our best, who failed to understand that Judaism never opposed the search for truth and that, on the contrary, disclosing the mysteries of creation leads only to the recognition of God's greatness.

We cited the opinions of Torah sages that resemble those currently fashionable among scientists. Of course, it would have been possible to marshal numerous references and citations on behalf of the dissenting opinions. The inevitable conclusion is that these questions will only be decided – if they can be decided – when the study of the natural world advances even further. Perhaps, in time, the veil will be lifted from these issues and the evidence will point clearly to one of the disputing views. But these proofs will be of the purely scientific variety. Only the tools of the natural sciences can produce answers to questions in the natural sciences.

Not even prophecy can transmit information that man is incapable of absorbing and understanding. The Sages said: "It is impossible to tell mortals of the power of the Account of the Beginning.

---

49. Mishna Avot 3:14.

For this reason, Scripture tells you obscurely: 'In the beginning God created....'"[50] Scripture did not come to teach us physics, biology, astronomy, or cosmogony, since it would be impossible to do so.

The Religious Value of Scientific Progress

Every advance in our understanding of nature's wonders opens new avenues for expanding our religious consciousness; the increase in the intellect's prowess and the discovery of truth both reinforce man's spiritual character and prepare him to realize his destiny.

> When a man contemplates these things and becomes familiar with all creations such as angels, spheres, man, and the like and sees the wisdom of the Holy One in every creature, his love for the Omnipresent will increase, and his soul will thirst and his flesh will yearn to love the Omnipresent.[51]

With respect to our topic, this is an extremely important principle. Scientific advancement is an important religious value – not because science can confirm what we already knew without it, but because each additional discovery of the secrets of creation reveals the wonders of the Creator.

We have already seen that scientific tools cannot undermine the "foundation of foundations and the pillar of wisdom" that the Holy One "brings into existence everything that exists."[52] On the other hand, we do not need science to prove this basic principle. This being the case, if one has strong faith in the world's Creator and Guide and desires to know Him, the road before him is open to contemplate His ways and be awestruck by His might and providence that are revealed in their full power and grandeur in the natural world that He created. The more one understands natural processes, the more he is aware of the greatness of the Creator.

---

50. Cited by Maimonides, *Moreh Nevukhim*, Introduction, p. 9.
51. *Hilkhot Yesodei HaTorah* 4:12.
52. Ibid. 1:1.

It makes no difference whether creation was a sudden or evolutionary process; either way, in the process of creation lies hidden the imprint of His wisdom.

The religious value of scientific advancement applies not only to the incremental accumulation of new details of scientific knowledge. Scientific revolutions – the rejection of old concepts in favor of the new – are also of religious value, because we can only understand that which we see through concepts with which we are already familiar.

Thus, for example, in ancient times it was thought that everything consists of a mixture of elements. Since those generations were familiar with processes like cooking, which is in essence an act of mixing, they tried to understand every phenomenon in the mineral, vegetable, and even animal world as acts of "cooking" and mixing.

Since the days of Newton, who sparked a revolution in all of the natural sciences, admixture has lost its centrality. Discoveries in the pure sciences were accompanied by a technological revolution; the era of automation arrived. This led to an attempt to reinterpret the motion of the celestial spheres mechanistically, as though the universe were a giant clock. Natural processes were understood not only according to the mixture paradigm, but also on the machine paradigm. The workings of the machine illustrated the workings of the forces of nature. Recently, after the discovery of radiation, the paradigm shifted again. The universe is no longer to be understood as a great machine. It is now the turn of new concepts, like fields and waves (in their modern scientific sense). Who knows what tomorrow will yield?

Maimonides, teacher of the generations, has described the great benefit of advancement through negation: "You come nearer to the apprehension of Him, may He be exalted, with every increase in the negations regarding Him; and you come nearer to that apprehension than he who does not negate with regard to Him that which, according to what has been demonstrated to you, must be negated."[53] The wisdom of the Creator is beyond our grasp, and the more we discern the extent to which it is inestimable and incomparable, the higher we climb on the ladder of knowledge. Thus, for the man of faith, science is doubly valuable.

53. *Moreh Nevukhim* I:59, p. 138.

> When a man contemplates His great and wondrous deeds and
> creatures and from them sees His infinite and inestimable wis-
> dom, he will immediately love, praise, and glorify Him, and he
> will passionately crave to know the great name. As David said:
> "My soul thirsts for God, the living God" (Ps. 42:3).[54]

Additionally, the practical benefits that are derived from the application
of science to solving life's ongoing challenges enable the formation of
the ideal society. Technology is a tool given to us by the Holy One; if we
use it to do as He commanded in the Torah, "He will remove everything
that hinders us from observing it, such as illness, war, famine, and the
like; He will bestow on us all the benefits that strengthen our ability to
observe the Torah, such as plenitude, peace…so that we do not spend
all our days working to meet our bodily needs. Rather, we will be free
to study Torah and observe the commandments."[55]

We can already envision the extent to which it is possible to realize the goal: "The good will be in bountiful supply, and all luxuries will
be as common as dust."[56] Nevertheless, we must remember that science
and technology cannot decide moral questions. Advanced technology
served the Nazi monster without any pangs of conscience.

God's loving-kindness toward us is great, and He has enabled us
to go forth from enslavement to freedom. Now we can look forward to
the days when "the sole occupation of the whole world will be to know
God."[57]

---

54. *Hilkhot Yesodei HaTorah* 2:1.
55. *Hilkhot Teshuva* 9:1.
56. *Hilkhot Melakhim* 12:5.
57. Ibid.

Chapter 9

Wisdom and Human Pretension: The Riddle of Solomon and Its Resolution

Introduction

Much ink has been spilled in the attempt to reconcile the description of King Solomon that appears in the Book of Kings with the description in the Book of Chronicles. It emerges from even a cursory reading that the Solomon of Chronicles is the paradigmatic king of the yearned-for kingdom. A prophecy proclaims the main features of his reign even before his birth:

> But you will have a son who will be a man of rest; I will give him rest from his enemies on all sides, for Solomon (Shlomo) will be his name, and I will confer peace (*shalom*) and quiet on Israel in his time. He will build a house for My name; he shall be a son to Me and I to him a father, and I will establish his throne of kingship over Israel forever. (I Chr. 22:9–10)

This is what Solomon was supposed to become, and this is what his reign should have been. The author of Chronicles then sets forth numerous episodes to demonstrate that it was indeed so; every detail of the prophecy was fulfilled, albeit in reverse order. **"I will establish his throne of kingship over Israel forever"** is fulfilled with: "Solomon, son of David, took firm hold of his kingdom, for the Lord his God was with him and made him exceedingly great" (II Chr. 1:1). **"I to him a father"**: God appears to Solomon as a loving father: "Ask, what shall I grant you?" (1:7). **"He shall be a son to Me"**: like an intelligent son who brings joy to his father, Solomon asks: "Grant me wisdom and knowledge" (1:10). **"He will build a house for My name"**: Solomon immediately undertakes the massive task of building the Temple: "Then Solomon resolved to build a house for the name of the Lord" (1:18). He did not let up until he saw that "the glory of the Lord filled the house of God.... Then Solomon declared: 'I have built for You a stately house, and a place where You may dwell forever'" (5:14–6:2). **"I will confer peace and quiet on Israel in his time"**: not only did peace and quiet prevail in Israel in his day, but all were "joyful and in good spirits" (7:10). **"I will give him rest from his enemies on all sides"**: not only did he have a respite from all his enemies, but "King Solomon surpassed all the kings of the earth.... All the kings of the earth came to pay homage ... in the amount due each year" (9:22–24). And ultimately, he became king over kings: "He ruled over all the kings from the Euphrates to the land of the Philistines and to the border of Egypt" (7:26).

As described with great specificity, every element of the prophecy was fully realized.

Yet this is not the entire chronicle of Solomon. More than is written here is written in the Book of Kings. There, other facets of Solomon and his reign are revealed – facets that are more shadow than light.

By comparing the descriptions of Chronicles with those of Kings, we find that with regard to everything relating to the realization of the prophecy, Chronicles repeats what was already stated in Kings, and even embellishes it – with one exception. In Chronicles, as in Kings, it is recounted that "wisdom and knowledge are granted to you" (II Chr. 1:12; compare to I Kings 3:12), to the extent that "All the kings of the earth came to pay homage to Solomon and to listen to the wisdom with which God had endowed him" (II Chr. 9:23; compare to I Kings 10:24). However, the wondrous tale of how Solomon's wisdom was first revealed to Israel, when "they saw that he possessed divine wisdom to execute justice" (I Kings 3:28), does not appear in Chronicles. The absence of the episode of the two mothers from Chronicles is perplexing, for there would seem to be no greater exhibition of Solomon's extraordinary wisdom.

In truth, the Sages have already addressed this problem and shown us that what seems to be the supreme expression of Solomon's "wise and discerning mind" (ibid. 12) was not just a divine gift but actually pushed him into the abyss. The Sages said: "Kohelet [=Solomon] sought to pronounce judgment based on intuition – without witnesses and without admonition. A heavenly voice issued forth and said to him: 'and that which He wrote is upright and true' (Eccl. 12:10) – 'by the word of two witnesses…' (Deut. 17:6)."[1] Solomon wanted to circumvent the Torah's demands with his wisdom. It was not divine wisdom that led him to do so; rather, it was the dark side that wisdom too contains.

The Sages even found fault with the wisdom of Solomon's judgment regarding the identity of the mother of the live child: "How did he know? Maybe she was duping him?"[2] The wisest of all men wished to go beyond the limits of human intelligence and liberate himself from the shackles of mitzvot, which are merely tools whereby the body controls the soul. But that was not the intent of the prophecy, and so there is no place for the story of Solomon's judgment in Chronicles. We must look to the Book of Kings to understand Solomon's seemingly split personality.

It is not easy to peer into the soul of an ordinary person, let alone into the recesses of the soul of King Solomon. Not every mind can discern the deeper meanings behind the biblical stories of Solomon. Therefore, the Sages induced us to follow them into the secrets of the soul by presenting us with beguiling parables and captivating tales. We will attempt to unravel the Sages' exposition, and we will see where it leads us.

A Sin Commensurate with His Greatness

Solomon's personality is an undecipherable conundrum. On one hand, Solomon was Israel's greatest king. It was to him that God said: "wisdom and knowledge are granted to you, and I grant you also

---

1. Rosh HaShana 21b.
2. Makkot 23b.

wealth, property, and glory, the like of which no king before you has had, nor shall any after you have" (II Chr. 1:12). That is, Solomon represents a historical peak; even the greatness of the anticipated King Messiah is measured with the yardstick of Solomon's accomplishments: "The king that arises will have his royal capital in Zion; his name will become great and will spread to the ends of the earth – even more than Solomon's reign did."[3] Furthermore, the eminence of the Messiah will, in essence, be Solomon's as well, for the Messiah will be a descendant of Solomon.[4] This is emphasized in the promise of the prophet Nathan to King David: "When your days are done and you follow your fathers, I will raise up your offspring after you, one of your own sons, and I will establish his kingship. He shall build a house for Me, and I will establish his throne forever.... I will install him in My house and in My kingship forever, and his throne shall be established forever" (I Chr. 17:11–14).

On the other hand, neither Scripture nor the Sages spare King Solomon from their criticism:

> King Solomon loved many foreign women…from the nations of which the Lord had said to the Israelites, "None of you shall join them and none of them shall join you…." Such Solomon clung to and loved…. His wives turned his heart away…. Solomon did what was displeasing to the Lord…. The Lord was angry with Solomon, because his heart turned away from the Lord, the God of Israel." (I Kings 11:1–9)

Just as his wisdom became a byword, so too did his sins, as Nehemiah reproved his contemporaries: "It was just in such things that King Solomon of Israel sinned! Among the many nations there was not a

---

3. *Commentary on the Mishna*, Introduction to the Tenth Chapter of Sanhedrin (*Perek Ḥelek*), p. 138.
4. See *Commentary on the Mishna*, Introduction to the Tenth Chapter of Sanhedrin (*Perek Ḥelek*), p. 145; *Moses Maimonides' Epistle to Yemen* (Halkin and Cohen, eds.), p. xv.

king like him, and so well loved was he by his God…yet foreign wives caused even him to sin" (Neh. 13:26).

The Sages scrutinized Solomon and found even more sins:

> Solomon said: Three things with which the attribute of justice makes sport – I desecrated: "He shall not have many wives" (Deut. 17:17), yet Scripture states, "King Solomon loved many foreign women" (I Kings 11:1)…. "He shall not keep many horses" (Deut. 17:16), yet Scripture states: "Solomon had forty thousand stalls of horses for his chariotry and twelve thousand horsemen" (I Kings 5:6)…. "nor shall he amass silver and gold to excess" (Deut. 17:17), yet Scripture states: "The king made silver as plentiful in Jerusalem as stones" (I Kings 10:27).[5]

The Yerushalmi explains that Solomon was punished and deposed because of his sins:

> The Holy One said to Solomon: "What is this crown on your head? Get off of My throne." R. Yosi b. Ḥanina said: At that moment, an angel that looked like Solomon descended, removed him from the throne, and sat down in his stead. [Solomon] circulated among the synagogues and study halls, saying: "I am Kohelet; I was king over Israel in Jerusalem" (Eccl. 1:12). They would say to him: "The king is sitting on his throne, yet you say, 'I am Kohelet'?" They beat him with a stick and fed him a plate of beans. At that moment, he said: "This was my lot" (Eccl. 2:10).[6]

The idea that Solomon was dethroned also appears in the Talmud Bavli,[7] which tells an extended story of his replacement. In my opinion, this story contains a remarkable theory for understanding Solomon's complex personality. It is one of the longest narratives in the entire Talmud (in printed editions, it stretches over almost an entire folio page), and it

---

5. Y. Sanhedrin 2:6.
6. Ibid.
7. Gittin 68a.

seems that it was copied from there into various midrashim. It is worth pointing out two literary features of the Bavli version.

The first pertains to the central idea of a substitute king. As we have seen, the Yerushalmi speaks of an angel, whereas the Bavli speaks of a demon (*shed*) – more precisely, the king of the demons. This fits nicely with the fact that the Yerushalmi never even mentions demons, whereas the Bavli frequently discusses them. The Talmud itself records a dispute between the Jews of Eretz Yisrael and the Jews of Babylonia about whether to explain a given verse in Ecclesiastes as a reference to demons. As will be explained later, this has major implications. This is no fantasy tale about demons.

The second observation is that Solomon's wisdom is characterized by parables and riddles, based on the verses: "He composed three thousand parables.... He spoke about the trees, from the cedar in Lebanon to the hyssop that grows out of the wall; and he spoke about beasts, birds, creeping things, and fishes" (I Kings 5:12–13) and "The queen of Sheba heard of Solomon's wisdom... and she came to test him with riddles" (10:1). Fittingly, the Talmud's story of Solomon is a parable in its entirety, built of layer upon layer of riddles. It is worthwhile, then, to attempt "to understand proverbs and parables, the words of the wise and their riddles" (Prov. 1:6).

To understand the meaning of this parable, one must first read the entire narrative and then attempt to understand each detail, until a whole picture emerges. The story is brought in response to a question about the interpretation of a verse in Ecclesiastes – we will cite this as well. To assist the reader, we will present the entire story, broken up into segments, so as to facilitate the subsequent discussion.

The Text of the Aggada
The Talmud[8] states:

> It is written: "I got myself *sharim* and *sharot*, and human pleasures, *shidda* and *shiddot*" (Eccl. 2:8). "*Sharim* and *sharot*" – these

---

8. Gittin 68a–b. This translation is based on the Koren-Steinsaltz edition (Jerusalem: 2015).

are types of musical instruments. "Human pleasures" – these are pools and bathhouses. "*Shidda* and *shiddot*" – here [in Babylonia] they translated this as "male demons" (*shidda*) and "female demons" (*shiddetin*). In the West (Eretz Yisrael) they said: carriages (*shiddeta*).… The Master said: "Here they translated this as 'male demons' and 'female demons.' What did he need male and female demons for?"

A. As it is written: "For the house (the Temple), when it was being built, was built of stone made ready at the quarry…." (I Kings 6:7). [Solomon] said to the sages: How shall I do this? They said to him: There is the *shamir*, which Moses used for the stones of the breastplate. He said to them: Where is it found? They said to him: Bring a male demon and a female demon and shackle them together. Perhaps they know and will reveal it to you.

B. He brought a male demon and a female demon and shackled them together. They said: We do not know; perhaps Asmodeus king of the demons knows. He said to them: Where is Asmodeus? They said to him: He is on such-and-such a mountain.

He has dug himself a cistern, filled it with water, covered it with a rock, and sealed it with his seal. Every day he ascends to heaven and studies in the heavenly yeshiva. Then he descends to earth and studies in the earthly yeshiva. Then he comes and inspects his seal, opens the cistern, and drinks. Then he covers it, seals it, and leaves.

C. [Solomon] sent for Benayahu, son of Yehoyada. He gave him a chain onto which God's name was engraved, a signet onto which God's name of God was engraved, fleeces of wool, and wineskins filled with wine. Benayahu went and dug a cistern lower down the mountain from Asmodeus's cistern, drained the water (from Asmodeus's cistern) into it, and plugged it up with the wool fleeces. He then dug a pit higher up the mountain from Asmodeus's cistern and poured the wine through it into Asmodeus's cistern. He then sealed the cistern, climbed a tree, and sat in it.

D. When [Asmodeus] arrived, he checked his seal, opened the pit, and found the wine. He said: "It is written: 'Wine is a mocker, strong drink is riotous; and whosoever wallows in it is not wise' (Prov. 20:1); and it is written: 'Harlotry, old wine, and new wine take away understanding' (Hos. 4:11). I will not drink this wine." When he became thirsty, he could not hold back. He drank, became intoxicated, and fell asleep. [Benayahu] descended from the tree, threw the chain around [Asmodeus], and bound him within it. When [Asmodeus] awoke, he began to struggle. [Benayahu] said to him: "The name of your Master is upon you! The name of your Master is upon you!"

E. As [Benayahu] took [Asmodeus] away, he reached a palm tree. [Asmodeus] rubbed up against it and knocked it down. He reached a house and knocked it down. He reached the shack of a certain widow. She emerged and pleaded with him. He inclined his whole height away from her shack, and one of his bones broke. He said: This is the meaning of the verse, "Soft speech can break a bone" (Prov. 25:15).

F. [Asmodeus] saw a blind man who lost his way; he guided him back on the right path. He saw a drunk who lost his way; he guided him back on the right path.

G. He saw a very joyous wedding ceremony; he cried. He heard a man say to a shoemaker, "Make me shoes that will last for seven years," and he laughed. He saw a fortune-teller performing divinations, and he laughed.

H. When Asmodeus arrived there [in Jerusalem], they did not bring him before Solomon for three days. On the first day he said to them: Why is the king not summoning me to him? They said to him: His drink overcame him. [Asmodeus] took a brick and placed it atop another brick. They went and told Solomon. He said to them: He was telling you, "Give him more to drink." The next day he said to them: Why is the king not summoning me to him? They said to him: His food overcame him. He took the brick off the other brick and placed it on the ground. They went and told Solomon. He said to them: He was telling you, "Take his food away from him."

I. At the end of three days, he came before him. [Asmodeus] took a rod, measured four cubits, and threw it before [Solomon]. He said to [Solomon]: When you die, you will have nothing in this world except four cubits. Now you have conquered the entire world, yet you are not satisfied until you also conquer me?

He said to him: I need nothing from you. I want to build the Temple, and so I need the *shamir*.

[Asmodeus] said to him: It was not given to me. It was given to the Prince of the Sea, and he only gives it to the wild rooster, the hoopoe, whose oath he believes.

J. And what does [the hoopoe] do with it? It brings [the *shamir*] to uninhabitable mountains, places it on the mountain's crag, and the mountain splits. Then it takes tree seeds, brings them over, and throws them in. And it becomes habitable. This is why [the hoopoe] is also called [in Aramaic]: mountain-cutter (*"negar tura"*).[9]

K. They looked around and found a hoopoe's nest in which there were chicks. They covered the nest with white glass. When the adult hoopoe came, it wanted to enter but could not. It went and brought the *shamir* and placed it on top. Solomon's servant shouted. [The hoopoe] dropped [the *shamir*]. Solomon's servant took it. The hoopoe went and strangled itself because of its oath.

L. Benayahu said to [Asmodeus]: Why, when you saw that blind man who lost his way, did you guide him on the right path? He said to him: They proclaim about him in heaven that he is completely righteous, and anyone who brings him comfort earns merit in the next world. He asked: And why, when you saw the drunk who lost his way, did you guide him on the right path? He said: They proclaim about him in heaven that he is a completely

---

9. See *Onkelos* to Deuteronomy 14:18. "It is called *dukhifat* (in Hebrew) because its glory is subservient (*hodo kafut*); it brought the *shamir* to the Temple" (Ḥullin 63a). It is also called *sekhvi* (see the *Targum* on Job 38:36).

wicked man. I gave him some pleasure so that he consumes his reward in this world.

M. Why did you cry when you saw that joyous wedding? He said to him: That man [the groom] will die within thirty days, and [the bride] will have to wait thirteen years for his little brother to become an adult [and perform levirate marriage or divorce]. Why did you laugh when you heard that man say to a shoemaker: "Make me shoes that will last for seven years"? He said to him: That man does not have seven days; he needs shoes that will last for seven years!? Why did you laugh when you saw that fortune-teller? He said to him: He was sitting above the royal treasury. Let him divine the fortune that is just beneath him!

N. [Solomon] detained [Asmodeus] until he built the Temple. One day he stood alone. [Solomon] said to [Asmodeus]: It is written: "He has the strength of a wild ox" (Num. 24:8), and we interpret this to mean: "the strength" refers to the ministering angels, and the "wild ox" refers to the demons. In what way are you greater than us? [Asmodeus] said to him: Take this chain off me and give me your signet, and I will show you my great strength. He removed the chain and gave him the signet. [Asmodeus] swallowed [Solomon]. He placed one of his wings in the heaven and the other on earth, and he spewed him a distance of four hundred parasangs.

O. Regarding that time, Solomon said: "What profit is there for a person through all of his toil under the sun?" (Eccl. 1:3). "And *this* was my portion from all of my toil" (ibid. 2:10). [The Gemara adds parenthetically:] What is the meaning of "*this*"? Rav and Shmuel – one says it refers to his staff, and the other says it refers to his jar.

P. Solomon went begging door-to-door, and everywhere he went, he would say: "I am Kohelet; I was king over Israel in Jerusalem" (Eccl. 1:12). When he reached the Sanhedrin, the rabbis said: A fool does not obsess over one thing. What is this? They said to Benayahu: Does the king summon you to him? He said to them: No. They sent word to the queens, asking: Does the king come to be with you? The queens sent word back to them: Yes, he comes.

[The rabbis] sent word to them: Check his feet. They sent word back: He comes in his slippers. He also demands [to have sexual relations] with us during our periods. And he also demands it of Bathsheba, his mother.

Q. They brought Solomon and gave him a signet and a chain on which God's name was engraved. When he entered, [Asmodeus] saw him and flew away. Even so, [Solomon] was terrified of him, and it is written: "Behold the bed of Solomon, surrounded by sixty strong men from the warriors of Israel, all of them holding swords and trained in war, each man with his sword on his thigh from fear in the nights" (Song. 3:7–8).

The Conduct of Asmodeus after His Capture

Let us first try to understand the meaning of Asmodeus's conduct after Benayahu captured him. We are first told of three incidents that Asmodeus is not asked to decipher (section E): 1. He comes to a palm tree, scratches himself against it, and knocks it down; 2. he comes to a house and knocks it down; 3. he comes to the widow's shack, she comes out and pleads with him, and so he inclines his whole stature away from the shack, thus breaking a bone.

After a quick glance at biblical and midrashic descriptions of Solomon, it dawns on the reader that these incidents allude to the first chapter of Solomon's reign[10] – the establishment of his rule and the elimination of his rivals.

The stately palm tree symbolizes a grand and boastful person: "Just as the palm and the cedar are the greatest of all trees."[11] In I Kings (1:5) we read: "Adoniya ben Ḥagit boasted, 'I will reign.'" We have there a confrontation between Solomon and Adoniya: "King Solomon dispatched Benayahu ben Yehoyada, who struck [Adoniya] down, and he died" (ibid. 2:25).

> 1. He comes to a palm tree, scratches himself against it, and knocks it down.

10. See I Kings 2:13 ff.
11. Numbers Rabba 3:1.

Solomon's second act, as recorded there (ibid. 27), was: "So Solomon dismissed Evyatar from being the priest of the Lord – thus fulfilling the word that the Lord spoke regarding the house of Eli at Shiloh". In the short passage about the prophecy on the **house** of Eli,[12] the term "house" appears ten times. This house is represented by Evyatar, the scion of the house of Eli. Thus, Solomon arrives at a house (the house of Eli) and demolishes it.

2. *He comes to a house and knocks it down.*

The next passages tell of what Solomon did to Yoav and to Shimi ben Gera, but these actions were not his initiative; he was carrying out his father's last will. Therefore, they should be addressed separately.

Thus, the third action that Solomon undertakes on his own, as recorded by Scripture, is: "Solomon allied himself through marriage with Pharaoh, king of Egypt. He married Pharaoh's daughter and brought her to the City of David" (I Kings 3:1). The Sages expounded on the juxtaposition of this episode with the one immediately preceding it, explaining: "One should always live in the same locale as his teacher, for as long as Shimi ben Gera was alive, Solomon did not marry Pharaoh's daughter."[13] According to this, at least three years elapsed between Solomon's coronation and his marriage to Pharaoh's daughter (see I Kings 2:39). According to other midrashim, cited below, Solomon married at the time of the Temple's inauguration.

There is no doubt that the purpose of this marriage was to strengthen Solomon's international alliances, as the preceding verse states: "Thus the kingdom was secured in Solomon's hands." However, it seems that the marriage had the opposite effect domestically; it caused a new wave of disapproval against Solomon, or the reawakening of a dormant opposition. Scripture does not specify when Solomon married Pharaoh's daughter, but it should be noted that this episode, in which "Solomon allied himself through marriage with Pharaoh, king of Egypt," appears at the end of the process by which Solomon eliminated opposition, but before the incident at Givon, wherein, "the Lord appeared to Solomon

12. I Samuel 2:27–36.
13. Berakhot 8a.

in a dream by night" (ibid. 3:5), which marks the beginning of Solomon's activities as a leader who shows concern for his people's needs and who wins the people's trust. Indeed, after his judgment of the case of the two harlots, it states: "When all Israel heard the decision that the king had rendered, they stood in awe of the king; for they saw that he possessed divine wisdom to execute justice" (ibid. 28). The placement of this episode intimates that Solomon's marriage to Pharaoh's daughter caused some opposition amongst the people and set off a series of rebellions against Solomon's rule, as explained in subsequent passages.

Right at the time of the wedding, a threat against the king emerged:

> R. Yoḥanan said: Why did Jeroboam merit becoming a king? Because he rebuked Solomon...as it states: "The circumstances under which he raised his hand against the king were as follows: Solomon built the Millo and repaired the breach of the city of his father, David." [Jeroboam] said to [Solomon]: Your father David made those breaches so that Israel could make festival pilgrimages. You fenced them in to collect tolls on behalf of Pharaoh's daughter!?[14]

A midrash states that Jeroboam rebuked Solomon for delaying the daily *tamid* offering on the morning after his wedding to Pharaoh's daughter:

> That day, Solomon slept until the fourth hour of the day, and the keys to the Temple were under his head.... Jeroboam b. Nevat entered and rebuked him.... This is the meaning of the verse: "When Ephraim spoke, there was trembling" (Hos. 13:1)... when Jeroboam spoke, Solomon trembled.[15]

In both accounts, Jeroboam appears to be a righteous man with pure intentions, to the extent that even his master, Ahija the Shilonite, misjudged his intentions.[16] And therefore the Sages commented:

---

14. Sanhedrin 101b.
15. Leviticus Rabba 12:5.
16. Sanhedrin 102a.

"Jeroboam said to himself" (lit.: "in his *heart*") (I Kings 12:26) –
on this the sages say: "Base silver laid over earthenware are ardent
lips with an evil *heart*" (Prov. 26:23). This refers to Esau and his
ilk. What is he like? An urn, which is gold inlaid with gemstones
on the outside, but earthenware on the inside. Thus, Esau –
"Esau said to himself" (Gen. 27:41) ... and similarly, "Jeroboam
said to himself." ... [As the verse teaches,] "Though his speech
is charming, do not trust him, for seven abominations are in his
heart!" (Prov. 26:25).[17]

Scripture obscures what exactly happened with Jeroboam. There
may have been an attempt to compromise with him. Perhaps this is
why Solomon "appointed him over all the forced labor of the House
of Joseph" (I Kings 11:28), a high office indeed. However, it is also
possible that Jeroboam "raised his hand against the king" (ibid. 27)
only after his appointment. According to the Sages, it is clear that
at some point a compromise was offered to him: "R. Abba said:
When the Holy One grabbed Jeroboam by his clothes and said to
him: 'Repent, and you, I, and the son of Jesse will walk together in
the Garden of Eden!' He replied: 'Who will be at the head?' [God
answered:] 'The son of Jesse will be at the head.' [Jeroboam replied:]
'If so, I do not want it.'"[18]

Accordingly, the third parable – the parable of the widow –
should be understood as relating to Solomon's rival. Scripture emphasizes Jeroboam's maternal lineage: "Jeroboam son of Nebat, an
Ephraimite of **Tzereda**, the son of a **widow** named Tzerua" (ibid. 26).
Of Jeroboam it is said: "Though his speech is charming, do not trust
him, for seven abominations are in his heart" (Prov. 26:25). Scripture
attests that Solomon sensed Jeroboam's treachery: "Solomon sought
to put Jeroboam to death" (I Kings 11:40), but he was prevented by
Heaven from doing so. Furthermore, it had already been decreed: "For
thus said the Lord, the God of Israel: I am about to tear the kingdom

---

17. *Yalkut Shimoni*, I Kings §198.
18. Sanhedrin 102a. It is also possible that the "son of Jesse" refers here to Reḥoboam,
not Solomon.

out of Solomon's hands, and I will give you ten tribes. But one tribe shall remain his" (ibid. 29–32).

The meaning of the parable is now clear: 3. *He comes to the widow's shack, she comes out and pleads with him, and so he inclines his whole stature away from the shack, thus breaking a bone.*

Solomon's Proverbs in Asmodeus's Mouth

More than Solomon was a man of action, he was a teacher of wisdom to the people. He scrutinized man's ways and preoccupations, and he responded with wisdom, inspiring people with his astute and biting aphorisms. Thus, after the first three episodes, the narrator presents two instances in which Asmodeus guides people who have lost their way (section F), and three proverbs that focus on the futility of man and his desires (section G). The narrator clarifies these meanings through Asmodeus's answers to Benayahu's questions (sections L-M).

We learn in a midrash:

> R. Abba b. Kahana said: This is like an old man sitting at a crossroads with two paths before him. One starts on a plain but ends up among brambles, cedars, and bulrushes; the other begins among bulrushes, cedars, and brambles, but ends up on a plain. He would caution passers-by, saying: "This one starts on a plain but ends up among cedars, brambles, and bulrushes, while this one begins among brambles, cedars, and bulrushes, and ends up on a plain." Don't people owe him gratitude for warning them for their sake, so they do not exhaust themselves? Similarly, don't people owe gratitude to Solomon, who sits at the gates of wisdom and warns Israel: "I have further observed under the sun" (Eccl. 9:11); "I observed all that is done beneath the sun, [and I found that all is futile and pursuit of wind]" (ibid. 1:14), except for repentance and good deeds?[19]

Thus we learn that Solomon guided those who lost their way.

19. Ecclesiastes Rabba 1:14.

[Asmodeus] saw a blind man who lost his way; he guided him back on the right path. He saw a drunk who lost his way; he guided him back on the right path.

Solomon did not save his wisdom for the righteous alone; he taught and instructed everyone. Scripture says so explicitly three times: "Men from **all peoples** came to hear Solomon's wisdom on behalf of all the kings of the earth, who had heard of his wisdom" (I Kings 5:14); "**All the earth** came to pay homage to Solomon and to listen to the wisdom with which God had endowed him" (ibid. 10:24); and "**All the kings of the earth** came to pay homage to Solomon and to listen to the wisdom with which God had endowed him" (II Chr. 9:23).

Benayahu said to [Asmodeus]: Why, when you saw that blind man who lost his way, did you guide him on the right path? He said to him: They proclaim about him in heaven that he is completely righteous, and anyone who brings him comfort earns merit in the next world.

That a "blind man" represents a righteous person is explicit in Scripture: "Who is so blind as My servant? ... Who is so blind as the one who is whole, so blind as the servant of the Lord? ... The Lord desires his vindication, that he may magnify and glorify the Torah" (Is. 42:19–21).

And why, when you saw the drunk who lost his way, did you guide him on the right path? He said: They proclaim about him in heaven that he is a completely wicked man. I gave him some pleasure so that he consumes his reward in this world.

This, too, reflects the Sages' interpretation of a verse in the Torah: "The prophets said to the Holy One: Why do you give benevolently to the nations of the world in this world? He replied: Have I not written to you: 'but Who repays those who hate Him to their faces (He repays them in this world), to destroy them' (Deut. 7:10)?"[20] And R. Ila expounded the

---

20. *Midrash Tehillim* 7:17.

verse, "He will not delay [repaying in this world] those who hate Him" (ibid.): "He never delays [repaying] those who hate Him, but He does delay the repayment of the completely righteous."[21] Likewise, the Sages explained[22] that Solomon's mother rebuked him: "Why do you frequent those kings who drink wine and get drunk?" Solomon taught wisdom to these kings as well.

We then read about how Asmodeus cried once and laughed twice:

> He saw a very joyous wedding ceremony; he cried. He heard a man say to a shoemaker, "Make me shoes that will last for seven years," and he laughed. He saw a fortune-teller performing divinations, and he laughed.
>
> Benayahu asked: Why did you cry when you saw that joyous wedding? He said to him: That man [the groom] will die within thirty days, and [the bride] will have to wait thirteen years for his little brother to become an adult [and perform levirate marriage or divorce.]

The Sages expounded:

> "His lips are like lilies, dripping with flowing myrrh" (Song. 5:13). Scripture should have said "myrrh that stays in one place." Because when Solomon built the Temple, the whole world was filled with the scent of fragrance. He saw that ultimately it would be destroyed, and he cried saying, "This fragrance is for naught."[23]

Other midrashim described the joy of the building of the Temple in greater detail:

21. Eiruvin 22a.
22. Sanhedrin 70b.
23. *Pesikta Rabbati* 20 (*Parshat Matan Torah*); p. 96b in the Ish-Shalom edition (Vienna: 1880).

The night that Solomon completed the construction of the Temple he married Batya, Pharaoh's daughter. There was the joy of the Temple and the joy of Pharaoh's daughter, and the joy of Pharaoh's daughter was greater than the joy of the Temple.... At that moment, the thought of destroying Jerusalem arose before the Holy One.[24]

At the very moment that "Solomon and all Israel with him ... [were] joyful and glad of heart" (I Kings 8:65–66), celebrating the inauguration of the Temple, it was decreed upon Solomon's dynasty and on all of Israel that they would have to wait for a long time, like a woman has to wait for a young levir: "I will chastise David's descendants for that, though not forever" (ibid. 11:39). For at the end of days, the redeemer will come, "and I will make them a single nation in the land ... and one king shall be king of them all. Never again shall they be two nations, and never again shall they be divided into two kingdoms. My servant David shall be king over them; there shall be one shepherd for all of them" (Ezek. 37:22–24).

> Benayahu asked: Why did you laugh when you heard that man say to a shoemaker: "Make me shoes that will last for seven years"? He said to him: That man does not have seven days; he needs shoes that will last for seven years?!

This parable, like the one preceding it, is explained by a verse from Ecclesiastes: "A man cannot even know his time. As fishes are enmeshed in a fatal net, and as birds are trapped in a snare, so men are caught at the time of calamity, when it comes upon them without warning" (Eccl. 9:12). However, it seems that the shoes allude to something more specific. Shoes are mentioned twice with respect to Yoav ben Tzeruya. It is written in Psalms: "Yoav returned and struck Edom in the Valley of Salt" (60:2). Of the same battle, it is written: "on Edom I will cast my shoe" (ibid. 10). Thus, the shoe symbolizes the powerful Yoav, whose victories in battle led to the defeat of David's enemies. The same symbolism emerges from a different verse: "Yoav ben Tzeruya ... staining the girdle

---

24. Numbers Rabba 10:4.

of his loins and the shoes on his feet with blood of war" (I Kings 2:5). The girdle and the shoe both indicate leadership and strength.

When Adoniyahu boasted, "I will reign," Yoav sought to ensure himself a position in the upper echelons of the kingdom after David's death, even though he certainly could have stood aside and not gotten involved: "He (Adoniya) conferred with Yoav ben Tzeruya and with the priest Evyatar, and they supported Adoniya" (ibid. 1:7). That is, Yoav wanted to make sure he had shoes for the long term, unaware that his fate was sealed in David's last will to Solomon. This, too, is implicit in a verse from Ecclesiastes (7:3): "Anger is better than laughter." The Sages expounded: "Solomon said: Had Father (David) gotten a bit angry at Adoniya, it would have been better for him than the Attribute of Justice laughing at him."[25] The Attribute of Justice laughed at Yoav, too.

The Sages said: "Every verse that Solomon prophesied has two or three meanings."[26] As such, this parable, too, has an alternate interpretation, according to which it is about Solomon himself. Solomon requested of King Hiram of Tyre: "Now send me a craftsman to work in gold and silver...and send me cedars, cypress, and algum wood from Lebanon" (II Chr. 2:6–7). He prefaced his request with an explanation, in which he emphasized that the building materials must be of exceedingly high quality: "I am about to build a house for the name of the Lord my God; dedicating it to Him...forever" (ibid. 3). Solomon repeated that expectation when he inaugurated the Temple: "Then Solomon said, '...I have now built for You a stately house, a place where You may dwell **forever**'" (I Kings 8:12–13). Here are the shoes meant to last for seven years! It was not long before God informed him: "I will tear the kingdom away from you and give it to one of your servants" (ibid. 11:11). "I will reject the house which I have consecrated to My name; and Israel shall become a proverb and a byword among all peoples" (ibid. 9:7).

> Benayahu asked: Why did you laugh when you saw that fortune-teller? He said to him: He was sitting above the royal treasury. Let him divine the fortune that is just beneath him!

---

25. Ecclesiastes Rabba 7:10.
26. Ibid. 7:46.

This question is essentially the same question that the Talmud asks: "What did he need male and female demons for?" Solomon sat atop the royal treasury. He was king of the world: "Wisdom and knowledge are granted to you." He was initiated into the secrets of the Torah and the mysteries of science, the wisdom of creation and of God's chariot! And he needs male and female demons?! It is laughable!

Thus, everything that Asmodeus did and said, from the moment that Benayahu captured him until he entered Jerusalem with him, is nothing but a synopsis of Scriptural and rabbinic stories about Solomon himself. Everything that happened to Solomon happened to Asmodeus, and everything that Solomon taught, Asmodeus taught.

This being the case, it behooves us to examine the tales about Asmodeus before his capture and after he arrives at the royal palace.

The Conduct of Asmodeus before His Capture

Let us return to the beginning of the story (section B):

> He has dug himself a cistern, filled it with water, covered it with a rock, and sealed it with his seal. Every day he ascends to heaven and studies in the heavenly yeshiva. Then he descends to earth and studies in the earthly yeshiva. Then he comes and inspects his seal, opens the cistern, and drinks. Then he covers it, seals it, and leaves.

Does this description not apply to the wisest of all men, to whom the reasons for the Torah were revealed? "There is no water but Torah, as it is stated: 'Ho, all who thirst, come for water' (Is. 55:1)."[27] And he drinks from these living waters and protects them so that they always remain pure and holy, free of any foreign admixtures. And just as he knows the ways of the earthly yeshiva, so too he knows the ways of the heavenly yeshiva.

How did Benayahu capture Asmodeus? The latter was particularly careful about wine. When he returned, inspected his seal, and found the cistern filled with wine, he held himself back and did not

---

27. Bava Kamma 17a.

drink. However, when thirst overcame him, he drank, became drunk, and fell asleep. He was then bound in a chain from which he could not break free.

> R. Yudan said: Throughout the seven years that Solomon was building the Temple, he drank no wine. Once he built the Temple and married Pharaoh's daughter – that night he drank wine.... That day, Solomon slept through the fourth hour of the day.[28]

The words of the Sages are indeed implied by the verses. The first time that Solomon's table is mentioned, it says: "Solomon's daily provisions consisted of thirty kors of fine flour, sixty kors of [ordinary] flour, ten fattened cattle, twenty pasture-fed cattle, and a hundred sheep, besides deer, gazelles, roebucks, and fatted geese" (I Kings 5:2–3). There is no mention of drink. However, when the queen of Sheba comes to visit, she is impressed not only by "the fare of his table," but also by his wines.[29]
The Talmud addresses this:

> "Wine is not for kings, O Lemuel, not for kings to drink" (Prov. 31:4). "Not for kings" – [his mother] said to him: "Why do you frequent those kings who drink wine, get drunk, and say 'Why do we need God?[30]'" "Or for rulers (*roznim*) to crave strong drink" (ibid.) – shall the one to whom all the secrets (*razei*) of the world are revealed drink wine and get drunk?![31]

Once again, we have the same astonishing parallels between Solomon and Asmodeus!

> Let us now turn to what happened after Asmodeus reached the royal palace (section H):

28. Leviticus Rabba 12:5.
29. See I Kings 10:5.
30. "*Lamah lanu El*" – a play on the name "Lemuel."
31. Sanhedrin 70b.

> On the first day he said to them: Why is the king not summoning me to him? They said to him: His drink overcame him. [Asmodeus] took a brick and placed it atop another brick. They went and told Solomon. He said to them: He was telling you, "Give him more to drink." The next day he said to them: Why is the king not summoning me to him? They said to him: His food overcame him. He took the brick off the other brick and placed it on the ground. They went and told Solomon. He said to them: He was telling you, "Take his food away from him."

Two points are especially conspicuous here: first, only one who is aware of the description of the vastness of "the fare of [Solomon's] table … and his wines," which left the queen of Sheba "breathless" (I Kings 10:5), can understand how it is possible for Solomon to be overcome by eating and drinking. Second, in contrast to the abstemiousness that characterized him earlier, we now hear: "His drink overcame him – give him more to drink!" This is explicit in the text as well: "I ventured to tempt my flesh with wine" (Eccl. 2:3).

Then: "Take his food away from him!" Does this not echo Solomon's own misgivings in response to his mother's rebuke? As the Talmud states: "R. Yitzhak said: How do we know that Solomon changed his mind and agreed with his mother? As Scripture states: 'I am more of a fool than any man (lit. 'than a man'). I do not have human understanding' (Prov. 30:2). 'I am more of a fool than a man' – more [foolish] than Noah, as Scripture states: 'Noah began to be a man of the soil [… and he drank from the wine and became drunk]' (Gen. 9:20–21)."[32]

> At the end of three days, he came before him. [Asmodeus] took a rod, measured four cubits, and threw it before [Solomon]. He said to [Solomon]: When you die, you will have nothing in this world except four cubits. Now you have conquered the entire world, yet you are not satisfied until you also conquer me? (See above, section I)

---

32. Sanhedrin 70b.

Is this not the basic idea of the entire book of Ecclesiastes slapping Solomon in the face? "All is futile and the pursuit of wind; there is nothing worthwhile under the sun" (Eccl. 2:11). "Even if a man should beget a hundred children and live many years – no matter how many the days of his years may come to, if he is not sated through his wealth, and he has no burial ... he departs into darkness, and his very name is covered with darkness" (ibid. 6:3–4). A midrash explained:

> Rabbi [Yehuda HaNasi] made a banquet in honor of his son....
> [Bar Kappara] went and wrote on the door: "After all your
> rejoicing is death; so what is the point of your joy?" ... Did not
> Solomon say: "What profit is there for a person through all of
> his toil under the sun?" (Eccl. 1:3)[33]

The mention of the "Prince of the Sea" from whom the elusive *shamir* must be obtained seems to be linked to Solomon's attempt to increase his maritime power: "King Solomon built a fleet of ships at Etzion Gever, which is near Eilat on the shore of the Red Sea" (I Kings 9:26). This, too, was because he was not satisfied with the riches he had already hoarded, to the extent that, "All King Solomon's drinking cups were gold" (ibid. 10:21).

With regard to the story of the hoopoe and its conduct (section J above), it seems that it is from a different aggada and was embedded here, because it is not related to the present passage. The Talmud states: "It was taught ... [it is called] *dukhifat* because its glory is subservient (*"hodo kafut"*); it brought the *shamir* to the Temple."[34] The hoopoe ends up strangling itself – which recalls the story of Ahitophel's end.[35]

Once the *shamir* was found, the situation did not improve; there is not even any mention of the *shamir* being used for its designated purpose. On the contrary, things began to deteriorate precipitously. There is a secret confrontation between Solomon and Asmodeus (section N), during which Solomon conceded to Asmodeus the means by which he

---

33. Ecclesiastes Rabba 1:4.
34. Ḥullin 63a.
35. See II Samuel 17:23.

controlled him – the signet and the chain on which God's name was engraved. Asmodeus then swallowed Solomon. At that point, Solomon was no longer recognized, except as a beggar, wandering from door to door, "obsessing over one thing" (section O). And now, free from the constraints imposed by the signet and chain bearing God's name, the code of conduct in the king's palace breaks all boundaries, to the point that demands are made of the king's wives to engage in intercourse during their periods (section O).

Yet the Sages attributed the same severe transgression to Solomon himself. Commenting on the verse, "King Solomon loved many foreign women," the Yerushalmi cites R. Shimon b. Yoḥai: "he literally loved them – for lewd purposes."[36] R. Eliezer b. R. Yosi HaGelili goes further in a midrash: "It is written: 'yet foreign wives caused even him to sin' (Neh. 13:26) – this teaches that he would have intercourse with them during their periods, and they would not inform him.[37]

The Meaning of the Aggada

What, then, is the meaning of this aggada, which equates Solomon with Asmodeus in all respects? A close reading of this aggada leads us to the conclusion that it is a parable for King Solomon's uniquely complex character. There was a deep split, a duality, in his soul. This was not the normal dichotomy of the good impulse and evil impulse (*yetzer*), which characterizes all human beings. Everyone is constantly in conflict with his *yetzer* and must do battle against it. However, in this story, Asmodeus does not just symbolize the evil impulse, as Solomon's benevolence and even his abstemiousness are attributed to Asmodeus as well; on the other side of the ledger, all of the evil perpetrated by Asmodeus has been attributed by the Sages to Solomon.

The Sages said: "One who is greater than another also has a stronger *yetzer*."[38] Solomon was greater than other men, not just quantitatively, in that he had more wisdom, insight, and knowledge, but qualitatively, in his essence. Consequently, it was as though two powerful souls were

---

36. Y. Sanhedrin 2:6.
37. Song of Songs Rabba 1:10.
38. Sukka 52a.

struggling within him, and it was impossible to tell which one was good mixed with evil, and which one was evil mixed with good. The Sages addressed this directly in a midrash, noting that Solomon had seven names, of which four can be expounded:

> Agur – for he amassed (*agur*) words of Torah; Yakeh – for he would spew (*meki*) words, like a cup is filled up and then emptied – so too, Solomon learned Torah at one point and forgot it at another point; Lemoel – for he said to God (*nam la-El*) in his heart: "I can increase [my wives, horses, and money] and not sin"; Itiel – for he said "God is with me (*iti El*) and I am able."[39]

Like a cup is filled up and then emptied, he is sometimes filled up, and then he is God-fearing in his rule. And sometimes, he is emptied, and then he is the demon king. This constant struggle stayed with him until the end, until, in his old age, it was impossible to know who exactly was on the throne. "Rav and Shmuel [disagree]: One says that he was a king, then a commoner. The other says he was a king, then a commoner, and then a king."[40] This dispute cannot be resolved: "The heart is the most devious of all. It is incurable. Who can know it?" (Jer. 17:9).

The Mitzvot and Human Pretension

We are left with a question that runs very deep: How could it be that King Solomon, the wisest of all men, could not recognize what was happening to him? How could he, who was so full of Torah, be so careless as to spit it all out? How could he not see the abyss gaping before him?

This, essentially, is the question that the Sages placed in Asmodeus's mouth: **"Now you have conquered the entire world, yet you are not satisfied until you also conquer me?"** Solomon responded: **"I need nothing from you. I want to build the Temple, and so I need the *shamir*."** Solomon's answer contains a world of meaning.

Solomon wanted to bring the Divine Presence, the *Shekhina*, down from the heavens and build a dwelling place for the *Shekhina* in this

---

39. Ecclesiastes Rabba 1:2.
40. Gittin 68b.

world. He wanted the entire Temple, not just the altar, to be the peak of perfection. The Sages explain "complete stones (*shelema*)" (I Kings 6:7) as "stones that cause peace (*shalom*)."⁴¹ How is it possible to bring large and precious stones without enslaving the masses to work the quarries? Without drafting slaves to split boulders that reflect the grandeur of creation? Without overworking prisoners who pick away at the rocks with iron tools, created to cut man's life short? Is it not forbidden to "wield something created to shorten [man's life] over something created to extend [man's life]"?⁴² **The path to becoming close to God is long and arduous, and the Torah safeguarded it with all sorts of prohibitions.** The *shamir* is the wondrous creature that can shape those stones, make them complete, and bring peace to a world that is so full of envy, rivalry, hatred, and strife. Where is the *shamir* to be found?

The Creator attests that all existence is "very good" (Gen. 1:31). Nothing in the world is evil in essence. Why, then, did the Torah forbid the things it forbids? Does a prohibition define something as evil? How can that be, if everything is ultimately good? Rather, the mitzvot were given in order to instill within man the proper character traits, which prepare him for the higher virtues of knowing God. But, Solomon reasoned, if one can go directly to the knowledge of God, there is no need for preparation! The Torah said: "He shall not keep many horses and send the people back to Egypt.... He shall not have many wives, lest his heart go astray" (Deut. 17:16–17). The increase of horses or wives is not an intrinsic evil. Rather, it is a safeguard against other things. Thus, Solomon thought he could increase their number without sinning. "God is with me and I am able!" "What does God care whether one slaughters an animal from the front of the neck or from the nape? The purpose is to refine people."⁴³ Since the purpose of the mitzvot is to refine people, one who has access to the wellsprings of wisdom and knows how to refine his soul with the fire of love for God, which "vast floods cannot quench"

---

41. *Mekhilta DeRabbi Yishma'el, Yitro, Masekhta Debahodesh* 11 (on Exodus 20:21; p. 244 in the Horowitz-Rabin edition).
42. Ibid.
43. Genesis Rabba 44:1.

(Song 8:7), does not need to perform the mitzvot: "Solomon said: I delved into and examined all of these,"[44] and once he became aware of the reasons and purposes of most mitzvot, he thought he could aim straight for the ultimate purpose and no longer needed safeguards and prohibitions. On the contrary, the superior man, who knows how to cleave to his Maker, can raise up all of existence along with him, without exception. After all, since in reality everything is good, and some things were prohibited not because they are intrinsically evil, but in order to train and refine people who need training and refinement, the truly wise man does not need all of that. And so, Solomon said: "I ventured to tempt my flesh with wine" without fear, because "my heart conducted itself with wisdom," and therefore I can "grasp folly so that I might see what is good for men." Since "my wisdom remained with me," "I withheld from my eyes nothing that they asked for," including "*sharim* and *sharot*, and human pleasures, *shidda* and *shiddot*."[45] Solomon even wished to conquer Asmodeus and harness his power to build a dwelling place in the nether worlds for the *Shekhina*. A Temple built with the power of both impulses, the good and the evil, would truly be complete. And so God's name and God's throne would be complete as well. The capture of Asmodeus would disclose the whereabouts of the *shamir*, thus realizing "the sanctuary, O Lord, that Your hands established" (Ex. 15:17). This is the secret of the *shamir*. Now the stones of the Temple would really be whole, as though they were created this way at the beginning of time. After all, this is the task of the *shamir*: to split mountains quietly, pleasantly, so that they become habitable settlements.[46]

It was not only the mitzvot that apply to individuals and kings that Solomon wished to circumvent, but also the laws that apply to judges, and to justice itself:

> Kohelet wanted to pronounce judgment based on intuition – without witnesses and without forewarning. A heavenly voice

---

44. Ecclesiastes Rabba 7:44.
45. Quotes are from Ecclesiastes 2:3–10.
46. See section J of the story.

issued forth and said to him: "and that which He wrote is upright and true" (Eccl. 12:10) – "by the testimony of two witnesses..." (Deut. 17:6)."[47]

All Solomon wanted was to arrive at the truth without troubling himself to penetrate the layers of human experience, which cloak the truth like a shell conceals the nut inside. To what can he be compared? To one who swallows a nut in its shell.

Solomon wished to conquer Asmodeus because he desired to build a Temple that would last forever. However, he made a terrible error when he thought that he could imprison the evil inclination by satisfying it. Asmodeus, imprisoned in the vaults of Solomon's heart, gained control over him and turned him into a laughingstock. He never had the *shamir*, for peace and perfection – *shalom* and *shlemut* – cannot be achieved by loosening restraints. The *shamir* must be sought from the wild rooster, which symbolizes wisdom.[48] "A man of understanding takes wise counsel" (Prov. 1:5).

Though he was the wisest of all men, Solomon paved the way for many who followed him throughout history, from early sectarians to contemporary groups, to make the same error. They think that the Torah can be divided into essential and inessential, primary and ancillary, core and husk, spirit and letter – and that one can keep the essence while dispensing with the rest. But this is not so!

> R. Shimon b. Yoḥai taught: The Book of Deuteronomy came and prostrated itself before the Holy One. It said: "Master of the Universe! You wrote in Your Torah that a contract that is annulled in part is completely annulled. Yet Solomon seeks to annul an iota of my content!" The Holy One said to it: "Solomon and a thousand like him will be annulled, and nothing of you will be annulled."[49]

---

47. Rosh HaShana 21b.
48. Job 38:36.
49. Y. Sanhedrin 2:6.

Yet even Solomon recognized his error when he declared: "The conclusion, when all has been heard: Fear God and observe His mitzvot, for this is the whole of man" (Eccl. 12:13). But it was too late, for the years had arrived "when you will say 'I find no pleasure in them'" (ibid. 1).[50]

Yet that heavenly voice continues to reverberate through the generations: "that which He wrote is upright and true" (Eccl. 12:10).

---

50. This accords with the statement of the Sages (Song of Songs Rabba 1:10): "R. Yannai, the father-in-law of R. Ami said: 'All agree that Kohelet was said at the end [of Solomon's life].'"

Appendix: Sources of Essays

"Halacha and Other Systems of Ethics – Attitudes and Interactions," in Marvin Fox, ed., *Modern Jewish Ethics* (Columbus: Ohio State University Press, 1975), 89–102.

"Torah and Science: Conflict or Complement?" in A. Carmell and C. Domb, eds., *Challenge: Torah Views of Science and its Problems* (Jerusalem: Feldheim, 1976), 44–52.

"Torah and the Spirit of Free Inquiry," in A. Carmell and C. Domb, eds., *Challenge: Torah Views of Science and its Problems* (Jerusalem: Feldheim, 1976), 54–67.

"Rambam, Science and Taamei Hamitzvot," in Y. Elman and J. S. Gurock, eds., *Hazon Nahum: Studies in Jewish Law, Thought, and History Presented to Dr. Norman Lamm on the Occasion of His Seventieth Birthday* (New York: Yeshiva University Press, 1997), 187–206.

"The Way of Torah," transl. Joel Linsider, *The Edah Journal* 3:1 (2003), 1–34.

"What is Emunat Hakhamim?," *Hakirah: The Flatbush Journal of Jewish Law and Thought* 5 (2007), 35–45.

‏"דרכה של תורה", מעליות י, תשמ"ח, מעליות, מעלה אדומים, עמ' 8–42.

"תורה ומדע, שותפות או ניגוד?", שמעתין 109, ניסן-אב תשנ"ב, בני ברק, עמ' 87–96.

"חידה ופשרה", מגדים כה, כסלו תשנ"ו, תבונות - מכללת יעקב הרצוג, אלון שבות, עמ' 91–110.

"אמונת חכמים מהי?", מעליות יז, שבט תשנ"ו, מעליות, עמ' 101–107.

"מה נורא בימים הנוראים", בהיותו קרוב: אסופת מאמרים לימים הנוראים לזכרו של יחיאל שי פינפטר הי"ד, עורך: אלחנן גנזל ואחרים, תש"ס, מרכז שפירא, המכון התורני שליד ישיבת אור עציון, עמ' 204–214.

"צווים, חיובים ומטרות", נחום אליעזר רבינוביץ, עיונים במשנתו של הרמב"ם, מהדורה שנייה מורחבת, ירושלים, מעליות, תש"ע.

The fonts used in this book are from the Arno family

Maggid Books
The best of contemporary Jewish thought from
Koren Publishers Jerusalem Ltd.